ISBN 978-1-331-90745-9
PIBN 10252479

This book is a reproduction of an important historical work. Forgotten Books uses
state-of-the-art technology to digitally reconstruct the work, preserving the original format
whilst repairing imperfections present in the aged copy. In rare cases, an imperfection in
the original, such as a blemish or missing page, may be replicated in our edition. We do,
however, repair the vast majority of imperfections successfully; any imperfections that
remain are intentionally left to preserve the state of such historical works.

1 MONTH OF
FREE
READING

at

www.ForgottenBooks.com

By purchasing this book you are eligible for one month membership to ForgottenBooks.com, giving you unlimited access to our entire collection of over 700,000 titles via our web site and mobile apps.

To claim your free month visit:

www.forgottenbooks.com/free252479

THE
MEDIEVAL EMPIRE

BY

HERBERT FISHER

FELLOW AND TUTOR OF NEW COLLEGE, OXFORD

VOLUME II

London
MACMILLAN AND CO., LIMITED
NEW YORK: THE MACMILLAN COMPANY
1898

GLASGOW: PRINTED AT THE UNIVERSITY PRESS
BY ROBERT MACLEHOSE AND CO.

CONTENTS.

CHAPTER VIII.

THE EXPANSION OF GERMANY IN THE NORTH-EAST.

CHAPTER IX.

THE EXPANSION OF GERMANY IN THE SOUTH-EAST.

CHAPTER X.

THE CHURCH IN GERMANY.

CHAPTER XI.

IMPERIAL LEGISLATION IN ITALY.

CHAPTER XII.

THE EMPERORS AND THE CITY OF ROME.

CHAPTER XIII.

IMPERIAL ADMINISTRATION IN ITALY.

CHAPTER XIV.

THE EMPIRE AND CULTURE.

CHAPTER XV.

CONCLUSION.

THE MEDIEVAL EMPIRE.

CHAPTER VIII.

THE EXPANSION OF GERMANY IN THE NORTH-EAST.

How was the monarchy to exploit and to control this dangerous military sentiment, this abundant human material of war? In the eighth century the problem was more difficult, for the military energy of the Germanic races was still fresh and exuberant, and the internecine strife of the Merovingian sovereigns had made every Frank a fighting man. Yet it was met for a time by the first sovereigns of the Carolingian house in a manner which was at any rate of transitory efficacy. They do not indeed organize professional armies like the armies of the early Roman empire or of the Byzantines. Their levies receive no state pay. There are no standing legionary camps, there is no state commissariat, no war budget, no code of military discipline. But just as Napoleon utilized the amazing energy created in France by the Revolution to spread French culture and dominion through Europe, so the early monarchs of the Caroling house utilize the amazing energy of the fresh Germanic peoples to diffuse through Europe the Christianity of the Latin Church. They employ all the races of the

Frankish empire in a huge but connected series of missionary wars.[1]

Now it was an integral part of the conception of the imperial office that the emperor should extend the boundaries of the Church and do battle against the heathen. In all the manuals written during the break-up of the Carolingian empire for the guidance of princes as well as in the prayer offered by the Church, this duty is enjoined with a mournful and a monotonous emphasis. At the coronation service of Otto I. in the Cathedral of Aix, the Archbishop of Trèves goes to the altar, takes thence a sword and a belt, and turning towards the king says to him, " Receive this sword, by which you may cast out all adversaries of Christ, all barbarians and evil Christians, since full power of the whole empire of the Franks has been given you by divine authority to the most firm peace of all Christians." And this missionary and military obligation is firmly enjoined in all the orders for the coronation service of a German king or a Roman emperor which have come down to us.

When the empire was transferred to the kings of the Saxon house it went to a quarter of Europe which was singularly fitted to be a basis for a series of effective crusades. The whole southern shore of the Danube, the whole region north and east of the Elbe, the whole of Denmark, Sweden, and Norway remained to be evangelized. The Baltic Slaves were divided into three great groups—the Obodrites, who occupied Holstein and Mecklenburg; the Wiltzi or Luticii, who formed a great block

[1] Frederick I. in the *Canonizatio Caroli Magni*, 1166, says, " In fide quo-que Christi dilatanda, et in conversione gentis barbaricae fortis athleta fuit, sicut Saxonia et Fresonia Hispanis quoque testantur et Wandali, quos ad fidem Catholicam verbo convertit et gladio " [Harz., *Conc.*, iii. 399, 400].

of tribes facing the Middle Elbe : and lastly, the Sorbs, in the upper valleys of the Elbe and the Saale.[1] But the line of Elbe was not a sufficient barrier. Slaves penetrated into the Altmark, as many place-names, such as Wendish-Apenburg, testify to this day, and there were Slavonian colonies in Swabia, in Hesse, in the Rhine land [2] To reduce their Slavonic neighbours to subjection, to colonize the Baltic lands with Germans and with Flemings, who could till the heavy soils neglected by the light and careless cultivation of the Slave, to obtain possession of the Baltic ports and the Russian and Swedish trade, to spread Church organization through the vast plain which stretched from the Elbe to the Vistula, was a mission which seemed naturally imposed upon the German monarchy. The task was not one of excessive difficulty. Cyril and Methodius had by their sweetness and intelligence converted the Moravians quietly, speedily, and without bloodshed, and if ruder methods were to be employed now, there was every prospect that these too would succeed. There was, indeed, a time in the ninth century when Europe was menaced with the consolidation of a great Slavonic empire in the east stretching from the Vistula to the Drave. But then came the Hungarians driving their Magyar wedge between the Slaves of the south and the Czecks of Bohemia. From that time onward the Baltic Slaves, placed between the German hammer and the anvil of Poland and Bohemia, seem incapable of forming any large or strong combina-

---

[1] Riedel, *Die Mark Brandenburg im* 1250, vol. iii., pp. 8-14 ; Meitzen, *Siedelung und Agrarwesen,* ii., pp. 475-93 ; Schulze, *Die Kolonisierung und Germanisierung der Gebiete zwischen Saale und Elbe.* For a picture of a Slavonic round village, Meitzen, ii., p. 485.

[2] For the various subdivisions of these tribes, cf. Hauck, *Geschichte der deutschen Kirche,* vol. iii., pp. 74, 7.

tions. Though they were numerous, according to Adam
of Bremen ten times more numerous than the Germans,
inured to all dangers, and not wholly uncivilized, for
they work hemp and linen, and possess towns, such
as the Slavo-Greek commercial city of Wollin on the
Oder, where freedom of access was accorded to German
traders, yet they show no political capacity or powers of
military organization. The only ties which bound these
peoples together seem to have been the oracular shrine
of Svantovit, in the island of Rügen, the Slavonic
Delphi to which all paid annual sacrifices, and the
temple of Radigost at Rethra, with its mailed and
helmeted gods.[1] But the settlements were sparse and
isolated, the lands of the village communities divided
up every three generations, their civilization stationary.
" In the midst of the greatest natural wealth, the men
of this land," says a German observer in the middle of
the twelfth century, " seem plunged in a general coarse-
ness and rusticity. The cities and castles are destitute
of walls and turrets, and are fortified alone by a wooden
palisade and a ditch. The churches and houses of the
nobles are lowly and mean. The people are given over
to hunting, fishing, and the tending of flocks, for in this
consists all their wealth, and agriculture is rare among
them. There is little of opulence or beauty in their
style of living or clothes, and our middle class is
glorious when compared with their nobility."[2] In the
eleventh and twelfth centuries the Baltic Slaves were,
in fact, very much in the same condition as were the
Croatians and the Slovenes, when they were described

---

[1] Thietmar, vi. 23, 24 ; Adam. Brem. ii. 18, 19 ; Helmold, i. 6, 36, 52.
It is probable that the Germans stimulated the formation of a Slavonic
priesthood in these parts, for elsewhere we do not hear of heathen
priests.

[2] *Herbordi Dialogus*, iii. 30 ; Jaffé, *Bibliotheca*, v., p. 822.

by Procopius and the Emperor Maurice towards the close of the sixth century. Excellent divers and swimmers, good bee-keepers, skilled archers and javelin-men, who could harass the march of an incoming force, and take advantage of natural cover of every description, but unapt for the invasion of a foreign territory; living in the rude democracy of their family communities, crowded together in wretched huts of wattle, hideous, dirty, and evil-smelling, but musical, sensitive, and hospitable, gentle and humane in their treatment of the decrepit and of prisoners of war; using small pieces of cloth as their internal currency, but for all that carrying on an extensive trade in wax and furs and honey; enduring of hard labour and long fasts, assuaging the paroxysms of religious terror by human or animal sacrifice, yet with no strong priesthood or robust religious creed, and with no central political authority whom they could obey or revere; at critical moments they fight with one another, when they should have been banded together to resist the Germans.[1] If the Christian missionaries had been spiritual or persuasive, or if the emperors had been strong, these tribes might have been rapidly absorbed or vanquished. In the latter alternative the emperors might have created in the northern plain of Germany the dominion which it afterwards fell to the margraves of Brandenburg and the dukes of Prussia to create, a dominion which was capable of strong centra-

---

[1] Procopius, *De Bello Gothico*, iii. c. 14 ; Mauricius, *Ars Militaris*, ix. 3, xi. c. 5 ; Ibrahim-ibn-Jakub [Jacob, *Ein arabischer Berichterstatter aus dem 10 Jahrhundert*, and *Arabischen Geographen*, ii.]; Jaffé, *Bibliotheca*, iii. 170 ; Widukind, ii. 20 ; Adam. Brem., ii. 19, iii. 21, iv. 18 ; Helmoldi, *Chron. Slav.* i. 82, 83, and *passim* ; Thietmar, vi. 17, 18, 24, 25 ; Krek, *Einleitung in die Slavische Literaturgeschichte*, pp. 246-473 ; Hauck, *Kirchengeschichte Deutschlands*, iii. pp. 69-86 ; Schulze, *Die Kolonisierung*, pp. 19-43, 86-116.

lization, because it was the military rule of a foreign
and energetic people, unprotected by natural frontiers,
and established in a conquered Slavonic land.   At the
outset it seemed likely that this would be the issue.
Henry the Fowler made his reputation in the Slavonic
wars.   He conquered Brandenburg, the capital of the
Hevellians, beat the Danes and Wends, and cleared
the whole line of the Elbe.   Otto I., aided by
two vigorous subordinates, Hermann Billing and Margrave Gero, continued this work, three times invading
the Slavonic territory—in 936, 939, and 955—and
forcing all the tribes from the Elbe to the Oder
to acknowledge his suzerainty.   Even the Duke of
Poland bowed down before him.   In Nordalbingia the
effects of the Ottonian peace made a deep impression.
The provinces of Wagria and Schlesvig began to be
covered with monasteries, villages, and towns, and
the Holsatian archaeologist of the twelfth century
found among his native forests, in the lines of furrows,
the embankments of streams, and the outlines of fortified places, signs of the activity of the Saxon colonists
two centuries earlier.[1]   The See of Magdeburg was
raised to archiepiscopal rank, in order that the boundaries of the Christian faith might be extended and the
untamed Slavonic races between the Elbe and the
Saale subdued to the Christian yoke.[2]   Six new bishoprics were founded—Oldenburg, Havelburg, Brandenburg,
Merseburg, Zeitz and Meissen—to co-operate towards
the same end.   The first archbishop of Magdeburg is
nominated to be " Archbishop and Metropolitan of the
whole race of the Slaves beyond the Elbe which has
either been already converted or which remains to be
converted to God."[3]   A Papal Bull enjoins upon him to

[1] Helmold, i. 13.   [2] Leibnitz, iii. 234.   [3] *Diplom. Otto.*, 366 ; Stumpf, 460

carve out the sees of his bishops in the trans-Elbine lands in conjunction with Otto, according as expediency may direct, and gives to him the right of consecrating the bishops of this region."[1] The archbishop is in fact to be the great ecclesiastical margrave over the six military marches which Otto set up on the north and north-east after Gero's death in 965.

The death of the valiant Margrave Gero marks an epoch in the history of these regions. Until Albert the Bear in 1134 received the Nordmark from the Emperor Lothair, there was not a stoppage of progress, there was actual retrogression. The margraves of the north-east seemed to have been for a hundred and seventy-nine years small, avaricious, and quarrelsome men. The emperors were chiefly occupied in Italy, and then with the Saxon Revolt and the War of the Investitures. The Saxon dukes were jealous of the great churchmen, and there was neither unity nor direction in attack or defence. The effects of the Italian wars were immediately felt.[2] After the defeat of Otto II. in South Italy in 983, there was a general explosion of revolt along the Saxon border. The Danes burst in from the north, destroyed Stade, one of the most convenient Saxon ports on the Lower Elbe, and burnt Oldenburg as Duke Bernhard of Saxony was wending his way to Verona. The Wiltzes, exasperated by the tyrannical government of Count Dietrich of the Nordmark, cast off Christianity, slaughter the garrison, and destroy the churches and towns of Havelburg and

---

[1] *Cod. Dipl. Sax.*, i. 1, 248 ; Jaffé, 3731 ; Hauck, *Kirchengeschichte*, pp. 109-132.

[2] Helmold, i. 15, " Eo quod . . . medius quoque necnon et tertius Otto bellis Italicis essent occupati, et ob hanc causam Sclavi temporis opportunitate freti non solum divinis legibus, sed et imperatoriis jussis cepissent paulatim obniti."

Brandenburg. A Bohemian force captures and plunders the Church of Zeitz, and levels the Monastery of St. Laurence in Kalbe to the ground. The **Abodrites** burn and devastate Hamburg, and German Christianity is rolled back again to the Elbe frontier, and almost half the province of the Archbishop of Magdeburg relapses into heathendom.

Henceforward the Saxons stand on the defensive. The Slaves and the Northmen plunder and ravage the land. The whole line of the Elbe with all the boats is in the hands of the heathen, whose inroads pierce almost to Hildesheim, so that Bishop Bernward has to build a fortress at the confluence of the Ocker and the Aller to repel the invader. Five campaigns, accompanied or directed by Otto III., are fruitless of any permanent result, and the policy of an alliance with Mesco of Poland leads to nothing but the recapture of Brandenburg. Henry II., Otto's successor, was a man of resource, full of energy, penetrated by the ecclesiastical ideas of his time, alive to the importance of Christianizing the Slave. He founds the Bishopric of Bamberg with a view to converting the Slaves of the Main. He marches an army now as far as Posen, now as far as Glogau. But the problem in his day is somewhat changed, for the real danger now was not so much the Wiltzes or the Abodrites as Poland. Here Bolislav Chabri had built up one of those ephemeral monarchies, which are so easily constructed and so easily dissolved in a great plain peopled by barbarians. His conquests stretched from the golden gates of Kiev to the waters of the Saale; his horsemen overran the March of Meissen. The Slaves of the Middle Elbe trembled before him. The situation was critical, and Henry even turned to his old enemies the Wiltzes, and played them against the Polish peril. He also detached Bohemia from Bolislav, and in 1013 obtained from the Polish king the recognition of German suzerainty. But the German border was not advanced eastward, and in Nordalbingia every trace of Christianity was extirpated. The cruelty and avarice of the German nobles, who wrung the utmost farthing from the miserable Slaves; the ill-judged imposition of tithe upon the half-converted heathen by Otto I.; an insulting word addressed by Margrave Dietrich to the Prince of the Winules, who asked the niece of Duke Bernhard of Saxony in marriage, and was told that the relation of a Saxon could not be wedded to a dog; the rebellion of Duke Bernhard himself against Henry, seem to have been the causes or occasions of the catastrophe.

The Franconian emperors were assailed by new dangers—the rise of the Lombard republics, the settlement of the Normans in southern Italy, the Saxon revolt, the ecclesiastical opposition. Their policy in these quarters was not calculated to secure any permanent advance. The main concern of Conrad II. and of Henry III. seems to have been to extract the recognition of imperial suzerainty from Poland, Bohemia, and Hungary, and to maintain a balance of power between the three eastern rulers. The main concern of Henry IV. was to obtain Slavonic aid against the revolting Saxons. The main concern of Henry V. was to recover the Saxon base of the earlier monarchy. The first policy was showy but futile, the second was treacherous, the third resulted in complete failure. The story of the Slavonic border throughout this period is one dreary tale of burning and hanging and slaying punctuated by great massacres, such as the annihilation of a German army at the confluence of the Havel and the Elbe in

1056, and the Slavonian disaster, or *Clades Slavonica*, ten years later, which ruined the whole province of Hamburg, and forced six hundred Holsatian families to cross the Elbe and emigrate to the Harz Mountains.

Yet far eastwards by the upper waters of the Elbe, in the bishoprics of Zeitz and of Meissen, the Sorbs had quietly accepted Christianity. If the same result was not achieved among the Abodrites and the Wiltzes, the cause is not to be found in the greater religious tenacity of these tribes. If the evidence of Thietmar and other contemporary German observers can be trusted, the Slave had lost confidence in his own deities, and perhaps, with the single exception of the inhabitants of Rügen, there was no single tribe which, if Christianity had been intelligently and mercifully offered it, would not have gladly burnt its wooden images and groves. The condition of the Slavonic population indeed seems to have been so miserable that they would have been willing to exchange it for even the most modest share of well-being. The settlements were sparse and isolated, the poorer people enslaved by a brutal and contemptuous nobility, and though the absence of a Slavonic monarchy made wholesale conversion impossible, the task which lay before the German missionaries was by no means desperate. But there was a tradition of war between Slaves and Germans (which certainly must have been intensified by the brutalities of the first two Saxon kings), such as to exclude every vestige of honour or mansuetude. " With the innate pride of Teutons," as Cosmas of Prague tells us, " the Germans always despised the Slaves and their tongue." [1] The Bishops of Hamburg and Bremen preferred the distant but more

[1] Cosmas, *Chron.* i. 40, SS. ix., p. 62.

honourable prospect of founding a patriarchate over the Scandinavian countries of the north to the humbler but more feasible task which lay at their doors, and although here and there a missionary acquired the Slavonic tongue, a long series of inhuman outrages impeded the work of conversion.   If there be any truth in Frederick Nietzche's view that most of the distinguished men in Germany have had Slavonic blood in their veins, the country has paid heavily for the barbarity of the Middle Ages, which stamped out of existence an artistic and impressionable people in Holstein, Brandenburg, and East Prussia.

It was left to the Saxon emperor Lothair, "the imitator and heir of the first Otto,"[1] once more to advance the cause of Christian civilization in these regions.   No emperor since the death of Henry II. had been so clearly marked out to achieve success in this direction.[2]   He had been a powerful Saxon duke before he became king, and as Duke of Saxony he had distinguished himself on more than one occasion in the Wendish wars.   A man of simple piety, he owed his elevation to the throne to Church influence, and was fortunate enough to preserve the friendship of the German Church and of the Papacy throughout his reign. The conquests of Bolislav III. of Poland about 1125 had broken up a confederacy of the Wiltzes, and the conversion of Pomerania was due to the assistance of the Polish duke.   The Concordat of Worms had brought a welcome though temporary solution of the ecclesiastical dispute, and at the same time events had taken a

---

[1] *Ann. Pallid.*, 1125, SS. xvi. 77.

[2] Helmold, i. 41, "Cepitque in diebus Lotharii Caesaris oriri nova lux non tam in Saxonie finibus quam in universo regno, tranquillitas temporum, habundantia rerum, pax inter regnum et sacerdotium."

favourable turn in Nordalbingia. In 1093 Henry, the son of Gottshalk, effected an entry into the country, treacherously murdered its heathen ruler, married his widow, and obtained possession of his principality. The new prince set to work to continue his father's policy. He made alliances with the Saxons, and in conjunction with Duke Magnus won a victory over the northern and eastern Slaves; reduced them to slavery; rooted out robbers from the land; encouraged agricultural labour; rebuilt houses and churches; gave the Saxon missionary Vicelin a church in Lübeck and attracted a large colony of merchants to the town; destroyed the power of the most warlike of Slavonic races, the Rani of Rügen; exacted tribute from all the peoples subject to them right up to the border of Poland; did, in fact, more for the civilization of those parts than anyone had done since the time of Otto I. In all this work he is vigorously aided by Christian missionaries, by Otto of Bamberg, Norbert of Magdeburg, and Vicelin. The chroniclers are struck with the revival of missionary interest.[1] It seemed as if the good days of Otto I. had returned. Norbert of Magdeburg, who is the close friend and constant companion of the emperor, resumes the buildings which had been left unfinished since Otto's death.[2] The heathen fortress of Rethra is destroyed; a timely campaign in 1131 reduces Magnus of Denmark to submission, and the Wendish princes of Nordalbingia, Nicklot, and Pribislaw. In 1134 the emperor meets Vicelin, the apostle of the Wends, at Luneburg, and, in compliance with his request, builds and garrisons the fortress of Siegeberg, together with

[1] Helmold, i., 54, "Factumque est misericordia Dei et virtute Lotharii Caesaris seminarium novellae plantationis in Sclavia."
[2] *Gesta Arch. Magd.*, SS. xiv. 414.

a monastery hard by, in order to guarantee the security of the mission.   In the same year he gives the Nordmark to Albert the Bear.   In 1137 he makes peace with Bolislav III. of Poland, who does homage for Pomerania and Rügen, and who had for many years paved the way for German expansion in the east by his victories over the Slaves of the Middle Elbe.   Yet we must not exaggerate the effects of the imperial authority in Nordalbingia.   On the death of the Abodrite Henry, Lothair handed over his kingdom to a Danish fugitive, Cnut, who not only aroused the jealousy of the Saxon court, but revived all those oppressions which had made alien rule so hateful among the Slaves.   Another effect of this unfortunate step was to involve the whole province of Nordalbingia in the fratricidal broils which form for so long a period the most important strand in Danish history.   And it is worth noting that the final conquest of this region was achieved not by the emperor but by Henry the Lion, Duke of Saxony.

After the death of Lothair the emperors do little or nothing in these Wendish parts.   The work of conquest and colonization falls from the hands of the Hohenstauffen into the hands of the clergy and nobility.   While Conrad III. is on crusade and Frederick Barbarossa fights in Lombardy, the Saxon nobles and clerks slowly but surely penetrate into the vast inheritance, which the emperors have tasted only to abandon.   For a time progress is slow.   It is delayed partly by lack of religious zeal, partly by the absorption of the leading nobles in German and in imperial politics.   The Wendish crusade of 1147 results in three ineffectual sieges, a few baptisms, and an inglorious retirement.   Albert the Bear, the founder of the March of Brandenburg, is too busy with his claims upon the

Saxon duchy to do much against the Wends. The smaller Saxon nobles anxiously watch the career of Henry the Lion, conspire against him, and finally, in 1180, effect his exile and the partition of his duchy. Still the foundations of a more permanent settlement of the North are laid in the twelfth century. In 1106 six Hollanders from the diocese of Utrecht came to Archbishop Frederick of Bremen, and petitioned for leave to settle upon the unoccupied marsh on the north of the city. The compact between the archbishop and the new settlers marks an epoch in the agrarian history of North Germany. The Hollanders were to retain their old laws and customs, and to settle their own disputes, upon payment of two marks a year from every hundred manses. They paid a mark yearly as rent from each manse, and corn, sheep, pigs, goats, geese, and honey were tithed.[1] The terms were favourable, and were substantially repeated in many subsequent contracts by which Hollanders and Flemings, Frisians and Brabanters were settled upon waste places. The immigration of these new settlers, accustomed to cope with flood and marsh, and practised in the ploughing of heavy soils, made the effective colonization of the East a possibility. The Slaves with their light ploughs had merely scratched the most worthless soils, but the strong ploughshare of the Hollander first revealed the agricultural possibilities of the heavy soils in the great North-German plain.[2]

---

[1] The contract is reprinted from the *Bremisches Urkunbenbuch* in Meitzen, *Siedelung und Agrarwesen*, ii., pp. 344, 5. For a map of a Dutch settlement, cf. the plan of Siebenhofen near Stade in Meitzen, i. 48. Meitzen's beautiful series of maps are the best commentaries upon the expansion of Germany.

[2] For the work of the Flemings, Schulze, *Die Kolonisierung*, pp. 129, 130, where full bibliographical indications are given. A charming Flemish

If the influx of the Flemish and Hollander colonists is one cause of the German acquisitions in the twelfth century, the introduction of the Cistercian Order is another.[1] Marsh and forest were the elements with which these Cistercian houses chose to surround themselves, and in which they preferred to work. The Christianization of Mecklenburg is effected by a Cistercian monastery founded about 1170 in the Wendish village of Doberan. In Pomerania the Danish monastery of Eldina is founded in 1199 on the Hilda, attracts colonists from Westphalia and the Rhine, the Netherlands and Friesland, and with their aid reclaims six square miles of waste. The monastery of Leubus, northwest of Breslau, founded in 1175, and protected by Duke Bolislav I. and his son Henry the Bearded, germanizes Silesia. A brother of the Order, writing at the beginning of the fourteenth century, describes in detestable verse the condition of the country on the first arrival of the Cistercians.[2] A land of forest, inhabited by poor and lazy Poles, who, with a wooden plough

---

emigrant song is printed by Willems, *Oude Vlämische Liederen*, p. 25. The first stanza runs :

> " Naer Oostland willen wy riden,
> Naer Oostland willen wy mêe,
> Al over die groene heiden
> Daer isser een betere stêe."

[1] For the work of the Cistercians, cf. Michael, *Geschichte des deutschen Volkes*, pp. 91-120, where full references are given.

[2] *Monumenta Lubensia*, ed. Wattenbach, p. 15 ; cf. Michael, p, 100.

> " Nam sine cultore tellus jacuit nemorosa,
> Et genus Polonie pauper fuit, haut operosa,
> Sulcans in sabulo lignis uncis sine ferro
> Et vaccis bobus nisi scivit arare duobus.
> Civitas aut opidum per terram non fuit ullum
> Sed prope castra fora campestria, broca, capella,
> Non sal, non ferrum, numismata nonque metallum
> Non indumenta bona sed neque calciamenta
> Plebs habuit ulla, pascebat sola jumenta."

drawn by two cows or oxen, lightly stir the sand.
Nowhere a town ; markets held in the open air by a
castle or a chapel.   The inhabitants without salt, or
iron, or coins, or metal-work, or shoes ; pitiably clothed.

The House of Leubus attracts colonists from Flanders
and Eastphalia, from Hesse and Thuringia, settles them
down on the land under favourable terms, and in thirty-
five years [1204-39] cultivates at least a hundred and
sixty thousand acres, and either founds or converts into
German colonies some sixty-five villages.

The nobles too take an active part in this work of
exploitation.   Watch the career of Adolph of Schauen-
berg, Count of Holstein, who sends to Flanders, Holland,
Westphalia and Frisia in search of poor colonists to till
the rich but desolate soil of his war-worn province, who
builds Lübeck, induces the Abodrite nobles to do him
homage and to cede estates to his colonists.   He has
struck out the way, which the Slavonic Prince Henry
had been the first to demonstrate, of harmonizing the
two races in the work of colonizing a half empty land.

Unfortunately the crusade of 1147—useless, impolitic, and cruel—spoils his plans.   Niclot, King of
the Abodrites, who was prepared to be Adolph's " eye
and ear in the land of the Slaves," rallied his race in
defence of their liberties and existence.   On June 26,
1147, a Slavonic fleet surprised Lübeck, slew more than
three hundred of its inhabitants, and discharged a band
of raiders into the country, who burnt down all the
Westphalian and foreign colonies beyond the Trave.
It was left to Adolph to attempt to repair the ravages
which the inconsiderate and unsuccessful crusade had
been the means of causing, to patch up again the alliance
with Niclot and the eastern Slaves, to redeem captives,
to repel the Danes, to tame the rude Holsatians, who, like

the Greeks of old, considered thieving a form of virtue. By 1150 the damage was repaired, the alliance with Niclot renewed. The navy of Lübeck rapidly increased. A Saxon colony was planted at Oldenburg. The castle of Plön was rebuilt, and a town and market attached to it. By degrees, says Helmold, the Slaves departed from the land. In 1164 this vigorous Saxon died in battle, coping with the last Slavonic rising in the land of the Abodrites. "When his good journey was done he obtained the palm, and bearing the standard in the camp of the Lord, he stood for the defence of his country and loyal adherence to the princes. Instigated by his example, his good and illustrious comrades, Guncelin, Count of Schwerin, and Bernhard, Count of Ratzeburg, did also good work fighting the battles of the Lord, that the worship of the house of God might be raised up in an incredulous and idolatrous race."[1]

A still greater figure is Henry the Lion, Duke of Saxony from 1139 to 1195.[2] He had moved in the large world of imperial politics, knew the great trading towns of South Germany and Italy, introduced some of the Italian machinery of war into his northern duchy. He was the first of the Saxon dukes who realized the immense revenue which might be gained from the encouragement of commerce, and he had the strategical eye of the commercial pioneer. From the beginning he saw the importance of Lübeck, and he never rested till he had wrung the island and the port from Adolph of Holstein. Then at once he sent envoys to Denmark, Sweden, Norway and Russia, offering freedom of traffic with the city, formed a mint, established an octroi, and guaranteed the town most ample privileges. The brilliant fortunes of Lübeck, with its colonies in Livonia

---

[1] Helmold, ii. 5. [2] Cf. Helmold and Arnold of Lübeck.

and Curland, its control of the Baltic trade, date from its second creation in 1158 by Henry the Lion, and there is another respect, too, in which Henry the Lion's tenure of the Saxon duchy marks an epoch. A fairly large though steadily diminishing Slavonic population under its own chieftain Niclot still remained among the German Holsatians and Dithmarschers in Nordalbingia. Owing to the policy of Count Adolph and the moderation and wisdom of Niclot these Slaves had ceased to present any formidable dangers. They were on their way to become Christianized; the worst customs of the race, such as punishment by crucifixion, were in process of disappearing; and there seems little doubt that the two races, if left to themselves, would have quietly fused together. But Henry the Lion was not a man to wait upon a process. In 1160 he devastated Nordalbingia with fire and sword, and divided the land of the Abodrites among his knights. The country was soon studded with German garrisons, and the population further recruited with Flemish settlers. The duke created the county of Ratzeburg, and obtained from the Archbishop of Bremen the investiture of the county of Stade. The three sees of Oldenburg, Ratzeburg and Mecklenburg were provided with bishops who received their investiture from the duke, and the efficiency of the churches was guaranteed by the payment of tithes—a burden which was borne alike by the surviving Slaves and the incoming Germans. The conquest then of Nordalbingia was definitely achieved by Henry the Lion, and it was not without significance that the stone lion before the palace at Brunswick was turned with its face towards the east. The northern danger appeared to be overpast. It was the east which beckoned to the German warrior and colonist.

East of Ratzeburg and north of the Elbe Henry founded the county of Swerin, deriving the name of the new area from the old capital of the Abodrite princes. Diplomacy too came to the aid of his arms. He gave his daughter Matilda in marriage to Henry Borwin, the Slavonic prince of Mecklenburg, and thus founded the half-German, half-Slave dynasty which rules in Mecklen burg to this day. The Slavonic dukes of Pomerania, who had conquered the eastern portions of the present March of Brandenburg, were forced to acknowledge his suzerainty. He joined hands with Waldemar of Den mark to sweep the Slavonic pirate from the Baltic, and he made the islands of the northern sea for the first time habitable. His name was a terror to the Slaves from the mouths of the Elbe to the furthest corner of Pomer-ania, and he was able to use them as the pawn upon a chess-board, moving them now against Saxon nobles, now against the Rugians, now against the pirates of Denmark. When Waldemar the Dane fitted out an expedition to the island of Rügen to destroy that famous seat of piracy and religion, Henry ordered his Slavonic subjects to help the Dane. The image of the oracular god of the Slavonic nations was trailed on the ground in the sight of its worshippers; the fane was plundered and destroyed, and twelve Christian churches were erected in the holy island, which was shared between Waldemar and Henry. So did the Baltic Slaves lose their religious centre. The last strong-hold of the old beliefs was utterly broken. The whole region from Egdor to Swerin was made a Saxon colony.

Such a figure as Henry's had not been seen in North Germany since Otto the Great. He was rapacious, jealous, and domineering, but he had the qualities of a master of men. A word from him spoken to the subject

Slavonic princes is sufficient to loose such a storm of pirates upon Denmark as shall force the Danish king to do his bidding.   Another word will seal up the river mouths, and not a Slavonic craft will infest the sea. He marries the daughter of Henry II. of England ; his own daughter is asked in marriage by the king of the Danes ; he receives an embassy from Byzantium at his court at Brunswick.   His private wealth was enormous, and excited a jealousy which proved fatal to him. Besides the properties which came to him from his ancestors, the Billungs, Nordheimers, Lothair, and Richinza, he absorbed the property and the commerce of his nobility with restless and imperious greed.   Learning that his own market at Bardwick was suffering from the competition of Adolph's port at Lübeck, and that his salt springs at Luneburg were inferior to those possessed by the Count Thodulo, he offered a choice of alternatives. Either the count must cede half Lübeck and the salt-works to the duke, or the duke will prohibit merchants from frequenting Lübeck.   The count refused to accede to these monstrous conditions, and Henry stopped the Lübeck market, ordered the merchandise to be transferred to Bardwick, and closed up the salt springs of his rival.   What wonder that he was hated as well as feared!   "He was the prince of the princes of the land. He crushed the necks of the rebels, and broke their fortresses, and made peace in the land, and had too great a heritage."[1]   Yet even his adversaries reluctantly admit his greatness.   "Henry the Lion, Albert the Bear, Frederick Barbarossa were three men capable of converting the world."

Albert the Bear and Henry the Lion and Wichmann, Archbishop of Magdeburg, the friend and counsellor of

[1] Helmold, ii. 6.

Barbarossa, were the last of the colonizing nobles of the North who took an active part in imperial politics.[1] If it had not been for a lucky accident—the conversion of Pribislav of Bohemia to Christianity and his nomination of Albert as his heir—the Ascanian Margrave of the Nordmark would hardly have been able to triple the area of his domains.[2] But the empire gradually lost its hold upon the energies and the imagination of the Germans of the north. The Margraves of Brandenburg were the chamberlains of the empire, and one of them, Otto III., even aspired to the imperial crown in 1256. But their policy was naturally governed by local rather than imperial interests. In the great struggle which succeeded the death of Henry VI. there are neither consistent Welfs nor consistent Wibelings. It is more important for them to know upon which side the Archbishop of Magdeburg or the King of Denmark may be, in order that they may choose the other, for these are their real adversaries, the one cleaving their territories in two, the other threatening their northern frontiers. Yet after all the empire is a shadow which it is always useful upon occasion to invoke. Again and again, out of the confusion of the north, voices come to the great Sicilian ruler who is battling in Italy, and who, if he cannot give effective help, can at any rate dispense charters. In 1235 Frederick II. confirms to the Margraves of Brandenburg, "out of his superabundant grace," the Duchy of Pomerania, a gift which the margraves are not slow to utilize. Lübeck, Goslar, Ratzeburg receive imperial privileges,

---

[1] For Wichmann's colonizing activity, cf. Lavisse, *La Marche de Brande-bourg*, p. 105.

[2] The House of Albert the Bear is called the Ascanian house, from the Castle of Aschersleben, which was latinized into Ascaria, and then corrupted into Ascania.

for the great ambition of a rising city is to become a
free town, under the direct protection of the emperor,
and liberated from feudal interference.   Even the
knights of the sword who are fighting pagans far away
in Livonia and Curland ask and obtain the "protection
and defence of the empire."   Even Hermann of Salza,
the Grandmaster of the Knights of the Teutonic Order
receives from Frederick II. permission to conquer the
heathen country of Prussia.[1]   The work of colonization
proceeded more rapidly than before.   The March of
Brandenburg was nearly doubled between 1170 and
1267.   In 1231 the long struggle between the German
knights and the Prussians began, which resulted in
making the Teutonic Order one of the powers of
Europe.   Between 1231 and 1233 Thorn, Kulm, and
Marienwerder were founded.   By 1283 the Prussians
are cowed, and these hard, rapacious, but valorous and
keen-sighted Germans rule supreme from the great
bend of the Vistula to the further shore of the Lower
Niemen.

The men who did these things were not diverted by
Italian wars and far-reaching diplomatic combinations.
The "great deed of the German people in the Middle
Ages,"[2] the conquest of three-fifths of modern Germany
from the Slaves, was not the work of the emperors
From 965 to 1134, a period of 179 years, hardly an
inch was gained in the north and north-east.   The
Saxon   wars   paralyzed   advance,   the   Italian   wars
diverted ambition, the ecclesiastical struggle perplexed
the motives of men.   The crown passed to a Middle-
German and then to a South-German dynasty.   From

[1] *H.B.*, ii. 549-52 ; iv. 940-1 ; ii. 768, 577, 625 ; i. 643 ; iv. 821 ; and
Lavisse, *La Marche de Brandebourg*, p. 152.
[2] Lamprecht, *Deutsche Geschichte*, iii. 349.

the beginning of the twelfth century Saxony, the
natural basis for a forward policy in the east, is prae-
tically what Gregory VII. hoped it might become, "a
regnum Saxonicum"; it is no longer the citadel of the
empire, but an outwork held by a jealous and more
than half-independent garrison.   The Hohenstauffen
try to recover their losses in Swabia and in Italy.
By a kind of tacit compact Frederick I. leaves Henry
the Lion to govern the north.   What South-German
knight, with the pride of race and the imperial idea
working in him, would abandon all the glories of Italy
to waste his prowess upon squalid Poles and Prussians,
in a dreary plain and under an inclement sky?   Frederick Barbarossa and his descendants conceived that
their duties lay elsewhere.   It was easy to grant
charters to Livonian and Prussian knights, as easy as
to send the Union Jack to an African chief.   Nothing
came of it.   The Teutonic Order regarded itself as
holding of the Papacy.   The Margraves of Brandenburg
went the way of the wind when it began to belly
the sails of Innocent IV., and they took care to make
their profit out of the weak and distracted empire of
William of Holland.   They might well have argued
that Frederick II. had sacrificed Germany to ambition
when he surrendered Nordalbingia to the powerful
Danish monarch in 1214, had they not themselves
subsequently espoused his cause.   Sensible men must
have understood that the empire was powerless in these
regions, and the decisive proof came in 1241.   The
Mongols who had ravaged Russia and sacked Kiev,
marched into the Polish and Hungarian gateways,
and all Europe was aghast at the hideous portent.
The Imperial Chancery wrote ream upon ream of
protestation, passionately, eloquently, with all its

southern exuberance of phrase ; the emperor sent brief and soldier-like rules for meeting the invaders, and it is possible that some horsemen, spared from the fevered struggle of Italian politics, rode up to check the foe upon the Danube. But the emperor, remembering how when he was away in Palestine the Pope had treacherously invaded his dominions, dared not leave Italy to his enemies. The Polish chivalry, fleshing their knightly swords in this their first achievement for Latin Christianity, helped to save the north from the Tartars but the days of Otto the Great were long gone by, and the emperor, excommunicated and deeply involved in Italian warfare, was not at hand to lead the hosts of Germany in the hour of her greatest peril.[1]

[1] *H.B.*, v., pp. 1139, 1143, 1148, 1215. The statement of Matthew Paris, *ed. Luard.*, iv., p. 131, that Enzio was sent from Italy with 4000 horse to join Conrad in Hungary, though accepted by Cherrier, *La lutte de la Papauté et les Empereurs de la maison de Souabe*, is elsewhere unsupported, is rejected by Wolff, and seems to me on many grounds to be suspicious. Cf. Howorth, *History of the Mongols*, ii., p. 55.

CHAPTER IX.

THE EXPANSION OF GERMANY IN THE SOUTH-EAST.

THE progress of German colonization in the south-east is almost wholly connected during this period with the fortunes of a single family, the Babenbergers. Geographical causes serve to explain why the history of this region is more simple and more continuous than the history of the north-east. The valley of the Danube piercing through difficult forest-clad hill country provided a solitary but a narrow outlet into the plains of Hungary. There was no large frontier to defend ; flank attacks from Bohemia were rendered infrequent by a screen of forest and mountain, and no Magyar forces cared to push through the Styrian highlands of the south. The German met his foeman face to face, and geography forbade a dispersion of his energies. Thus it is that a single family posted in a confined strategical position is enabled to dominate the politics of the Middle Danube for two hundred and seventy years. It is not necessary to enter into the elaborate archaeological discussions which centre round the origin of the Babenbergers. Two modern authors derive them from Bavaria, others from Swabia, others from Franconia.[1] The fact

[1] Otto of Freising, *Chron.*, vi. 15 ; *F.D.G.*, xii., pp. 113-36 ; *Mitt. d. Inst. Oest. Gesch.*, vi., pp. 385-88 ; Riezler, *Gesch. Baierns*, i., 360 ; Stein, *Gesch. Frankens*, i., p. 107. 11 ; ii., pp. 299. 3, 301 ; Schmitz, *Osterreichs Scheyern*

is that in the Middle Ages there was little knowledge professed upon this subject. The Babenbergers have no good biographer or family historian. A short history of the first Babenbergers written in Melk in the second half of the twelfth century, a short biography of Margrave Henry, a history of Leopold III. and his children written in Kloster Neuburg, a few jejune monastic annals make up the tale of literary evidence. The historian of Melk, the ducal monastery, writing a history of the dynasty by special ducal request reveals little but his own entire ignorance. The best writers fly at higher game—the ecclesiastical struggle or the crusades. The only author of real talent who might be expected to have special knowledge, Otto of Freising, tells us little even of his own family. He has been educated in Paris in the latest philosophic mode ; he has joined the Cistercians after the last religious fashion, he frequents the court and the camp of Barbarossa, he moves in the brilliant whirl of imperial politics. Of the inner history of the march he is ostentatiously careless. What can be the human interest of obscure strivings with marshes and backwoods, and Slaves and Magyars ? He has left us to conjecture the real history of the Austrian land from charters and laws or the manifest tokens of achieved progress.[1]

Yet this Babenberg family laid the foundations of the modern Austrian empire. It is possible from the charters to trace the steps by which the Babenbergs slowly carved themselves a way down the valley of the Danube. At first the capital of the margraves is at Pechlarn ; then,

Wittelsbacher oder die Dynastie der Babenberger ; Juritsch, *Geschichte der Babenberger*, p. 13.

[2] Redlich, " Die Osterreichische Annalistik bis zum Ausgang des dreizehnten Jahrhunderts" (*Mitt. d. Inst. Oest. Gesch.*, vol. iii., pp. 497-538). The chronicles are printed SS., vol. ix., pp. 474-843 ; vol. xxiv., pp. 69-71.

under Henry I., it is at Melk ; later we find it at Tulln ;
finally, under Leopold IV., it is at Vienna. We can
also trace, though more obscurely, the steps by which
the great Bohemian forest, the north wood or Riedmarch, was penetrated by German settlers, who made
their clearings and built their villages along the northern
bank of the Danube.[1] Before the dynasty died out in
the middle of the thirteenth century, how great a change
had come over the land ! Vienna was a large and
thriving city, second only, it was said, to Cologne. The
Russian trade passed up and down the Danube, bringing
grist to the custom officers of the duke. The men of
Venice brought the spices of the east, the men of
Bremen the herrings of the Baltic to the mart of
Vienna. The Regensburg traders in the march were so
important a body that they were protected by special
privileges. The Jews, led by their keen business instinct, had settled in great numbers in the land, and
were said even to exercise an influence over ducal policy.
They too, like the Regensburgers, were safeguarded by
special legal provisions in the town law of Vienna.
Literature too had begun to make itself heard. One of
the fathers of South-German poetry sang to his viol in
the brilliant ducal court at Vienna, and the praises of
that city are celebrated by the much-travelled Walther
von der Vogelweide, the least insipid of the Minnesingers.

In 976 a certain Leopold, count in the Donnegau,
brother of Bertold, who already, under Otto I., had
been named count in the Nordgau, is found described
as Marchio, that is to say, as Marquis of the Ost-mark.
This mark, first in 996 named Osterrichi or Austria,

---

[1] There is a valuable series of antiquarian maps of the Riedmarch, the
Ostmarch and Machland in Hasenöhrl's excellent article, " Deutschland's
Südöstlice Marken in 10, 11 und 12 Jahrhundert " (*Archiv. f. Oest.
Geschichte*, vol. 82, p. 419).

stretched from the Inn and the great Rodel [north-west of Linz] to St. Polten on the Traise and to Spitz on the Wachau. Its eastern border lay somewhere between Melk and Mautern, so that the whole march west to east would not have measured more than sixty miles.

Of this first margrave, who died at Wurzburg one July morning in 994 of an arrow wound while playing with his knights after matins, we know but little. "None more prudent," says the chronicler, "or better in all his actions did he leave behind him "[1] He must have borne himself well in many nameless struggles with the Hungarians and in the rough battle of the agricultural settlement, for as late as 985 the diocese of Passau is described as a solitude, so destitute of serfs that the freemen had to turn villeins in the places belonging to the ecclesiastical patrimony.[2] Under his guidance the Germans pushed on to the Viennese forest, and partially settled it; the Church of Passau began to lift up her head, to claim the devastated monasteries of St. Florian, of Kremsmünster, of St. Polten, to acquire imperial confirmation of her pious forgeries.[3] Between 983 and 991 the Duke of Bavaria held an assembly of the bishops, counts, and inhabitants of the march to determine the claims of the Church and of individuals on the newly acquired lands, and to settle the payments which were to be made by the families of bishops and abbots to the margraves. At this assembly the places which belonged to the See of Passau were determined and enumerated. They were found to stretch right up to the Viennese forest.[4] It

[1] Thietmar, iv. 14.   [2] Meiller, *Regesten*, p. 1, No. 3.

[3] In 991 when Pilgrim of Passau died the land between the Enns and the forest appears to have been partially recovered.

[4] Meiller, *Regesten*, p. 2, No. 4.

is ample evidence that the first Babenberg margrave had not been idle.

We know nothing of the second margrave, Henry I. [998-1018]. It is only possible to catch from the charters of his time some indications of German colonization. We find that the great ecclesiastical foundations are recovering or acquiring possessions in the march, possessions which, with the singular tenacity of pious foundations, they managed to preserve into the present century.[1] Now, too, for the first time, German squatters are settling on the eastern border of the Viennese forest, the greatest part of which, a territory some eighteen miles square, is granted to the margrave, and is destined to be the source from which in after days the abbeys of the Holy Cross and Maria Zell were so richly endowed.

But the advance of the Germans was slow and difficult. Vienna was built only to be recaptured by the Hungarians.[2] Under Margrave Adalbert [1018-1055], an imperial army led by Conrad II. was forced to retreat ; a tract of land on the eastern border was restored to Hungary, and a period of confused and active struggle began which has left a splendid imprint upon the greatest of the Medieval German Epics. From 1038 to 1077 Hungary was torn by the dissensions of rival competitors to the throne, one of whom was supported by the native aristocracy, and the other by the German king. Again and again German lines cross the frontier, and turn back baffled by marsh and forest and the difficulties of commissariat. Only a few scraps of authentic history survive to us

---

[1] Thus Freising acquires Ulmerfeld on the Ips in 996, which it retains till 1802. Thus too Tegernsee acquires in 1002 Unter Loiben [between Stein and Durrenstein], which it retains till 1806. Meiller, *Regesten*, p. 2, No. 2 ; and p. 191, No. 7 ; p. 3, No. 6 ; and pp. 192-3, No. 14.

[2] *Ann. Alt.*, 1030 ; SS. xx. 791.

concerning the margraves of this time, but these are illustrative of their gallantry and devotion. Both Adalbert and his son Ernest [1067-74] are closely connected by ties of friendship and common perils with the emperors of the Salian house. The charters tell us how Henry III. loaded Adalbert with gifts of land to reward his service and fidelity, how Henry IV. describes Ernest as "our knight," and gives him as a reward for true service land amounting to forty manses in the forest of the Raab.[1] The Hungarian wars of the eleventh century in every way fortified the position of the Babenberg house. In 1043 the land between the Leitha and the march, which had been won from the Germans by King Stephen, was restored to them by King Ava, and twenty years later the freshly ceded territory became incorporated in the east march. The wars too had the effect of bringing the margraves into close connection with the monarchy, of stimulating the stream of royal benevolence to the Babenberg house, and of founding that tradition of loyalty which was one of the secrets of its strength. Margrave Ernest—"The most illustrious man in the realm, and renowned for many victories against the Hungarians"[2]—remains true to the imperial side during the War of the Investitures, and dies loyally at the battle of Hohenburg [June 9, 1075], fighting in the second division with the Bavarians under Duke Welf.

Margrave Leopold II. [1075-1096] at first follows his father's example; he is loyal to Henry; Henry is generous to him. But the storms of the great ecclesi astical struggle sweep fiercely through Southern Germany. A noble Westphalian, once chaplain to Henry III. and his pious wife Agnes, is promoted to the See of

[1] Meiller, *Regesten*, p. 6, No. 10 ; p. 6, No. 11 ; p. 9, No. 10.
[2] *Lamberti Annales*, SS. v., p. 227.

Passau. He preaches the celibacy of the clergy to a degenerate and dissolute crew of clerks and monks. He expels the clerks of St. Hippolytus, abandoned to drunkenness, lust, greed, and usury. He makes a clean sweep of the monks of Kremsmünster. He summons men of high character and strict discipline into his diocese; he finds almost all the churches of wood, he leaves them almost all of stone; he finds them bare of adornments, he decorates them with frescoes and pictures and books; he finds many of the monasteries ravaged by the Hungarians or fallen into disrepair, he restores them. In all this work he encounters great persecution from the clergy who wish to keep their wives, who regard him as violating the custom of the land, and from the imperial party. He is driven from Passau, for the emperor descends upon the diocese, restores the ejected monks and clerks, and the "See of Passau becomes the See of Satan." He retires to Saxony, he visits Rome, is made papal legate, and ultimately takes refuge in the east march with Margrave Leopold.[1]

Long before this, Altmann of Passau had made efforts to conciliate the margrave. He had chosen him to be advocate and protector of the land belonging to St. Nicholas of Passau in the march; he had given him a benefice of three manses and seventy slaves in one of the little islands on the Danube near Kloster Neuburg.[2] How far Leopold was affected by these advances we are unable to say. At any rate, in 1078 he quarrels with the emperor, and leaves the court at Regensburg never to return. But the defection of Leopold to the ecclesiastical party did not exercise any enduring influence over the fortunes of his line. The emperor indeed made a successful foray into the march; his

[1] *Vita Altmanni*, SS. xii., pp. 226–43. [2] Meiller, *Regesten*, p. 10, n. 2.

ally Wratislaw of Bohemia, aided by Slaves and Bavarians, devastated the land with fire and sword, and defeated the margrave in a pitched fight [1082]. But the margrave was too powerful to be ousted, and Henry was too feeble to do much against him. Although "he was very true to the cause of the Holy Peter against the Schismatics," the emperor made no effort to contest the succession of his son.[1] When Leopold III. [1096-1136] succeeded his father, the religious war in Germany was dying of exhaustion, and the east was beginning to lay its powerful spell upon the western mind. The South-German knights, with their customary vigour and love of adventure, threw themselves energetically into the crusades, and the Babenbergs, planted on the extreme eastern frontier of Germany, become in time a famous crusading dynasty. Leopold's mother Ita found a tomb in Central Asia following the crusade of Duke Welf, but Leopold himself had no time for the east. He throws himself energetically upon the side of Henry V. in his base but successful revolt against the old emperors; he becomes Henry's brother-in-law; he participates in imperial affairs, and on the death of Henry in 1125 there was even a question of conferring the throne upon the margrave. We do not know how much support Leopold could have obtained. His piety, his loyalty, his connection with the sister of the late emperor, would have constituted a powerful claim. But there were strong reasons why both Leopold and the princes should decline the prospect. The princes may have reflected that the Babenberg dynasty had been posted on the eastern frontier; that it had been a military and colonizing dynasty; that it had been the bulwark of

---

[1] *Bernold ad* 1095, SS. v., p. 463.

Germany against the Hungarians, the protector of German civilization in a difficult land ; that as late as 1118 there had been a serious and successful Hungarian inroad into Austria ; that the Babenbergs had played but a small and subsidiary part in German affairs ; that they possessed little wealth outside the march ; that it would be dangerous and impolitic to distract their energies. On the other hand Leopold felt himself to be old. He reflected that he had many sons who, upon his death, would bring discord into the empire, and it seems likely that the adhesion of the ecclesiastical princes was only offered upon the understanding that he would concede to the Church upon the question of Investiture. But, whatever may have been his real or assumed motives, he declined the offer, and more than a hundred and fifty years elapsed before the imperial crown went to Vienna.[1]

The piety of Leopold was rewarded in the fifteenth century with the honours of canonization, and is evideuced in his own age by several monastic foundations, and by a long succession of gifts or "restorations" to Austrian monasteries. He sent his fifth son, Otto, afterwards famous as the historian of Barbarossa, to study theology in Paris, and appears himself to have attached an importance to literature. He also introduced the Cistercian monks into the east march at the instance of his pious and more learned son, and it was he who founded the Cistercian House of Heiligenkreutz, where the statue of the last prince of the Babenberg house may still be seen.[2]

[1] Simeon Dunelm, *Hist. Cont.*, SS. xiii. 125 ; *Narr. de Election. Lothar.*, SS. xii. 510 ; Huber, vol. i., p. 241 ; Giesebrecht, *KZ.*, iv., pp. 416, 19. Juritsch, pp. 137, 8. Leopold had eighteen children. Six sons and five daughters survived him. The two most distinguished were Otto of Freising and Conrad, 1149 Bishop of Passau, 1164 Archbishop of Salzburg.

[2] Meiller, p. 22, Nos. 57, 58.

Leopold III. had declined to stand as a serious candidate for the German kingship.   But another honour was in store for his house.   His son, Leopold IV. [1136-47], became Duke of Bavaria, and it was his son's Duchy of Bavaria which ultimately led to the creation of the Duchy of Austria.   Of this Leopold IV. we know little, for he died before his prime.   That he was the friend of the Emperor Conrad, who found him a useful lever against the Bavarian Welfs, gave him their Bavarian duchy, and utilized his Austrian forces in the Saxon war, that he was pious and brave, that he encountered great opposition in Bavaria, and found his duchy anything but a pleasant and profitable gift, when we have said this we have said all.

Leopold IV. was childless, and he was succeeded in the march by his brother Henry [1141-77], who had been Count Palatine of the Rhine, and who now resigned that dignity for the Austrian margraviate and the Bavarian duchy.   He too found the Bavarian duchy to be a gift that was no gift.   Despite the fact that his wife was the widow of Duke Henry the Welf, that his brother was Bishop of Freising, his hold upon Bavaria was always of the slightest.   Wars with the Church of Regensburg, with the Margrave of Styria involved him in trouble and the papal ban until St. Bernard swept Germany into the Second Crusade. Then Henry and his brother Otto followed the emperor to the east, sharing in the one inglorious achievement of that most calamitous expedition, the siege of Damascus.

The crusade, however, had postponed, it had not settled the Bavarian problem.   The young Henry the Lion was laying claims upon the duchy, which had been snatched from his family by the merest pretext. It was the interest of Frederick Barbarossa, who had

been raised to the throne for the express purpose of
terminating the strife of Welf and Wibelin, to satisfy
the rival house with whom he was connected by
marriage.   But for four years the obstinate margrave
resisted all proposals of accommodation.   It was not
until September, 1156, at a crowded meeting at
Regensburg, that a settlement was finally made.   Henry
of Austria restored to the emperor the Duchy of
Bavaria.   With seven banners the emperor gave it
as a fief to Henry the Lion.   Then Henry of Austria
restored the March of Austria, and three counties,
which the Margrave Leopold had held as fiefs of the
Bavarian duchy [probably between the Traun and the
wood of Passau] to the emperor, with two banners.
Then with the counsel and advice of the princes, declared by the Duke of Bohemia, the emperor raised
Austria and its appendant counties to be a duchy,
and conferred it with two banners, not only upon his
uncle Henry, but also on his wife Theodora.[1]   A
privilege too was given to Henry and his wife, which
raised Austria to a special position among the German
principalities.   The duchy was to descend not only
to sons, but to daughters.   If Henry and his wife
were to die childless, they could propose a successor
to the emperor ; no one, great or small, was to exercise
jurisdiction within the duchy without the duke's consent.   The duke should not be bound to render any
imperial service, except to appear when summoned at
the imperial court days in Bavaria, and to send his
contingent to every imperial expedition undertaken in
the lands bordering upon Austria.[2]

[1] Theodora was the niece of the Byzantine Emperor Manuel.   Juritsch,
p. 187.

[2] Otto Fris., *Gesta*, ii. 32.   For the *Privilegium Minus*, cf. Wattenbach,

This privilege of 1156 marks an epoch in the history of Austria. The march had long been faced with special problems, military and colonial. Its inhabitants had had to win their way across the great north wood, to fight Slaves and Hungarians and Czecks, to build castles and towns, and fortify islands. Its organization was something special ; simpler, and more centralized than the organization of the older, safer parts of Germany, for it was not divided into counties ; or, if it was so divided, the counties had long been absorbed by the margrave. It had no imperial towns or imperial churches, and the power of the margrave was not broken by such powerful ecclesiastical organizations as confronted the secular princes in Bavaria or in Franconia. For nearly two hundred years it had been ruled by members of a single family. It had stood in a way apart from the central life of Germany. But the margraves seem at some periods to have been dependent upon the Duke of Bavaria. They were technically bound to attend all the imperial courts and hosts ; they were liable to have their office taken from them by the emperor. In the reign of Henry III. the imperial armies, headed by the emperor, cross the march again and again. The land which is won from the Hungarian is ceded to the emperor, who makes an independent march of it, and twenty years elapse before this march becomes absorbed by the Babenberg family.[1] So too all land wrested from the Slaves and Hungarians is deemed imperial land, and though the emperor's influence in the march is

---

Archiv. f. Oest. Gesch., viii. 10 ; Brunner, "Das Gerichtliche Exemtions-recht der Babenberger" [Sitzungsbericht der Kais. Akad., vol. xlvii.]

[1] I prefer to follow Hasenöhrl in this point. Archiv. f. Oest. Geschichte, vol. 82, p. 419.

intermittent, there is no recognized limit to its possible extent.[1]

But now that the march has become a hereditary duchy, that the obligations of its dukes to the empire are narrowed and defined, that the highest constitutional sanction has been procured for the unimpeded jurisdictional authority of the duke within the limits of the duchy, Austria starts upon a new way. She is still part of the empire, and the Austrian dukes still take their share in imperial politics. Henry the first duke appears at Barbarossa's court, does military work in Italy, swears adhesion to the Wurzburg decrees of 1165, accepts an embassy to Constantinople in 1166. When Henry the Lion ten years later tries to win him from the emperor, the duke declines the peril and the temptation.[2] In spite of the fact that his brother and his nephew were on the Alexandrine side, that he was personally appealed to by Alexander, that the whole ecclesiastical influence of South-Eastern Germany was Alexandrine, Henry will not break with Frederick.

But the connection with the empire henceforth brings strength, not weakness, to the duchy. The emperor no longer limits the jurisdictional power of the duke by the grant of immunities. On the other hand the duke will appeal to the emperor to settle a boundary dispute between Bohemia and Austria, just as the duke's mediation is invoked to settle the issues between the

---

[1] It is significant that pending the inquiry held by the Duke of Bavaria into corporate and individual claims in 985, the land was held in the possession of the emperor [Meiller, *Reg.*, p. 1, No. 4].

[2] Yet Henry of Austria had in 1174 alone of all the princes declined to consent to the deposition of Adalbert, Archbishop of Salzburg, Barbarossa's chief ecclesiastical antagonist in Germany, at the Council of Ratisbon. *Chron. Reicherspergense ad* 1174 ; cf. Harz., *Conc. Germ.*, iii., p. 406.

emperor and Milan.[1] But Austria goes her own way.
The duke busies himself with the consolidation of his
power in the duchy ;[2] he is involved in conflicts with
his brothers, the Bishops of Freising and Passau, about
jurisdiction and about dues ; he is involved in a great
border quarrel with Bohemia, for Czeck and German
backwoodsmen are at last coming into touch with one
another in the Nordwald, and sixty thousand Bohemians
and Moravians invade his land. At the same time he is
pushing eastward. He makes his capital at Vienna,
being the first of the Austrian dukes to date documents
from that town. "In our estate in the territory of
Favia, which is called by modern men Vienna," an
abbey is dedicated to the Virgin and St. Gregory, and
served by a band of simple Irish monks. This abbey,
the Scot-Cloister, is to be the burial place of the ducal
house.[3]

The second duke, Leopold V. [1177-94], has gone
down to fame as the crusader who imprisoned King
Richard of England. He was in fact one of those
enthusiastic South-German knights who were idealized
by Tyrolese singers, generous and enterprising and
pious, a crusader even in extreme old age, but withal
shrewd and politic in his management of affairs. His
rule is rendered remarkable by the peaceful acquisition
of Styria. In 1184 Ottocar IV. of Styria, who was
childless, announced that he had determined to give the
land of Styria to his beloved relation Leopold, Duke of

---

[1] Meiller, *Regesten*, p. 56, No. 8 ; p. 115, No. 122.

[2] A story in the *Regesten* illustrates the man. A ducal *ministerialis* had
sold a mill to the Abbey of Admont. "Quod quia sine permissione
domini sui ducis praesumpserit, indignatum et iratum Ducem pro eadem
re fratres cenobii tribus marcis et uno equo placuerunt" [*Reg.*, p. 52,
No. 89].

[3] Meiller, *Regesten*, pp. 43, 44, Nos. 51, 52, 53.

Austria, with all its appurtenances except 500 manses[1]
Two years later, in 1186, Ottocar IV. makes a treaty
with Duke Leopold of Austria, which illustrates the
extreme independence of these south-eastern potentates.
After consulting with his chief men he designs "the most
strenuous, most noble, most faithful Duke of Austria" to
be his successor, for the two provinces being contiguous
will best be governed under one peace and one prince.
The rights and franchises of the Styrian *ministeriales*,
clerks and inhabitants are expressly guaranteed, and appear to have been already consigned to writing. The
advocacies of monasteries and the advowsons of churches
held by the predecessors of the Styrian duke were now
to be transferred to the Duke of Austria. Even if the
successors of the Duke of Austria were to lose the favour
of the empire they were still to be lords of the human
beings transferred to them under the contract,[2] and it
was provided that the Duke of Austria for the time
being should be Duke of Styria as well.[3]

No more striking instance can be given of the free
manner in which a German prince disposed of what
was really not his to give, for the government of Styria
and the ducal title were imperial fiefs.[4]   It was, of

---

[1] Meiller, *Reg.*, p. 61, No. 25 ; Frölich [*Diplom.*, ii., 311, No. 43]. Huber
rejects this *diploma* on the ground that Styria was not Ottocar's to give.
The *terra* and the *ducatus* were imperial fiefs, and not to be confounded
with the *hereditas* [cf. *Cont. Zwet.* i. 11, p. 543, *ad* 1186]. But Ottocar
was no observer of forms. He cedes the *ducatus* in 1186 [Meiller, p. 62,
No. 29].

[2] This sentence is considered by Huber to be an interpolation of the
time of Frederick II.

[3] This *Erbvertrag* or contract of inheritance is contained in two documents, dated August 17, 1086, given in Meiller, *Reg.*, pp. 62, 63, Nos. 29,
30. Cf. also *Urk. d. Steiermark*, i. 651. The facsimile is in Muchar's
Gesch. der Steiermark.

[4] Up till 1180 Styria had been a march held in subjection to Bavaria.
The margrave held fiefs of the Bavarian duke, and had to attend his

course, necessary to negotiate with the emperor for formal investiture. But could that investiture have been refused ? Ottocar could in fact transfer to Leopold the substance of power. He could give him his own Styrian allods, his own very numerous advocacies, his own rights over the *ministeriales.* Once in possession of these advantages Leopold could have made it unpleasant for any incoming duke, could have made it impossible for him to secure a foothold in the duchy. On May 24, 1192, not a fortnight after Ottocar's death, Frederick invested Leopold of Austria and his son with the Duchy of Styria, and but for a brief interval [1192-1198] the two duchies remained united together, according to Ottocar's disposition.[1]

Then came the double election which followed after the death of Henry VI., the importance of which can scarcely be over-estimated. The downfall of the imperial power in Germany, the ecclesiastical emancipation of Bohemia and its elevation to the dignity of a kingdom, the interference of foreign powers in German electoral concerns, the development of a thoroughly unscrupulous electoral policy, the re-assertion of ultramontane influence in German capitular elections, the formal recognition on the part of the empire of the privileges usurped by the princes, the formal abandonment of the control over the Church

course days [cf. Huber, p. 215 ; *Hermann. Alt. Ann. S.S.*, xvii. 382 ; *M.B.*, xxix. 6, 260 ; Meiller, p. 35, No. 23] ; but Frederick I. in 1180 separated Styria from Bavaria and made it a duchy held immediately of the empire. The transfer of Styria to Austria was confirmed by the Emperor in 1187.

[1] On Ottocar's death Leopold holds a great meeting of Styrian *ministeriales* at Steier, and decides to resume all donations made by Ottocar to churches, which might be shown to be detrimental either to the cities or to the ducal government [Meiller, *Regesten*, p. 70, No. 55].

which had been so closely exercised by Barbarossa ;
all these events are ultimately traceable to this period
of discord.   Austria too aspired to profit by the occasion.   Leopold VI., "the Glorious, a most eloquent
and literate man, the father of the whole country, the
ornament of the land, and the solace of the clergy,"
attempted to secure some measure of ecclesiastical independence for Austria by founding a bishopric at
Vienna,[1] but the resistance of the See of Passau frus-
trated the attempt, and the pious Leopold acquiesced
in defeat.   Yet the reign of the last but one of the
Babenbergs brought prosperity and distinction to the
duchy.   Austrian knights followed Leopold's banner
against the Albigensians of Toulouse, and the Saracens
of Calatrava.   The valour of the duke was exhibited
beneath the walls of Beaufort in Palestine and Damietta
in Egypt, and the confidence of Pope and emperor alike
was reposed in the wealthy potentate, the husband of
a Byzantine princess, who had so generously endowed
the German Order, and who was so perfect a mirror of
the conventional and easy virtues of medieval chivalry.
The daughter of Leopold was married to Henry VII.,
the son of the emperor, and the Austrian duke was
chosen to mediate between Frederick and Pope Honorius
in 1228.   The Pope was convinced that so pious and
prosperous a noble could not fail of an eternal reward,
and solaced his widow with the most confident assurances.
His heir should have been grateful to him for some
extensive and provident purchases of land, while Vienna
had every reason to regret the prince who was so
generous a patron of the lyre, and under whose pacific
rule she received her first code of municipal law, and
became for a while the most brilliant capital in Germany.

[1] Meiller, p. 96, No. 64.

The reign of Leopold VI., was in after times looked back upon as the golden age of the Babenbergs. To the men of the last decades of the thirteenth century in Austria he was what Edward the Confessor was to the men of the twelfth century in England, and when the customs of the land were committed to writing they were drawn up as they were conceived to exist in Duke Leopold's day.[1]

The last of the Babenberg dukes, Frederick II., dealt a serious blow to all this prosperity. His nickname, "the Quarrelsome," is justified by the fact that his country enjoyed the blessings of peace for one year only during the sixteen years of his rule. But it is inadequate to describe all the aspects of his character. He was a wild, impudent, tyrannical savage, with fits of rollicking generosity, but at the same time fundamentally cruel, avaricious, and lawless. Wars with his own nobles and *ministeriales*, with Bohemia and Moravia and Hungary and Bavaria, make up the staple of his existence. His taxation wrung a rebuke even from a servile rhymster ; his constant wars dragged the peasant from the plough and made his name odious in the land ; his tyranny drove many of the nobles beyond the border, while he confiscated the property of princes and of churches to support quarrels in which no one but himself had any conceivable interest.[2]

Here was clearly a case in which the moral and material force of the Holy Roman Empire should be invoked, and the story of the imperial intervention

---

[1] The numerous German critics who have devoted themselves to the Austrian Landrecht do not seem to have observed this.

[2] Estimates of Frederick's character may be found in SS. xix. 374 ; xvii., 392, 845 ; xvi., 30 ; ix., 637, 732, 596, 635. *H. B.*, iv., 855. Ficker has attempted to whitewash him. Cf. also Röthe, *Die Geschichte Reinmars von Zweter.*

is so typical both of the strength and the weakness of
the imperial fabric that it may be told in some length.
As in the case of Henry the Lion, indignation gathers
among the neighbouring nobles and princes.   There are
loud complaints at an imperial diet, a campaign is undertaken, the land is ravaged, castles are besieged, the
emperor for a time triumphs absolutely.   But then
comes the reaction.   The duke has all along managed
to hold out in a few castles, and when the emperor departs he re-emerges, rapidly reconquers the
land, and in a few years he is more firmly seated in the
saddle than ever.   Pope and emperor compete for his
favour; the popes offer the independent bishopric of
Vienna, after which Leopold had aspired; the emperor
promises to raise Austria to the dignity of a kingdom,
and, but for the mere accident of the religious scrupulosity of a girl, one of the very worst and most rebellious
of the many bad and rebellious princes of Medieval
Germany would have been made by the emperor, whom
he had insulted, defied, and fought, the first king of
Austria.[1]

In one respect the oppressed subjects of the Austrian
duke were happy in their opportunity.   No emperor
held a more exalted view of his own prerogative than
Frederick II.   As early as 1217 he had affirmed that
the jurisdiction or *Landgericht*, the compositions, the
bans, the marchfodder, the mines of the duchy belonged to him, though they were held by the duke in
virtue of a special privilege of the empire.   He sum-

---

[1] The stipulation was that the duke's niece Gertrude, aged nineteen,
should marry the emperor, aged fifty-one (1245).   The Genoese chronicler
[SS. xviii. 216] says that the duke refused to acquiesce in the arrange.
ment because the emperor was under the Papal ban.   Matthew Paris,
however, says that it was Gertrude who felt the scruples, and on many
grounds this seems the more probable account.   Juritsch, p. 643.

moned the duke to Italian court days, and paid little regard to the *privilegium minus*, and in executing justice upon his contumacious vassal, he was assisted by the general sentiment of the duke's neighbours. Bavaria was jealous; the King of Bohemia, the Margrave of Moravia, the Archbishop of Salzburg, the Bishops of Bamburg and Passau and Regensburg and Freising had revenues and rights in the duchy, and they complained that the duke had taken them away. The Austrian *ministeriales*, who had been crushed in a revolt of 1231, complained of tyranny and violated rights, and in 1235 at Mainz these recriminations were loudly uttered. The duke was summoned to appear before a meeting of the princes three times, but he disregarded the call, and in 1236 Frederick determined to declare him an outlaw, and to deprive him of his principalities. The emperor issued a long and serious requisitory against the duke; the duke had refused to respond to the summons to Ravenna; he had impudently demanded 2000 marks of the emperor that he might make war on Hungary; repulsed in his petition he had declared that he would no longer serve the emperor; he had invaded Hungary; he had deprived princes of their rights and revenues in Austria and Styria; he had oppressed the poor, the widows, the orphans; he had corresponded with the Milanese, with the Old Man of the Mountains; he had chased his mother from Bohemia.[1]

The duke prepared for defence. In one day he laid hands on all the hoards of all the Austrian monasteries; he raised a tax of sixty pence upon the *huba*, and he prohibited, with the counsel, it was said, of the Jews, the importation of corn into the duchy. But for the

[1] *H.B.*, iv., p. 882.

moment all was in vain. Most of the *ministeriales* of
Austria and Styria rose against him. Most of the
towns followed the *ministeriales* ; even Vienna deserted
its patron. The King of Bohemia invaded the land from
the north ; the Duke of Bavaria and the Bavarian
bishops invaded it from the west ; the Bishop of Bamberg and the Patriarch of Aquileia fell upon Styria. Then
the emperor came over the mountains from Italy, taking
castles, capturing the duke's wife, and the Austrians
and Styrians flocked to his court at Vienna. He freed
the Bishops of Freising and Passau from the duchy ; he
declared the two Austrian duchies to be immediate
dependencies of the empire ;[1] he declared Vienna to be
an imperial town ; he gave it a constitution, according
to which the town judge was to be appointed every
year by the emperor like the judges in the South-
Italian towns ; he confirmed and expanded the ancient
franchises of the *ministeriales* and the unfree knights of
Styria ; he confirmed and expanded monastic privileges ;
he took many of the most important monasteries under
his special protection ; he drew up a valuable list of
privileges for the Jews ; he probably stimulated the codification of the Austrian Landrecht, reasserting therein
the time-honoured barriers which fenced in the liberties
of the Austrian aristocracy. In one winter he had ex
hibited in a most signal manner the omnipotence of his
office. He had come, he had fought, he had conquered,
he had legislated. But then came the *peripateia*. The
emperor could only be a bird of passage. He could
assert a theory but he could not establish a practice.
He had never really conquered the country, for siege

---

[1] *Chron. Regia Colon.*, 1237, p. 271. The best account is to be found in
the *Continuatio Sancrucensis Secunda*, SS., ix., pp. 638-9, and in *H.B.*,
vol. v., pp. 1-66.

work was tedious, unfruitful, perilous to dignity. A winter of feasting in Vienna, a few scrolls of parchment, this was all that was apparently signified by the emperor's stupefying descent. It left no more permanent imprint upon the country than does some eagle which alights upon a Styrian rock. In 1239 the duke was back again in full possession of his duchy and his rights. He had starved the burghers of Vienna to submission and reduced the imperial charters to waste paper, and six years later the emperor is offering him a crown, and the imperial chancery has actually prepared the document, which is to give to Austria the dignity of a kingdom and to the Austrian king the full power to outlaw his nobles, his *ministeriales*, and his knights.[1]

The Babenberg dynasty suddenly died out in 1246, for Frederick had no male heir. It was a dynasty of knights and pious founders, in the main very loyal to the empire, but, notwithstanding, keeping on good terms with the pope ; some of them bitten with the crusading zeal, but all of them chiefly occupied in obscure fights and purchases, in the reclaiming of land, the deciding of disputes, the keeping of order.

It was apparently with grief that the Austrians learnt the death of the last duke, for all his savage ways. In beauty equal to Paris or Absalom, in courage to Hector or Gideon, in wisdom to Solomon : such is the strain of the flattering dirges composed in the Austrian cloisters, which owed so much to the vanished house.[2] In the troubled times which succeeded the disappearance of the last male Babenberger, it may

---

[1] Wurdtwein, *Nova Subsidia Diplomatica*, xii. Böhmer-Ficker, 3484.

[2] Four poems on the occasion are given in SS. xi., pp. 50, 51. Some of the verses are above the average :

"Austria diviciis omnibus fecunda
Sola jam in pulvere sedet gemebunda,

have been that Frederick's faults were forgotten, and the land only remembered that it had lost a line of strong rulers.

Under these Babenberger dukes the march obtains a special character of its own. It is still indeed part of the empire. The dukes are expected to receive investiture of the emperors, and to attend imperial court-days. Appeals to the empire are recognized even in the later version of Austrian Landrecht, which belongs to the time of Ottocar. The count, the Free Knight, the Dientsmann, can appeal to the Reich from the Landesherr, and it is with the Reich also that the ultimate decision on all feudal questions lies. The emperor will intervene to decide a vexed question of boundary, as Frederick Barbarossa decided the boundary between the March and Bohemia in 1179, to fix the relations between the duke and another prince of the empire, as Frederick II. fixed the relations between Leopold V. and the See of Passau. There were, too, imperial fiefs in the march,[1] and sometimes the emperor might descend upon the land, and legislate as Frederick II. legislated, for the land looked up to the emperor as its supreme lord, and when the last Babenberg duke fell in a skirmish, the inhabitants applied to the Wonder of the World to supply them with a prince.

Yet these ties were weak and of increasing weakness. and Henry III. was the last emperor who was much seen

> Parvipendit Styria quelibet jocunda,
> Quamvis in militibus nulli sit secunda.

> " In diversa spargitur terre dominatus,
> Propriis in sedibus regnat incolatus,
> Agnus ovem devorat, lupus est beatus,
> Cattis atque muribus par est principatus."

[1] Meiller, *Reg.*, p. 41. 44.

in Austria. As the Bohemian forest becomes reclaimed, as the borders on the north and the east become fixed, the imperial donor, who had once been so lavish with virgin forests, withdraws from the cartularies.

After 1156 we hear of Duke Frederick holding the "Monarchy of Austria"[1] Nor is this a mere empty phrase. Tried by the most substantial tests, the duke is a sovereign prince. He makes treaties with foreign powers, as with Hungary in 1225,[2] or with German princes, as with the Bishop of Passau in 1240.[3] He negotiates ambitious marriage alliances with England, with Constantinople, with the imperial family. He enjoys large revenues, regulating as he does the brisk trade of the Danube, taking toll of merchants at his three toll-stations,[4] exacting marchfodder, selling or letting fishing and mining rights, succeeding to the goods of intestates, raising purveyance, living at free quarters on his nobles, pocketing all the judicial fines, plundering Jews.[5] When the revenues of the German princes came to be estimated, the Duke of Austria stood equal second. He was as rich as the Archbishop of Cologne and the Margrave of Brandenburg. He was more than twice as rich as the Duke of Bavaria or the Archbishop of Salzburg ; more than seven times as rich as the Archbishop of Mainz or the Duke of Saxony; more than ten times as rich as the Archbishop of Bremen. He was inferior only to the King of Bohemia.[6]

---

[1] Meiller, *Rg.*, p. 77. 2.   [2] Meiller, *Rg.*, p. 136. 200.
[3] Meiller, *Rg.*, p. 161. 58.   [4] Meiller, *Rg.*, p. 165. 76.
[5] Meiller, p. 83. 15 ; p. 161. 57 ; p. 89. 37 ; p. 59. 15 ; p. 94. 54 ; p. 104. 86 ; p. 133. 191 ; p. 158. 45; p. 179. 136.
[6] *Descriptio Theutoniae*, SS. xvii., p. 238. The King of Bohemia is given a revenue of 150,000 marks. The Archbishop of Cologne and the Margrave of Brandenburg 50,000, the Archbishop of Mainz 7000, etc.

Then again his judicial authority is great and profit-able.[1] If the march was ever divided into counties, then the margrave was count in each of the three counties into which it was divided. He holds his provincial court or *Lanteiding* three times a year at Mautern, at Tulln and at Neuberg respectively. He tries in person all causes affecting the property, the lives, or the honour of his nobles or freemen or *ministeriales*. He has three salaried provincial judges, to whom he pays £300 each a year, who represent him on the judgment seat, and who pay into his treasury the penalties and compensations levied by their court. He has inferior judges officiating in inferior courts, the whole *personnel* appointed by and removable by himself. It is true that there are immunities in Austria and Styria, but these immunities affected in a diminishing degree the jurisdictional rights of the duke. In the first place clerks could not hear capital charges, and the list of capital charges was in Austria and Styria long, vague, elastic. In all grants to ecclesiastical foundations these are reserved to the duke in person. Capital offences go to the duke alone.[2] Again the monasteries here as elsewhere are attempting to limit the jurisdictional rights of their advocates. They are saying to them, "You may try serious offences, homicide, larceny, theft, rapine, arson, rape. You may try anything which may come under the conception of a breach of the peace. But you must go no further. Minor cases must go to the abbot, the prior or the cellarer,

---

[1] For this, cf. Brunner, "Das Gerichtliche Exemptionsrecht" (*Sitzungs-bericht d. Kais. Akad.*, vol. xlvii.), and Hasenohrl, *Oesterreiches Landrecht.*

[2] Meiller, *Reg.*, p. 89. 36 ; p. 79. 12 ; p. 103. 83 ; p. 129. 173 ; p. 134. 192; p. 164. 72 ; p. 140. 220 ; p. 168. 90 ; p. 152. 19 ; p. 159. 50 ; p. 161. 56 ; p. 171. 101 ; p. 172. 107.

or the proctor of the monastery "[1]   The monasteries, in other words, are drawing up a rough list of graver crimes, and at the same time they are petitioning the duke against the oppressions of their advocates.   The duke is already from the first advocate of many monasteries, and in this capacity he or his agent exercises criminal jurisdiction over the men of the monastery. In other cases his intervention is sought and he intervenes.   He takes a monastery under his special protection, he decrees that the proctors and the villeins shall not plead except before his own agent.[2]   It is the privilege of the Cistercian houses that they shall have no advocate except the emperor.   At the ducal court at Mautern the question was gone into, and the court awarded that the Cistercian houses could have no advocate except the " Prince himself, who is the head of the land in which they are situated."[3]   The award sweeps all the Cistercian advocacies into the ducal net.   It almost implies that the duke is emperor in Austria.

The duke in fact is a king all but in name.   If the life, honour or property of the count, the freeman, the Dientsmann or the Landherr is concerned, the duke himself does justice.   In other cases he is represented by the judge.   His court is modelled on the imperial court.   He legislates with the counsel and consent of the better men of the land.[4]   The Jews are his Jews, the Jews of his chamber.   The villeins upon his domain

---

[1] Meiller, *Reg.*, 163. 63.

[2] Meiller, 163. 63 ; p. 71. 56.

[3] Meiller, p. 100. 73 ; p. 165. 75 ; p. 66. 40.

[4] By a law of Philip, 1205, the princes can only legislate. " Communicante sibi meliorum terrae baronum et ministerialium consilio." Cf. Furth., *Ministeriales*, p. 60 ; *L.L.*, iv., p. 283 ; and Meiller, 78, 85, 88, 33, 97, 66, 101, 75, 113, 115, 131, 160.

have a privileged position.[1]   He has wide tracts of
forests governed by salaried foresters.   He has complete
control of the commerce of the land.   He can forbid the
exportation and importation of corn and wine.   He does
forbid the exportation of gold and silver.   Although
theoretically his land is part of the empire, yet practically he treats it as a separate kingdom.   If a
citizen of Vienna die intestate, and his heir be an
" extraneous," that is to say a non-Austrian, then his
heir must come and settle permanently in Austria.
Otherwise the property is escheat to the duke.[2]   So too
the law administered in the courts is the custom
of the land, "terrae nostrae consuetudo."[3]   To determine the constituent elements of this custom, to
evaluate the importance attached to imperial laws or
decisions in Austrian courts with any degree of exacti-
tude would be a task exceeding the ingenuity even of
the German professor.   It is clear, however, that there
would be no objection to receiving imperial edicts.
The first written draft of the Austrian law probably
dates from Frederick II.'s temporary occupation of
the land in 1236 and 1237.[4]   It would seem that
it was composed at the instance of the Austrian
nobles who wished to shelter themselves behind the
trenches of custom from the tyrannous onslaughts of
their duke, and some of its clauses are based upon the

---

[1] This is clear from Meiller, p. 139. 192.

[2] Cf. "Oesterreichische Stadtrechte und Satzungen aus der Zeit der
Babenberger" (*Archiv. f. Ost. Gesch.*, x., pp. 148-159); *Wiener Stadtrecht*,
1221 ; and *Stadtrecht* for Enns, 1212.

[3] Meiller, *Reg.*, p. 100. 75.

[4] Opinions have been much divided on this point.   Peter von Ludevig
assigns it to 1190 ; Schmoller not later than Leopold VI. ; Senkenberg,
temp. Albert and Rudolph ; Rauch and Hormayer, Leopold VII. ; Würth,
Albert I. ; Rössler, 1295-8 ; Zöpfl after 1328 ; Zieglauer, 1287-95 ;
Schröder, 1236, 1237.

Mainz Landpeace of 1235. Since the Austrian margraves and dukes were almost consistently loyal to the emperors, and by no means generally abstained from attendance upon the imperial court, it is probable that they were familiar with the principles upon which imperial justice was conducted, and that this experience would in some measure affect the decisions given in the Austrian provincial courts. But the greater part of the custom of the land must have been a local growth upon a Bavarian or Swabian basis.[1] It would grow partly out of the accumulated decisions in the provincial courts, partly out of the privileges accorded by ducal charter to corporations or classes of men, partly out of ducal edicts and acts of legislation. The custom of the land was doubtless tolerably uniform, so far as concerned penal law, though here and there towns like Vienna or Enns would enjoy a privileged position. But in various other respects the custom would differ from place to place. In the mountains of Styria the *ministeriales*, originally unfree servants of a lord or corporation, had conquered for themselves an exceptional status. They could hand down their fiefs to daughters in the lack of sons, could sell them or give them to other Styrians. If they died intestate their inheritance could pass to collaterals. They were exempt from trial by battle, and their privileges were guaranteed by a written charter.[2]

[1] There is evidence to prove that the Babenbergs originally lived Swabian law. *Ughelli Ital. Sacra.*, iv., 781 ; Meiller, p. 222, n. 197 ; *Mitt. d. Inst. Ost. Gesch.*, vi., pp. 385-388 ; and the *Swabenspiegel* had great vogue in Austria. Thus it is one of the fountains of the *Wiener Stadtrechtbuch* (Schröder, p. 665, n. 93). On the other hand most of the settlers in the march were Bavarians.

[2] Luschin in *Beitrage z.k. Steir. Geschihtsq.* vol. ix., p. 7, and Zallinger, "Die Ritterlichen Klassen im Steirischen Landrecht" (*Mitt. d. Inst. f. Oest. Geschtsf.*, iv. 393-433). It seems possible from the *Vita Altmanni* that there was a special custom affecting the heritability of fiefs in the dioceses of Passau.

The Flemings in Vienna, the traders from Regensburg, Cologne, Aix, and Ulm,[1] the Jews could bring written evidence into court of ducal favour.   The later Babenberg dukes too had legislated generously for Enns, for Vienna, for Vienna Neustadt, for Hamburg.[2]   They had created an independent body of town law, of Stadtrecht, which embraced civil and criminal and constitutional provisions, and which henceforth exempted the towns from the Landrecht.   It is impossible now to trace the various influences which presided over these legislative experiments.   The most natural course would have been either for the citizens of the town in quest of privileges to have presented to the duke a draft scheme based upon the practice of other cities, or else for the duke and his advisers to have procured information about municipal privileges in other parts of Germany, and to have selected the provisions which they thought suitable. There is some reason for thinking that the Austrian town privileges were affected by Flemish usage, and if this is the case it is possible that the town legislation of the Babenbergs was based either upon the reminiscences of the Flemish settlers in Vienna or else upon the copies of charters supplied by them to the legislative advisers of the duke.[3]

We have dwelt at length upon the history of the Babenbergs, in order to illustrate clearly the extent of the power of the emperors in the March and the Duchy of Austria.   The two powers which, in the present century, disputed the hegemony of Germany, were both of them formed during this period.   Both of them were marches, both of them colonies.   The

---

[1] *Archiv. f. Kunde Oest. Geschichtsq.*, vol. x., p. 92.
[2] *Archiv. f. Oest. Gesch.*, x., pp. 148-159.
[3] Huber, i., p. 488.

historical office of Brandenburg has been to stay the advance of the Slave, the office of Austria to keep first the Hungarian and then the Turk out of Western Europe. The empire did nothing to assist the formation of these states, and the conjunction of the imperial crown at a later date with the Archduchy of Austria and the kingdoms of Bohemia and Hungary dissipated the attention and the energies of the Hapsburgs. The brutality of the Germans, who extirpated the Slaves in Brandenburg and Prussia, and the inviting simplicity of the great northern plain prepared for the northern march an easier political destiny than was possible amid the heterogeneous races and broken geography of the Austrian dominions. Yet a series of calamities, the dying out of the Ascanians and the weakness of their successors, arrested the growth of Brandenburg until the fifteenth century, while the Duchy of Austria, after a brief Bohemian interregnum, regained its lost position under Rudolph of Hapsburg, and grew in power and prestige under the rule of his dynasty.

CHAPTER X.

THE CHURCH IN GERMANY.

THE downfall of the Medieval Empire has been very generally attributed to the action of the Church. Now this appears at first sight to be one of those rare statements which are at once simple and correct. We see the empire engaged in a huge running conflict with the papacy, which covers about a hundred and eighty years. There are indeed breathing spaces between these papal-imperial wars, and there are a variety of issues involved, but in the main the struggle is one struggle, and involves one issue—was the Church to be dependent on the empire or independent of it? And we find that in this struggle the empire is beaten, and that all the causes for which it fought, such as the control over the German Church and the incorporation of Sicily in the empire, are lost, and that one of the chief causes for which the papacy fought, the foundation of a papal state in Italy, is gained. Further, if we look more closely into the details of the struggle, the same fact seems to emerge everywhere. The opposition of the Church appears to sap not only the political strength of the monarchy, but the very theory upon which it was built. Examine, for instance, the accounts given by contemporary writers of the motives which led the

princes to proceed to the momentous step of deposing Henry IV., and of raising Rudolph of Swabia to
the throne. "They said that he could not rule any
longer without great loss to the Christian religion,
that he had been guilty of crimes which, if they
were judged by law ecclesiastical, would be regarded
as involving abdication of marriage, and of the belt
of knighthood, and of all enjoyment of the world,
how much more of a kingdom." "They had pledged
their faith to him by an oath, but only if he would
be king for the edification, not for the destruction,
of the Church of God." It is plain that men wanted
a religious sanction to back them before they could
reconcile it with their consciences to break the oath
of allegiance. Unless they had been able to find such
a sanction the princes would never have proceeded to
so extreme a step as the deposition of the king, and
they would hardly have found a sanction of sufficient
force unless the pope had actually absolved Henry's
subjects from their allegiance. As has been very
sensibly said by a German writer, "When Gregory
VII. cut the Gordian knot of difficulties and doubts
which surrounded the oath, he practically completed
the deposition."[1] Now the significance of such an
act as the deposition of a king does not depend upon
the qualities of the king himself. A king may be
sensationally vicious or cruel or lazy or incompetent,
but it does not follow that his deposition will have
far-reaching consequences. It will be more beneficial
than the extinction of an ordinary criminal, but it
may not differ in kind from any one of the acts by
which society protects itself against the vagaries of a

---

[1] Victor Domeyer, *Die Päbste als Richter*, p. 18 ; Gierke, *Untersuchungen*,
vol. liii.

lunatic, or the fraud of the company-promoter, or the violence of the cut-throat. The real significance of a deposition depends, not so much upon the character of the person deposed, as upon the character of the forces which depose him. If the deposition of a sovereign indicates a change in the intellectual atmosphere, if it is an extraordinary act accomplished by extraordinary machinery, worked by extraordinary passions, and in defiance of great obstacles, then it is important. It sets one of those political precedents which stamps an idea into many generations of ordinary men. Now the deposition of Henry IV. was important just for this reason. It did not affect the permanence of the Salian dynasty, for Henry was deposed and succeeded by his own son. It did not, so far as we can see, alter the material resources at the disposition of the monarchy. It did not immediately create any new constitutional machinery whatever. But it marked in a very significant way the partial triumph of a new idea about the basis of sovereignty. It asserted the idea that sovereignty was based upon contract, that if the king broke his oath to his people, his people were absolved from their oath to· him. Against the view that the king was the irresponsible vicegerent of God upon the earth, it asserted the view that the king was a responsible agent, who could be deposed for ignoring his responsibilities. A large pamphlet literature which has now been published in three volumes of the *Monumenta Germaniae* was produced in German and Italian monasteries to support this theory, which has been the political theory of the papacy ever since, which was destined to fill the minds of Bellarmine, Mariana and Suarez, and to direct or stifle the consciences of the men who aimed at the

murder of Queen Elizabeth, and who accomplished
the murder of William the Silent and of Henry III.
of France.

We must not assign too much importance to pamphlets. They seldom convert people, unless they become
the programme of an organization. But it was the
peculiar fortune of these pamphlets that not only did
they become the programme of an organization, which
was in relation to other organizations existing at the
same time with itself, one of the most powerful known
to history, but that the doctrine expressed in them was
intimately associated with the interests and prerogatives
of a strong aristocracy. They lay down the theoretical
basis of the political programme of the Catholic Church.
They safeguard the electoral rights of the German
princes.

And hence this idea of sovereignty slowly gets hold
of the German mind. It had indeed many obstacles
to conquer. The Germans were proud of their emperor
as well they might be, and when Alexander III. excommunicated and deposed Frederick Barbarossa, the
thunders of the Vatican hardly evoked an echo north
of the Alps. Again, of all medieval churches, the German
Church was least ultramontane in temper and habit
of mind, and most closely associated with the fortunes
of the monarchy. But the idea made its way for all that.
If we read the *Sachsenspiegel* which was antipapal,
so much so indeed that many of its provisions were
subsequently condemned by the pope, we find that
"no one can be king who is under the ban of the Church,
and the ban of the Church may be lawfully imposed
if the emperor break his promise or abandon his lawful
wife, or destroy God's house." Now if the *Sachsenspiegel*
says this, it is clear that the doctrine of the contract

has made a very considerable impression upon men's minds. The *Sachsenspiegel* is not stating the papal claims as the papalists would have stated them. It is restating the limits within which patriotic Germans were willing to admit those claims. As a writer upon the deposition of Otto IV. puts it, "The emperor can only be excommunicated for three causes: Desertion of his wife, diminution of imperial honour, heresy."[1]

Again, if we turn from the history of political theory to the history of political fact, the influence of the Church in procuring the destruction of the empire seems to outweigh any other influence. It was Alexander III. who encouraged the Lombard towns to assert and defend their independence; it was the resistance of the Lombard towns which led to the Peace of Venice and to the Peace of Constance—the Peace of Venice which advertised the humiliation of the empire before the most brilliant diplomatic congress which had yet met in Europe, and the Peace of Constance which practically guaranteed the substantial autonomy of the Lombard League. So too on the death of Henry VI., who had come nearer to forming a united Italy than any sovereign since the days of Berengar of Friuli, the papacy profits by the occasion of the minority permanently to weaken the hold of the Hohenstauffen both in Germany and in Italy, so that if Gregory VII. may be called the true heir of Henry III., Innocent III. may with still greater justice be called the true heir of Henry VI. The pope reconquers the patrimony of St. Peter, drives the imperialists from Ancona and Spoleto, and the Matildine lands, and founds that papal state which had long existed in writing both forged and genuine, but which

---

[1] "Disp. carm. conscript. inter Romam et Papam de Ottonis IV. destitutione," Leibnitz, *Rer. Bruns.*, SS. ii. 530.

had never yet enjoyed more than a fragmentary, inter-mittent, and contested existence in the world of fact. He is regent in Sicily for the young Frederick IL, and contemplates in the Sicilian kingdom the pro-spect of a subject state ruled by a dynasty more docile than the Normans. He intervenes decisively in German affairs. When some of the princes elect Philip of Swabia, the brother of the late emperor, who had been put under the ban of the Church for his vigorous measures in Tuscany, Innocent sets aside the election. He decides for Otto, who represents North Germany and the trade interests of Cologne, and the dynastic pretensions of the Welfic House. Then when it is clear that Otto is too true to the imperialist tradition to abandon Italy and Sicily to the pope, Innocent turns round against him. He absolves the princes and barons and *ministeriales* of the empire from their oath to the young emperor. He sends Frederick II. his Sicilian protegé to contest with him the devotion of the German princes. He stirs up the King of France against Otto, who is the nephew of the King of England and supported by English gold, and so he helps to ruin in 1212 the emperor whose coronation he had helped to secure in 1204. Then again, disposing as he does of the empire, he is able to extract terms from the candidates; the recognition of the papal state, the abandonment of the right of spoils, the recognition of papal appeals, the abandonment of the incorporation of Sicily and the empire, the abandonment of the right of enjoying ecclesiastical revenues during a vacancy.

Further, to buy the support of the German Church Frederick II. has to throw away, one after another, the most precious prerogatives of the crown, and to abandon the towns, which are in the first decades of the thirteenth century waging active war against their bishops, and who might have given him a measure of help in Germany which would have secured the continuance of the Swabian dynasty. Then, again, Frederick's scheme for the consolidation of Italy and Sicily is ruined by the alliance of the papacy with the Lombard cities. The emperor is kept fighting in the Lombard plain and in central Italy, when his heart is set upon making the "regno" a model for all Europe to emulate. The most gifted administrator of the Middle Ages, with an incomparable grasp of detail, a passionate enthusiasm for civilization, a wide intellectual curiosity, a singular detachment from all superstitions except astrology, and a consuming thirst for work, is wasted upon a continuous war of sieges and skirmishes in central and northern Italy, which take the heart out of him, and steep his temper in a kind of bitter extravagance.[1] Then the emperor is, in 1245, formally deposed by the pope at a Council of Lyons, and, while he still maintains the struggle, aided by all the outcasts and desperadoes of Italy, a succession of counter kings are elected in Germany, whose shadowy half-acknowledged authority only assists the growth of the German principalities. Then, finally, the whole family of the Hohenstauffen is rooted out from Italy. The papal Curia, after sixteen years of almost unexampled duplicity, destroys the brave and accomplished Manfred, the bastard son of the great Frederick, by the aid of the French in 1266, and with Manfred's death the last hope of Italian unity vanishes for many

---

[1] Salimbene, *Chron. Parm.*, p. 68, " Igitur cum Fridericus imperator esset depositus ab imperio ab Innocentio Papa Quarto erat amaro animo veluti si ursa raptis catulis in saltu saeviat. Et convenerunt ad eum omnes qui erant in angustiis constituti et oppressi aere alieno et amaro animo et factus est princeps corum."

centuries.   The papacy which wrecked the Lombard
monarchy in the eighth century by invoking the Frank,
wrecks the Hohenstauffen monarchy in the thirteenth
century by an appeal to the same quarter.   As Stephen
invoked Pippin against Aistulf, and Innocent III. invoked Walter of Brienne against the officers of Henry
VI., so Alexander IV. and Urban IV. invoke Charles of
Anjou against Manfred.

The appeal was heard.   The Frenchman came down
with a strong force ; he got himself elected senator of
Rome ; he defeated Manfred at the battle of Benevento,
and four years later crushing Conradin, the boy grand-
son of the great Frederick, at Tagliacozzo, he established a tyranny in southern Italy.   But the spirit
which had arisen to the invocation could not be so
easily laid.   As the popes of the eighth century had
to bow the neck to Charles the Great, so the popes
of the thirteenth century had to bow the neck to
Philip le Bel.   The papacy had guided a long train
of events from the death of Henry III. in 1056 to
the death of Conradin in 1268.   The chain led to the
conquest of the empire, but it led to something else as
well.   It led by a necessary sequence to the degradation
of the papacy in the eyes of Europe and to its humiliation before the strong French monarchy, which had
inherited the claims and aspirations of the Carolingians.[1]
Yet a bare recital of these facts suggests a limitation to
the extent of the papal influence in securing the down
fall of the Medieval Empire.   The scene of the later and

[1] When Innocent III. invoked Walter of Brienne the Abbot Joachim of
Flora saw the full significance of the act. " Videat Romanum capitulum si
non fiat eis arundineus baculus potentia Gallicana, cui si quis innititur per-
forat manus ejus....Alamannorum enim Imperium quasi stimulum Francia
sentiet, adeo ut, si recalcitret vulnera in ecclesiae subventionem reponet"
(*In Jeremiam Interpretatio*, c. 2, ed. 1577, p. 46).

most decisive stages of the conflict was Italy, where the
popes could rely upon the strong Lombard towns, upon
the Franciscan order, upon the traditional dislike of
German brutality among the Italian populace, where
they could and did appeal to a nascent Italian political
sentiment. But what was the real influence of the
Curia in Germany? How far was it able to detach the
German clergy from the imperial cause and to penetrate
it with cosmopolitan theological sentiment? To what
extent was the victory of the popes over the Hohenstauffen due to the alliance of the Church in Germany?

We shall attempt here to explain the ways in
which the emperors controlled and utilized the Church
machinery; to describe the composition and the intellectual and moral character of the German Church
which was thus worked into the imperial system; and,
finally, to trace the attitude of the Church leaders in
Germany towards the popes on the one hand and the
emperors on the other.

When the first seeds of the Catholic Church were sown
in Germany, Boniface the first sower consecrated the crop
to the service of the Church of Rome. The oath of obedience which he took to the Roman see was most ample
and unreserved, but the dream of the missionary was far
from immediate fulfilment. The German mission of the
eighth century was very unlike any mission carried on by
the Catholic Church at the present day among disheart-
ened aborigines or placid and contemptuous Chinese.
The patients were barbarous, rude and vigorous, extremely resentful of discipline and disinclined to the
payment of tithe or tax. The Church was not assisted
by the many subtle agents of demoralization which
accompany the white missionary into Africa and sap
the strength of the heathen. It was not backed by the

Maxim gun. The mission was at once more difficult and more promising; more difficult because the peoples were fresh and vigorous and the material resources of the Church more slender, more promising because the bars of race and culture and clime were infinitely slighter and more fragile. The consequence of this was that the Church was at every turn dependent on the State. The words of the English and Irish missionaries had to be supported by the arms of the Franks, and the popes of Rome were unable to do more than to encourage or direct. From the time of Clovis onwards the Church looked to the Frankish monarchy to protect and promote its interests.

There was another fact which tended in the same direction. It was, as we have already said, the fashion of the eighth and of succeeding centuries to make large grants of land to the Church, and of all investments this seemed the most profitable, whether the contemplated reward was to be reaped in time or in eternity. Charles the Great complained that in his day gifts to the Church were so frequent that men were thereby reduced to poverty and compelled to take to a life of crime.[1] In 817 Lewis the Pious was obliged to legislate to prevent clerks from taking gifts, which might disinherit the children or near relations of the giver, and the enactment was re-enacted by Lewis II. in 875.[2] Nothing however is more vain than to legislate against timidity, especially when all the forces of culture are inculcating fear. The emperors themselves were the greatest offenders. The donations of Charles the Great, Lewis the Pious, and Lewis the German were lavish, and it was not until the beginning of the tenth century that any check was placed to this stream of beneficence. But the

---

[1] Boretius, p. 163.   [2] *Ib.*, p. 277.

Saxons reverted to the ancient ways. These four pious emperors pile donation upon donation. Whereas we have forty-two charters of donation proceeding from Lewis the German and thirty-seven from Arnulf, we have one hundred and fifty-two from Otto the Great. Again, the grants of market rights and toll-rights made during this one reign to ecclesiastical foundations exceed all the grants taken together made by Otto's predecessors.[1] The munificence of the Saxon emperors builds up the territories of the great Rhenish sees, creates the archiepiscopal see of Magdeburg, invests the Bishop of Wurzburg with ducal powers, creates the new see of Bamberg, endows and founds numerous Saxon abbeys and nunneries, and heaps political and judicial powers upon ecclesiastical foundations. It would probably be unfair to the memory of these sovereigns to refer their donations merely to spiritual insecurity. As the Church required aid of the civil power, the civil power required aid of the Church. The state demanded cultured and docile human instruments. and the Church alone could supply them. The state required a fund out of which to salary and reward its servants, the benefices of the Church alone constituted such a fund. The state required agents who would not found formidable families and create hereditary interests. Such agents were alone to be found within the Church. The king desired the development of his estates, and no bailiff was so good as the capable abbot. Charles the Great, who saw so many things, saw these things. He made large use of the Church as

---

[1] Hauck, *Kirchengeschichte Deutschlands*, vol. iii., pp. 57-9. For calculations as to the extent of clerical wealth at the end of the Carolingian period, cf. Waitz, *D.Γ.G.*, vii., p. 186; Inama-Sternegg, *Wirthschaftsgeschichte*, i., p. 291; *Grossgrundherrschaft*, p. 32; Lamprecht, *Deutsches Wirthschaftsleben*, i. 703. For a specimen of an ecclesiastical estate, see the beautiful map of the estates of Prüm (Lamprecht, *D.W.*, vol. ii.).

an instrument of government, perceiving that in the
protracted agony of the Merovingian age the bishops
had actually governed the French cities, and his
example was followed by Otto I.

So, too, the real control of episcopal elections lay
always with the emperor.   The chapter and the people
made a manifestation of sympathy; they proceeded
either before or after the royal will had been expressed
to a formal election, but the emperor really nominated.
It was no new practice.   The Merovingian kings had
entirely disregarded the freedom of capitular and
popular elections.   Charles the Great had allowed elections to be free, but had exacted royal confirmation,
and the arrangement was confirmed by his successor
Lewis in 816.   But even Lewis frequently violated the
concordat, and the later Carolings always secured the
appointment of their nominees.   There were only a
few specially privileged churches which maintained
their old electoral liberties.   Otto and his successors
stood in the old ways.   When the representatives of
the people and chapter came to the court with the
staff of the deceased bishop, the king would give it to
his nominee with the words, " Accipe Ecclesiam,"
" Receive the Church."   Nor did any fine distinction lurk
beneath the phrase.   The German king was not merely
conferring land and buildings, but a high spiritual and
political office.

This led straight to simony.   It was an old German
custom that no one should appear before the king
without a gift.   As early as the first quarter of the
sixth century the clerks of Auvergne come to the king
with gifts of money to obtain the election of St. Gall,
and Gregory of Tours remarks upon the origin of that
brisk traffic in benefices, which, like the astrologers in

Rome, was so often forbidden and so continuously retained. The practice, which was protested against by Gregory the Great [590-610] and by the council of Toledo in 633, was formally renounced by Pippin in 755, and it is to the lasting honour of Charles the Great that during his reign no bishopric was bought or sold. But with the death of Lewis the Pious this scrupulosity vanished. The later Carolings succumbed to temptation, and in 877 Hincmar of Rheims complained, possibly with some slight exaggeration, that hardly any one could obtain any honour or preferment without paying a price. The Saxons were far above the average of their time in piety, and resolution, and intellectual endowments. Yet although Henry the Fowler is said to have promised to abandon simony, if he should succeed in vanquishing the Hungarians, it is clear that the promise was not observed.

The reports of the synod of Ingelheim [998] and the chronicle of Thietmar of Merseburg show us that the Ottos were not immaculate. Conrad the Salic professed virtue, but lapsed from his professions, and of all the German emperors since Lewis the Pious, Henry III. alone seems to stand quit of the common accusation.[1] It was no part of Henry's scheme to relinquish his control over ecclesiastical nominations,[2] but his pure and enthusiastic nature revolted against a traffic which his clerical advisers pronounced to be sinful. In Italy and Germany he waged war resolutely against the prevailing vice, which, according to Desiderius of Monte Cassino, had left scarcely a man uncorrupted with its contagion.[3] In

---

[1] Wipo, *Vita Cuon.*, c. 8, "In omni vita sua pro omnibus dignitatibus ecclesiasticis unius oboli precium non dicitur adhuc accepisse." SS. iv. 85.

[3] Mabillon, *Acta*, SS. ; *Ord. S. Ben. Saec.*, iv., p. ii., p. 451.

1046 he summoned a synod at Pavia, and addressed them in the following words: "It is with grief that I speak to you, for as Christ of his own grace and goodness consented to come to redeem us, so he gave orders to his own ' Ye have received of grace, give of grace.' For you, corrupted by avarice and cupidity, who ought to confer blessing, by transgressing thus in your giving and in your receiving are cursed according to the canon. My father exercised overmuch the same damnable avarice during his lifetime. Verily, I fear for the peril of his soul. Whosoever among you then is conscious of being contaminated by this blot must be removed from the sacred ministry according to the disposition of the canons." The bishops were stupefied, knew not what to answer, and finally threw themselves upon the mercy of the king. Henry consoled them in the following words: " Go," he said, "and strive to spend well what you have received unlawfully, and remember to intercede the more zealously for the soul of my father who, together with you, is found in this fault." Then he issued an edict for the whole of the empire that no clerical rank or ministry should be acquired by money. If any person should presume to give or receive money for such a purpose, he should be deprived of all office, and visited with excommunication.[1] The decrees of Pavia were brought home to the world by the deposition of three popes, and by the appointment to the papal see of a series of men who at last cleansed the Augean stable of Roman ecclesiastical politics, and restored the prestige of the Curia. The emperor who in 1046 received from the Roman people the dignity of patrician, which was supposed to carry with it the first and decisive voice

---

[1] *Rod. Glab.*, p. 5, SS. vii., p. 71; cf. Steindorff, *Heinrich III.*, pp. 309, 311; No. 2., 897, and Giesebrecht, ii. 5, 659.

in papal elections, used his privilege to enthrone the extreme ecclesiastical doctrine of the Cluniac puritans in the chair which had been sullied by so many crimes of lust and violence. In so doing he prepared the way for the independence of the papacy. The popes henceforward recover the leadership of the Catholic Church which had fallen to the Ottos, which had been shared between Henry II. and Benedict VIII., and which had been exercised so enthusiastically and forcibly by Henry III.

Henry cleansed Rome and revived the papacy, but he could not bind his successors. The spiritual advisers of Henry IV. threw the decrees of Pavia to the winds, and the War of the Investitures illustrates nothing so clearly as the reluctance of the German Church to consent to reform.[1] When the war closed with the concordat of Worms in 1122, it seemed as if the honours of the struggle were divided. Free canonical election and free consecration were granted to all the churches within the kingdom or the empire. The investiture by ring and staff was handed over to the spiritual authority. On the other hand, it was conceded that the elected person should receive his regalia by the sceptre from the emperor, and should do homage to the emperor; that elections of such bishops and abbots in the German kingdom as held their regalia direct of the emperor should be conducted in the emperor's presence without simony or any violence, so that if any discord should arise, the emperor might support the saner party with the counsel of the

---

[1] For Henry IV.'s attitude, cf. Ebbo, *Vita Ottonis*, c. 7, 8 (SS. xii., pp. 827-8), "Quantum profectui et honori aecclesiae Babenbergensis congratuler, hinc advertite, quod cum tot magne et alti sanguinis persone episcopatum hunc a me precio comparare temptarent, ego illum potius ... vobis eligere malui."

metropolitan and the bishops of the province.[1]   It is
said that these terms were subsequently changed to the
advantage of the Church by Lothair ; that he promised
to give up the right of being present at elections ; that
he consented to allow consecration to precede temporal
investiture, and contented himself with the looser bond
of fealty instead of the stricter bond of homage.   The
statement is only contained in one narrative, and its
correctness has been suspected[2]; but whether Lothair
made the promise or not, nothing is clearer than that
both the concordat of Worms and the engagement of
Lothair were from the beginning treated by the emperor
with supreme contempt.   We know that Lothair himself, that Frederick I., and that Philip of Swabia were
present at elections ; that Conrad III. and Frederick I.
were invested with the temporals before consecration ;
and that both emperors and patrons unblushingly
trafficked in ecclesiastical patronage,[3] and as few
elections passed without a dispute in the chapter, the
emperor almost always appointed as he chose.

At the very beginning of his reign Barbarossa tried a
fall with the papacy and won.   Exercising pressure upon
part of the chapter of Magdeburg, the emperor caused
the election of his friend Bishop Wichmann of Zeitz.
It had been apparently held by Gregory VII., and it was
common doctrine in the Church, that translations from
one see to another could only be accomplished through
the medium of the pope, and two popes, Eugenius III.
and Anastasius IV. protested that the election was contrary to the canons.   But Wichmann travelled to Rome,
supported in his candidature by the recommendations of
the German prelates.   The timid Anastasius fled from

[1] Weiland, i., No. 107, 108.   [2] *Narratio de Electione Lotharii.*
[3] Bertold, *Entwickelung der Landeshoheit*, p. 59.

Rome to salve his conscience, leaving, however, the pallium upon the altar.[1] The bishop hesitated to take it in the absence of the pontiff, but his attendants were troubled with no such scruples. They picked up the pall, and Wichmann returned to Germany a complete archbishop. From that moment Barbarossa's control of the Church was complete. He nominated laymen to important sees[2]; he utilized two archbishops, Rainald of Cologne and Christian of Mainz to fight his battles in Italy, and to go upon diplomatic missions. He gave to Henry the Lion, the right of investiture to Oldenburg, Mecklenburg and Ratzeburg, and to all Slavonic bishoprics which might be founded in the future. He dispensed similar rights over the sees of Lausanne, Geneva, and Sitten to Bertold IV. of Zähringen, and such was the prestige of Barbarossa that some chapters, recognizing that their electoral rights had been whittled away to a formality, voluntarily surrendered them to the emperor.

Henry VI. was equally firm and equally corrupt. He sold the bishoprics of Cambrai and Liége. He appointed his vice-chancellor, Henry of Maestricht, to Worms, and when a bishop protested that he held his office not from the emperor but the pope, the pale electric little Swabian ordered his attendants there and then to beat him and to pluck out the hairs of his beard.[3]

Habits of long standing are not easily uprooted, and the old practice of simony and imperial control survived

---

[1] Otton. Fris., *Gesta Frid.*, ii. 6 ; *Dictatus Greg.*, vii., ed. Jaffé, *Bibl.*, ii., p. 175.

[2] *Chron. Reg. Col.*, 1149, " Interea legati Coloniensium Italiam venerunt domnum Reinoldum cancellarium sibi in pontificem deposcunt. Gavisus ergo imperator quod locum honoris deferendi ei invenisset, grato animo Coloniensem episcopatum et quae sui juris erant tradidit."

[3] Innocent III., *Reg. de Negot. Imp.*, ep. 29.; Migne *Patr. Lat.*, vol. 216, col. 1029.

the renunciations of Philip of Swabia, of Otto IV., and
of Frederick II. It is clear that Frederick II. demanded
ِinvestiture before consecration.[1] The *Sachsenspiegel*
holds to the old law,[2] and even the *Schwabenspiegel*,
which was papalist, admits that no bishop, abbot, or
abbess can dispose of a fief until the king has conferred
upon them the regalia.[3] The emperors did not only
appoint the leaders of the ecclesiastical army. They
freely helped themselves to the war chest. The
property of the see was held to be conferred by
royal investiture, and the consent of the empire was
required before it could be lawfully alienated.[4] During
a vacancy, which it was within the power of the king
to prolong, he disposed of the diocesan revenues. But
he was not content with this. There was an old and
barbarous practice, which yet was not without a justification, of despoiling the house of a deceased bishop.
Bishops and priests, it was argued, were made to serve
spiritual ends ; it would be intolerable if they were
allowed to build up and to bequeath private fortunes ؛
and the most effective steps to prevent the perversion of
a spiritual office was that a hungry crowd should invade
the bishop's house before the corpse was cold and carry
off every shred of the furniture. The premise was pious,
but the conclusion was indecent. The procedure, which
had originally been patronized by clerks, spread to the
laity, who may be excused for forgetting its original
justification. Yet there is no evidence that any German

---

[1] *Sententia de Regalibus non infeodandis* (Weiland, ii., No. 212).

[2] *Ssp.*, iii. 59. 1.   [3] *Swsp.*, 110, sct. 3.

[4] Weiland, vol. i., Nos. 148, 328, 336 ; vol. ii., Nos. 187, 227, 282, 289.
As Henry II. sensibly remarks, "Oportet ut in aecclesiis multae sint
facultates ... quia cui plus committitur, plus ab eo exigitur. Multa enim
debet (Fulda) dare servitia et romanae et regali curiae propter quod
scriptum est : Reddite quae sunt Caesaris Caesari et quae sunt Dei
Deo."

emperor exercised the right of spoils before Frederick
Barbarossa.[1] Frederick may have reflected that the continuance of the imperial government depended upon the
control of the ecclesiastical princes. The lay princes had
become hereditary, and practically independent. If the
ecclesiastical princes, who were so much more numerous,
followed their example, the power of the emperor would
be reduced to a phantom. So Frederick determined to
emphasize the difference between the fiefs of the lay and
the ecclesiastical princes. But at the same time he was
willing to offer a compensation. In defiance of the
customary law of Worms he decided, relying upon
Roman precedent, that the clerks might have testamentary rights. In other words, he prohibits the
exercise of the right of spoils against the lower clergy.
He reserves its exercise against the bishops. The *jus
spolii* is to be an imperial right, limited both as to the
person who was entitled to use it, and as to the persons
against whom it was to be used.

Vain precautions! How could the emperor, making
in his own person so many signal manifestoes of
rapacity, hope to restrain the greed of his subjects by
a quotation from the Latin laws of his "sacred" predecessors? The *jus spolii* was exercised by patrons and
by *ministeriales* despite the denunciations of councils
till the end of the fifteenth century. The Church indeed
often exacted a promise to abjure the practice. Otto
IV., Philip of Swabia, Frederick II. all surrendered the

[1] Frederick seems to speak of it as an old custom. Cf. Lacomblet, *Urkb.*,
i. 417, " Cum itaque constet et ex antiquo jure regum et imperatorum
atque ex cotidiana consuetudine manifestum est quod episcopis in imperio
nostro constitutis ab hac vita decedentibus episcopales redditus et bona
deputata usibus eorum, annona videlicet et vinum, et cetera hujusmodi
victualia seu servitia . . . fisco regali universo jure debeant applicari."
The words, though they may cover the *jus spolii*, seem chiefly to refer to
the right of enjoying the regalia during a vacancy.

jus spolii, but the value of this surrender is sufficiently attested by the fact that Frederick II. subsequent to all these renunciations granted an exemption from the right by way of special privilege to the Archbishop of Tarentaise in 1226, and to the Bishop of Hildesheim in 1228, that even small princes, such as the Counts of Henneburg, Hohenlohe, and Nassau exercised it with the utmost freedom.   Few things did more to alienate the German Church from the empire than this ill-judged application of a most vexatious practice to archiepiscopal and episcopal sees by Frederick Barbarossa.

This was not all.   Not only does the emperor appoint the bishops and archbishops, take the fruits of the see during vacancies, pillage the episcopal palace, compel his prelates to follow him to Italy to attend his councils, to go his errands to Rome, Constantinople, Rouen, London, to provide men-at-arms, and to lead his armies, but he also becomes their feudatory.   He condescends to accept, he even extorts, ecclesiastical fiefs from the prelates who receive their regalia from him.   Now, this was not in accordance with the strictest conceptions of German feudal law.   There was a time when men believed that if a lord held a fief of his feudal peer or of his feudal inferior, he lowered his Heerschild, and sank in the feudal scale.   This, too, is the general doctrine in the thirteenth century, but it is qualified by one exception.   The king may be the man of an ecclesiastical prince.   Now the lawyers do not attempt to give a reason for this exception.   They cannot say why the king may be the man of an ecclesiastical prince but not of a lay prince.   The symmetry of their feudal hierarchy is spoiled, but they accept the fact and suppress apologies.   The truth is that the king found the ecclesiastical fiefs too tempting to be resisted.   There seems, indeed, to be evidence that for a time appearances were saved. Lothair and Conrad III. transferred their inherited fiefs as soon as possible to their heirs, but then all disguise was thrown off. Frederick I., who tries to build up in Swabia and Franconia a royal domain, such as his predecessors had tried to build up in Saxony, keeps his ecclesiastical fiefs after his accession to the throne, steadily acquires others, and, though apparently avoiding the ceremony of homage, receives investiture openly of the bishops. If Henry VI. had lived to a ripe old age and left a full-grown successor, the hold of the Hohenstauffen family upon the property of the Church might have become too strong even to be shaken off. The princes of the church saw this. Many of their fiefs had been seized against their will, and they had grown restive under the hand of these powerful vassals. Here and there a *ministerialis* of a see, waxen powerful and ambitious, had built a castle, and bought imperial acquiescence by surrendering it to the emperor and holding it of him as a fief.[1] And so during the struggle between Philip and Otto the prelates make a resolute effort to liberate themselves. We see how Philip, in 1199, has to renounce the fiefs which his father and brother had held of Strassburg ; how, in 1201, he renounces the fiefs which he himself held of Wurzburg. When Frederick II. comes to Germany and has to beg for ecclesiastical support, he must pay the same price. In 1212 he renounces all the property which his progenitors and other emperors and kings held of Mainz, and all his fiefs from Worms and Lorsch.

---

[1] Conrad of Wittelsbach when he returns to the see of Mainz [1187-1190] complains "Oppressa etiam fuit [ecclesia Mog.] per novas municiones sicuti fuit Wizenowe [Weissenau] quam Tuto tunc camerarius aedificaverat et regio dominio subdiderat" [Stumpf, *Acta Mog. sec.*, xiii., pp. 114-117].

In 1220 he has to consent to the provision that in "whatever way any fief belonging to an ecclesiastical prince shall fall vacant, we will never invade it on our own authority, still less by violence, unless we are able to obtain it of the good-will and free grant of the prince." A most pregnant clause, for it reveals the unpopular methods of the emperors, and in them one of the most potent clauses for the decline of imperial influence in Germany. We do not know whether Frederick and his sons respected their promise to abstain from violence. We can only say that the Church was never able to shake off the Hohenstauffen feudatory. In 1237 Frederick II. is again found in possession of the Mainz fiefs. There was a long struggle over the Wurzburg fiefs which ended in a compromise in 1225. The renunciation of the Strassburg fiefs by Philip of Swabia was hotly contested, and Bamberg, Spires, Metz, Basle, Chur, Passau, Kempten, Marbach, and Ottobeuern can be proved to have numbered either the emperor or else one of his sons among their vassals. Thus the independence of the German ecclesiastical princes could only be fully secured by the fall of the Hohenstauffen dynasty.[1]

During the reigns of Barbarossa and Henry VI. the Church, though subject to the emperors, entered keenly

[1] Some of the bishops in the twelfth century were trying to get rid of their feudatories altogether—cf. Frederick I.'s diploma for Bamberg, 1160 (Ussermann, No. cxxiii), "Eximimus ab omni jure feodali castra que in tuo dominio absolute habere dinosceris . . . [13 castles named]. Hec igitur et alia si qua pro necessitatibus ecclesie tue, cuius bona late dispersa sunt, vel edificaveris vel aliter opitulante Domino adeptus fueris, ecclesie tue ea lege speciali et vinculo juris innodamus, ut nulli successorum tuorum potestas et licentia sit aliquid de his infeodare aut sub colore castrensis beneficii, vel aliquo quolibet malo ingenio a privatis usibus episcopii alienare." For the whole question of imperial church-fiefs, cf. Ficker, *Von Heerschilde*.

into all the affairs of the empire. The council of princes,
which in reality governed Germany, was mainly composed of ecclesiastics, and as the appeal to Rome was a
long, costly, and dangerous affair, as the Pope was
prevailingly hostile to the emperor, and as the relations
of the German clergy with Rome were closely watched,
the grievances and doubts of the Church were generally
laid before the imperial Curia. Can a bishop enfeoff or
alienate from a church a tithe which is not forthcoming
in his own time? If a bishop gives leave to a man to
build a house in a public square or place, is the bishop's
successor bound to respect the act? A *ministerialis* of
a church marries a freewoman. Is the offspring of the
marriage free? Can a bishop enfeoff or alienate goods
which belong to his kitchen or to any of his offices?
Has an advocate any rights over the dower of a church
or of a clerk alive or dead? Is the will of a clerk made
on a bed of sickness, and disposing of goods above the
value of five shillings without the consent of his natural
heirs, to be held valid or invalid? Is an ecclesiastical
prince bound to pay the debts of his predecessor? Is a
bishop bound to give the heirs of his predecessors his
predecessors' furniture? Such questions are referred to
the imperial court under Barbarossa and his son, and so
strong is the tendency to appeal to this quarter, that
the Bishop of Spires complains to Henry VI. that
appeals are made even before sentence is given in the
episcopal court. It would even seem that the judges
from whose decision the appeal was made, were not
bound to be present themselves before the princes so
long as they made clear in writing the facts of the case,
the manner of the appeal, and the term within which
an appeal was legitimate.[1] But when Innocent III.

[1] Weiland, ii., Nos. 328, 329, 336, 235, 227, 300, 336, 335.

ascended the papal throne to profit by the dissensions between the Welfs and the Wibelins, and to apply systematically to Germany the principles of papal autocracy which had always been theoretically acknowledged, this intimate connection between the German Church and the emperor gradually dissolved. Burdened, sometimes almost ruined by the Italian wars, vexed by the regalia and the right of spoils, compelled to enfeoff the members of the imperial family either as vassals or advocates, the faithful German Church wavers in its allegiance, takes advantage of a disputed election to extract a kind of magna charta of liberties from the emperor, and ultimately consents to allow the destruction of the imperial dynasty at the hands of the pope. When Conradin in 1268 led his forlorn hope to fight the papalists at Tagliacozzo, only three thousand Germans followed him into the field.

All through German history, from Rabanus Maurus to Gerhoh of Reichersberg, voices were raised within the Church to protest against the secular functions which the imperial policy had thrust upon it.[1] The voices are not many, nor are they influential, but they serve to remind us that from the ninth century onward there were always witnesses in Germany to the ideal of the spiritual life. Yet it would be unfair to tax the Ottos or their successors with the charge of wilfully or consciously degrading a noble instrument of civilization. Otto I. perceived that under his father the Church of Germany was fast becoming the prey of the nobility. The Bavarian duke had obtained from the Fowler the right to nominate to the Bavarian sees. If the example spread, the Church in Germany would split into a number of tribal organizations, which would intensify national

---

[1] Rabanus, *Opp.*, v., p. 795 ; Hauck, ii. 573 ; *ib.*, iii. 74.

differences, and possibly destroy the free circulation of talent through the kingdom. Otto was not choosing between a spiritual church on the one hand and a political church on the other. The alternative was be-tween a Church dominated and bullied by dukes and counts, and a Church controlled and utilized for the service of the nation by the king. Even if there were no other implications, the Church gained by the change of patron. With the single exception of Conrad II. all the emperors from Otto the Great to Frederick II. were lettered men. In an age when it was said that pictures were the literature of the laymen—"pictura est laici litteratura"—these laymen stand out above others as representatives of culture. They were not deeply read in theology, but some of them were better read than their own divines With the exception of Frederick II. there was no man of commanding intel-lectual gifts among them, and there were only two religious enthusiasts, Otto III. and Henry III. But in the main, the emperors stand forth as representatives of civilization, and though they took money from eccle-siastics in search of promotion, and allowed the princes at their courts to be bribed as freely as themselves, Frederick I. was probably justified in saying that royal appointments turned out better than capitular elections.[1] It is true that the highest posts generally went to men of noble extraction, and that the chroniclers are careful to mention the fact.[2] Otto I. cannot be acquitted of

---

[1] "Sciatis tamen quia dum pro voluntate imperatorum ista dispensaretur plures justi inventi sunt sacerdotes quam hoc tempore dum per electionem intronizantur" (Arnold Lub., iii., c. 18).

[2] Gudenus, *Sylloge* [1728], remarks bitterly, *apropos* of Christian II. of Mainz [1249, 50], "Admiranda res! per integrum seculi xiii. decursum vix ullus occurrit in Germania episcopus cujus natales decantati non sunt, et tamen supremi electoris ecclesiasti cognomen nondum potuit exquiri."

nepotism, or Henry II. of having unduly favoured Bavarians. It is true also that the clerkly warriors outnumber the clerkly theologians. But we cannot conclude from this that most of the German church patronage was wilfully exercised with a corrupt design. The interests of many institutions are often best secured by the alternate appointments of men of very various gifts. The scholar allows the neighbouring nobility to tyrannize over his flock; the soldier must be chosen to succeed him. "I must send a man," said Henry II. to his brother-in-law, Adalbero, who had turned the town of Tréves into a solitude, and driven the archbishop to Coblentz, "who can put a stop to your wild deeds." The emperor chose Poppo of Bamberg, young, robust, and descended of a fine fighting stock, to be the new archbishop, and he proved the man for the occasion. He distributed sixty prebends to as many knights, and then began to besiege the neighbouring castles and eventually rid the city of Trèves from the bird of prey.[1] In the Rhenish bishoprics, surrounded by the turbulent nobility of Lotharingia, the art of war was a necessary episcopal accomplishment. Many of the prelates may have sought their quarrels; many may have bought their way to a bishopric with a view to carrying out some family vendetta; some succumbed to the tempta-

---

The appointment of Willigis of Mainz [985] was resisted by many "ob vilitatem sui generis" (*Ann. Hild.*, SS. iii. 62; cf. Will., *Regesten von Mainz, passim*). Norbert was condemned at Fritzlar in 1118 for discarding fine clothes, since the custom of the land was to wear them, especially among the nobles, of whom he was one (*Vita S. Norberti*; *Acta*, SS. *Boll*. i. 826; Harz, *Conc. Germ.*, iii. 272, 3).

[1] *Vita Adalberonis*, ii., c. 27, SS. iv. 668. The desolation of Trèves is thus described: "Urbes certe depopulatae, vici et villae incensae omnes, viri omnes et feminae et totum promiscuum vulgus ferro, fame, igne pestilentiaque consumptum : multi etiam nobiles in paupertatem et magnam miseriam devoluti : multi gladio perempti."

tions of military display,[1] and squandered the revenues
of their sees in the collection of a small army.   But
upon many war was forced as an imperious necessity,
and the exercise of royal patronage cannot be condemned solely on the ground that it emphasized the
military character of the Church.

Still the emperors cannot be acquitted of having
made the Church an instrument subservient not only
to their civil, but also to their military needs.   But if
they may be accused of having steeped the Church in
secularity, they might reasonably reply not only that
they thereby helped to unify the state, to transcend
provincial antagonisms, and to crush feudal anarchy,
but that by the use of the resources of the Church
they were enabled to prosecute ideal objects and large
policies.   They might also reply that in binding the
Church to a long term of imperial servitude, they were
in reality conceding to it an ampler sphere of activity
and the highest liberty of which it was then capable.

We must remember too that nothing is so difficult as
to form a strongly-marked professional class in a semi
barbarous society, where there is little differentiation of
functions, and where the whole structure of civilization
is constantly being threatened by elementary perils.
It is questionable whether, if it had not been for the
highly specialized discipline of the monasteries, the
clerical profession would ever have obtained the distinctness of outline which in Catholic countries at the
present day so effectually marks it off from all other
callings.   The monasteries performed many useful
functions in society.   They preserved a tradition of
learning, they showed a pattern of self-denial, they did
much for education and agriculture ; but perhaps the

[1] *Gesta Trevirorum*, c. 22, ad ann. 1102.

most important of all their services was that they
maintained the distinction between the lay and the
clerical profession.   Whenever the clerical profession
in the Middle Ages showed signs of losing tone and
distinctness, it was rescued by a monastic revival.   But
nothing is more remarkable in medieval history than
the extreme difficulty which was found in maintaining
even a moderate standard of clerical morals.   The
clergy, in fact, were too large, too important, and too
highly-privileged a class to escape the dangers of partial
secularization.   Even in the thirteenth century, German
councils had to legislate to enforce the tonsure upon
clerks.

It is indeed looseness of thought which prompts us to
speak of the secularization of the clergy in the Middle
Ages.   The phrase postulates a golden age of ecclesiastical history which had as little real existence as the
state of nature prior to the social contract.   It is truer
to history to imagine that after the barbaric invasions
the influence of the Roman Church was extended partly
by pure missionary enthusiasm, partly by the superstitions or enlightened self-interest of barbarous kings,
until it drew recruits from all classes of society ; and
being therefore stocked with men in every stage of
culture from the unlettered rustic to the subtle meta-
physician, it could not help reflecting, like every other
large profession, the manners and opinions of society
around it ; was fuller of barbarians than of scholars,
of sensualists than of saints, of half-pagan superstition
than of enlightened belief; that consumed by debasing
avarice, racked by mean ambitions, largely given to
childish parade and old wives' gossip and morbid
sentiment, it yet had moments of true religious ex-
altation, of the highest self-surrender, of serious and

heroic study, of enlightened statesmanship, of brave
conflicts with temptation, of ardent and humorous and
tender sympathy.

The German Church in the Middle Ages presents
these contrasts.   There are famous clerical generals like
Rainald of Cologne and Christian of Mainz; there are
skilled architects like Bernward of Hildesheim and
Benno of Osnabrück; missionaries like Anschar, who
converted Denmark and Sweden; like Adalbert, who
met with death in Prussia; like Otto of Bamberg,
builder and administrator, whose curious and thrilling
experiences in Pomerania are so vividly narrated by
his biographer Herbord.   Great things are done for the
colonization of waste lands by the Cistercian monks and
by prelates such as Frederick, Archbishop of Bremen,
and Wichmann, Archbishop of Magdeburg.   There are
canonists like Regino of Prüm and Burchard of Worms;
clever and faithful historians like Adam of Bremen;
scholars like Rabanus Maurus, "the first preceptor of
Germany," and William of Hirschau; and one great
philosopher towering above all others, Albertus Magnus,
the creator of the Aristotelian theology of the Middle
Ages, and the master of Aquinas.   The Church too
supplied many statesmen.   No one, perhaps, of the
eminence of Abbot Suger of St. Denis or of Archbishop Lanfranc of Canterbury, but Willigis of Mainz
governs the country during the minority of Otto III.,
and Engelbert of Cologne during the minority of
Henry VII.   The founder of the Carthusian Order,
which, by combining the ideals of the common and of
the eremitic life, and by restricting the acquisition of
property, preserved its early purity longer than any
other monastic order in the Middle Ages, was St.
Bruno, a German from Cologne.   The saintly Norbert

of Xanten was the chief adviser of the Emperor Lothair, and the founder of the Premonstratensian Order of Clerks, which was distinguished as being the first attempt to combine the monastic ideal with pastoral activity. Many rude, violent, and treacherous figures pass across the stage, such as Adalbert of Bremen and Adolph of Cologne, and one of the darkest pages in German history is the treatment of the northern and middle Slaves by men who were professing to spread a gospel of peace and good-will. Strange contrasts were often united in the same person. The two most conspicuous forgers of ecclesiastical documents in this period, Pilgrim of Passau and Adaldag of Hamburg, were otherwise noted for the zeal with which they promoted the spread of the gospel among the heathen, and for the vigour of their administration. The vivacious and witty Adalbero of Trèves, whose charmed life during the war of the Investitures gives rise to many a pleasant saga, finds nothing in the world amiss except the prospect of a poor archbishopric. A brave captain in war, he yet has pleasure in the converse of the learned. An ardent papalist, he is yet the most daredevil Burgundian knight in Europe. A founder of monasteries and a patron of learning, he keeps the state of a mighty prince, sailing to the imperial court at Frankfort with a fleet of more than forty ships, and attended by the Dukes of Lorraine and Limburg, by eight counts, and two French philosophers.[1]

---

[1] *Vita S. Bernwardi*, SS. iv., pp. 757-82 ; *Vita Bennonis*, SS. xii., pp. 58-84 ; *Vita S. Anskarii*, SS. ii., pp. 683-725 ; *Passio S. Adalberti*, SS. v., pp. 706-8 ; *Vita S. Adalberti*, SS. iv., p. 577 ; *Vita Ottonis*, SS. xii., p. 728 ; *Vita Burchardi*, SS. iv., p. 829 ; *Burchardi Decretorum libri*, *ap*. Migne, *Patr. Lat.*, cxl., pp. 537-1038 ; *Reginonis libri duo de synodalibus causis et disciplinis ecclesiasticis*, *ap*. Migne, *Patr. Lat.*, cxxxii., pp. 185-370 ; *Vita*

Still, while we must acknowledge that the Church in Germany contained many eminent men of various gifts, it was yet on the whole far less conspicuous in culture and learning than the Churches of France and of England, and if we deduct Lotharingia and Burgundy, the balance will be still more heavily inclined against it. The Rhenish districts were no doubt more advanced in civilization than the rest of Germany, yet with the single exception of Albert the Great, who, however, received his schooling in Italy, there is no name of more than respectable importance associated with this region. A diligent collector of educational facts like Specht can tell us very little about the Rhenish schools.[1] It is true that Bishop Burchard of Worms [1000-1025] collects all the Carolingian rules for the education of the clergy. No illiterates are to be ordained; every ordinand is to know the mass, the pericopies, the baptismal rite, the psalter, the homilies for Sundays and feast days, the penetentiaries, the rules for determining ecclesiastical dates, the portions of the canon law which are essential to his profession. Every parochial priest is to have a clerk, who can sing, and read the epistle and lessons, and keep school, and admonish his parishioners to send their sons to the Church to be instructed. It also seems to be the case that the Salian emperors encouraged the cathedral school at Spires, and that this school was at one time largely attended. A few letters written by ecclesiastics of Worms in Henry II.'s reign

Willigisi, SS. xv., pp. 743-5 ; *Vita S. Engelberti*, *ap.* Böhmer, *Fontes*, ii., pp. 294-329 ; Ficker, J., *Engelbert der Heilige* ; *S. Brunonis Acta*, *ap.* Migne, *Patr. Lat.*, clii., pp. 1-631 ; *Vita S. Norberti*, SS. xii., pp. 662-703 ; Winter, *Die Prämonstratenser des 12 Jahr. und ihre Bedeutung für das nordöstliche Deutschland* ; Dümmler, *Pilgrim von Passau und das Erzbisthum Lorch* ; *Gesta Adalberonis*, SS. viii., p. 236. For further references, cf. Potthast, *Bibliotheca Historica medii aevi.*

[1] Specht, *Geschichte des Unterrichtswesen in Deutschland*, pp. 329-37.

prove the existence of a moderate standard of culture in a small circle at that time.[1]   Yet even when these facts are stated, when in addition it is shown, that Hildebrand at one time studied in Cologne, that Marianus Scotus was summoned to Mainz [1059-84], that Gregory V. was probably trained at Worms, little has been done to vindicate the ecclesiastical culture of the Rhineland.   In the eleventh century inquisitive Germans were going to Paris or Chartres or Angoulême for instruction,[2] and in the twelfth and thirteenth centuries the vogue of Paris-made scholarship and philosophy was even still higher.   The general illiteracy of the Rhenish clergy is clearly proved by a chapter in the Council of Cologne in 1260, which runs as follows, "Also concerning clerks who have been noted for insufficiency of learning, that is to say illiteracy, as we do not require eminent knowledge of all men, but that they should know how to read and sing competently at the ministration of the divine office ; so we order that those who cannot in person do their duty in the way of singing in the choir and reading, should employ a suitable person to do it for them according as shall seem good to the discretion of the Dean."[3]   Here then in Cologne, the most important commercial town in Germany, in the last half of the thirteenth century, clerical illiteracy is formally sanctified by a provincial council.   To those who know the disturbed political condition of the Rhine valley in the thirteenth century, the struggles between the bishops and the crafts on the one hand, and the bishops and the nobility on the other, the result is not wonderful.

[1] Pflugk-Harttung, *Iter Italicum*, p. 382 ff.

[2] Hauck, *Kirchengeschichte Deutschlands*, iii. 932.

[3] Harzheim, *Concilia Germaniae*, iii., p. 590.   Clerical illiteracy was, however, by no means confined to Germany.   Cf. the remarkable passage in Roger Bacon's *Compendium Philosophiae*, SS. xxviii., p. 580.

Nor again was the intellectual condition of the rest of
Germany very far different.   The two famous south
German monastic schools of Reichenau and St. Gall
had seen their best days before the close of the eleventh
century.   The war of the Investitures ruined them; the
papalist abbots of Reichenau fought out a long and
bitter feud with the imperialist abbots of St. Gall, and
all the lamps of learning went out in the course of this
obscure and tedious conflict.   The cathedral school of
Freising, famous in the ninth and tenth centuries for its
music, recovered for a moment some of its prestige
under Otto of Freising (1137-57), who introduced
disputations after the Parisian method, and has the
credit of having educated Ragewin, the spirited con-
tinuator of the bishops' history.   But the revival was
short-lived; the school rapidly declined in reputation,
and did not succeed in educating a single man whose
literary achievements have survived to posterity.   Of
the other south German centres of culture few were
more important in early times than the Benedictine
monastery of Tegernsee.   The calligraphy of its scribes
and the excellence of the materials, with which and upon
which they worked, were famous throughout Germany.
Henry III. and Frederick I. ordered books to be transcribed there, and the monastery seems always to have
been actively engaged in the useful art of multiplying
manuscripts.   Yet the original literary achievements of
Tegernsee are not remarkable.   The *Ruotlieb*, one of
the most curious monuments of early German poetry,
was possibly written by Abbot Fromund.   The *Ludus
de Antechristo*, and the *Odae Quirinales* and *Bucolica
Quirinalia* of Metellus were produced in the monastery
in the middle of the twelfth century.   But the surviving original labours of an imperial abbey which had

been singularly sheltered from invasion and violence by its situation on an island in the Lake of Constance, and which had occupied itself with literature for several centuries, do not amount to more than a clever school-boy could produce in a fortnight.

The school of St. Emmeran of Regensburg was more productive. From the middle of the tenth to the end of the eleventh century it produced several men who played a part in the religious and literary movements of their time. Balderich of Liége, Poppo of Trèves, Wolfgang of Regensburg, all came from this school. A catalogue of the library composed between 975 and 1000 shows it to have contained three hundred volumes, and an ignorant enthusiast of the eleventh century has ventured to compare the quality of its studies, and to prefer the truth of its philosophy to the studies and the philosophy pursued in Athens. The Aristotle of " this second Athens" was Othlo, "the first voluminous German writer," whose piety and conceit induced him to compile a book of Proverbs with a view of extirpating the study of the Latin classics. The Plato of Regensburg was William of Hirschau, the protagonist of classical learning, and a vigorous writer on grammar, dialectic, rhetoric, and astronomy, the creator of many monasteries in the Black Forest and in Bavaria, and the unresting protagonist of the Hildebrandine cause in Germany. But the bishops of Regensburg were cursed with ambition. In the twelfth century we find them engaged in active feuds with the neighbouring nobles, and the Italian wars of Barbarossa must have drained the resources of the see and deflected the energies of the chapter. It was an ancient privilege of the greater church of Regensburg that no one should be received into the chapter unless he were either a noble or a literate. The

privilege itself is significant of the way in which ecclesiastical patronage was exercised, and in times of local
feud or imperial war service we may suspect that
a noble would have more chance of obtaining a stall
than a "literate or one sufficiently exercised in the
divine offices." In any case the school of Regensburg
declines, as all the south German schools had declined
before it. There is not a single well-known name or
book connected with it in the twelfth and thirteenth
centuries.

Nothing is so difficult as to estimate the degree of
culture obtaining in a large profession many centuries
ago. Yet all the evidence obtainable concerning the
culture of the German Church, from the beginning of
the tenth to the end of the thirteenth century, tends to
show that it was inferior both in quality and amount to
the contemporaneous culture of France, England, and
Italy. It is perhaps only during the Ottonian period
when Germany could show an historian like Widukind,
a theologian like Ratherius, and a humorist like Bruno;
when she afforded a shelter to the witty Luitprand
of Cremona, and attracted the omniscient Gerbert of
Rheims, that she was in the van of progress. But even
then classical culture met with the usual ecclesiastical
obstacles. John of Gorze, who is held up to our
special admiration as a model of the intellectual virtues,
"heard the first elements of grammar and the first part of
Donatus, and, content with that introductory aspersion,
completely betook himself to the divine scriptures."[1]
The foreign scholars, attracted to the court of Otto I.,
were looked upon with jealousy and suspicion,[2] and the
pious Hrothsuitha, while properly despairing of emulating
the artistic virtues of Terence, trusted that her insipid

---

[1] *Vita Johannis Gorziensis*, SS. iv., p. 340.   [2] Hauck, iii., p. 333.

Christianity might provide an improving substitute. During the same reign a clerk saw in a dream Archbishop Bruno of Cologne arraigned before the throne of God for his devotion to the classics, and the elaborate apology for classical education which is prefixed to the astronomical works of William of Hirschau illustrates the strength of the forces which were making for devout obscurantism in the middle of the eleventh century. A trick played by Henry II. upon Bishop Meinwerk of Paderborn reflects as much discredit upon the emperor who conferred, as upon the clerk who accepted the bishopric. The emperor erased the initial syllable "fa" from the words in the mass for the dead, and the bishop, whose ignorance of Latin is only partially excused by his ability to read, innocently offered up a prayer for he and she mules [*pro mulis et mulabus*].[1] The reign of Henry III. promised to usher in a new order of things. The emperor himself was skilled in letters, and his wife, Agnes of Poitou, brought with her an influx of French manners. The old-fashioned Germans saw with regret the introduction of many "ignominious French follies," such as the shaving of beards and the shortening of tunics, which had been strictly forbidden in the days of the Ottos and the Henries, but even before this the most enterprising of the Germans had recognized the superiority of French learning, and schoolmasters were eagerly sought for from the Rhenish districts and from France. But then came the wars of the Investitures which arrested the Latin education of Germany, as the Danish wars arrested the Latin education of England. And the wars of the Investitures were followed by the crusade of Conrad III. and the Italian campaigns of the later

[1] *Vita Meinwerci*, SS. xi., p. 150.

Hohenstauffen. The fate of the famous Abbey of Fulda, which was founded in 744, which trained Walafrid Strabo, and Hartmuth of St. Gall, and Otfrid of Weissenburg, and Servatus Lupus the first German humorist, may serve to illustrate a process which affected most of the German abbeys. The *ministeriales* and military vassals of the see became too powerful for the monks. They controlled the revenues of the house and mastered its policy, and the neighbouring princes, seeing in the territories of Fulda a mere collection of feudal castles, ravaged them without scruple. The plate even of the abbey was pledged to meet the obligations of imperial war service, and by 1150 the house was almost ruined.

The German Church then was not conspicuously a literary Church. It was on the whole an ignorant, worldly, military Church. " Lo," wrote Richard of Cornwall to Prince Edward of England in 1257, " what spirited and warlike archbishops we have in Germany. It would not be a very bad thing for you if you could create such archbishops in England."[1] The general causes of this secularity are sufficiently obvious—the comparative barbarity of the whole German people, the lack of good roads, the inferiority both in size and number of German to French and Italian towns; the absence of a Latin element in the population ; a succession of wars, first the war of the Hungarians and Normans, then the wars of Investiture, then the Italian wars of the Hohenstauffen, then the civil wars of Germany between Welfs and Wibelins ; the lack of a strong central government, which throws every bishop and abbot upon his own resources in a disordered land ; the policy of the emperors, who make the Church the chief political, financial, and military instrument of their rule.

---

[1] *Annals of Burton*, SS. xxvii., p. 480.

While the universities of Salerno and Bologna, Paris and Oxford were flourishing in the twelfth century, no university was created east of the Rhine and north of the Alps until the University of Prague in 1447. It follows from this that the German Church was a highly political Church. The obverse side of its literary and theological ignorance is its vigorous political activity. In spite of the fact that an exceptional field of missionary enterprise lay open before it on the eastern border, it was the least professional and the most vulgar branch of the Catholic Church of the west. Whatever test is applied, this will be found to be the case.

The councils of the Church were not purely ecclesiastical councils. A diocesan synod at Cologne in 1077 was attended " by all who had the care of souls, both monks and clerks. Besides that there were counts and other noble persons from the people in great numbers." [1] At a diocesan council at Quedlinburg in 1085 a layman stands up to refute a clerk upon a point of ecclesiastical law.[2] At a provincial synod of Magdeburg in 1135 there are present five bishops, six princes, three nobles, five *ministeriales*.[3] At a synod of Cologne the friars of Steinfeld appeal to the archbishop, his priors, and the barons of the land.[4]

Every abbot and bishop governs his territory by the aid of a little parliament of nobles and *ministeriales*. Again the participation of the people in episcopal elections continues longer in Germany than in other parts of Europe.[5] As the Bishop wielded political power

---

[1] Harzheim, *Concilia Germaniae*, iii., p. 187.   [2] *Ib.*, iii., p. 200.
[3] *Ib.*, iii., p. 329.   [4] *Ib.*, iii., p. 866, 7.
[5] Cf. Innocent III., *Ep.*, ii., 54, 1199, " Laicis sub poena excommunicationis firmiter inhibentes ne amplius quam consensum debitum in electione praesumant aliquatenus usurpare." Cf. also the " Dialogus clerici et laici contra persecutores ecclesiarum ": ed. Waitz, *Chronica Reg. Col.*, p. 315 ff.,

it was only natural that his election should be a matter of general interest in the town which it was his duty to defend and to govern. The avidity of the nobles and *ministeriales* for episcopal fiefs, and of clerks for preferment, combined with more respectable motives to produce a paroxysm of excitement and corruption, whenever a bishopric was vacant; for it was well understood that a German bishop, like an American president, must reward his supporters. In 1124 Godfrey, dean and archdeacon, having amassed a large fortune from pluralities, bought the archbishopric of Trèves for a hundred thousand or more marks of silver from Henry V. The men of Trèves had in vain objected to the foolishness of this servile noble from the province of Liége, and no sooner had he been appointed than the knights rose against him. They claimed that he had promised them benefices and that it was by their favour that he had obtained his election. The archbishop was timid and the knights were strong, and though the bribes of Godfrey were lavish, the fields of his province were ravaged by his dissatisfied supporters.

It remains now to consider the attitude of the Church in Germany towards the popes on the one hand and the emperors on the other.

When, in the eleventh century, the papacy began to recover power and to formulate anew the principles which had been laid down by Gregory the Great and Nicholas I., it did not find an over-zealous ally in the German Church. If English historians choose to call the medieval church in England a national church, and French historians choose to find in the policy of a Hincmar, or in the resolutions of the councils

where the question is discussed in reference to the election of Bruno of Cologne, 1205.

of St. Bale, a premonition of the Gallican liberties,
Germans may with still greater reason contend that
of all the branches of the medieval Catholic Church,
theirs was the least ultramontane. The Germans,
always scared by the thought of taxation, looked upon
the English tribute of Peter's pence as an intolerable
burden of servitude ; the Italian journeys of the three
Ottos revealed the degradation of papacy ; the policy of
the emperors worked the Church into the general fabric
of the national government, while the vast size of the
German provinces stimulated the temporal ambitions
of the prelates who ruled them. Less disciplined and
less civilized than the French or the Normans, the German churchmen received the programme of reform with
something like an indignant protest. Yet the movement
was not initiated from Rome. It was Henry II. who
first opened in Germany the campaign against simony
and the marriage of priests. He began by carrying out
a monastic reform, abolishing small monasteries, or
consolidating them, sweeping away abuses, confiscating
monastic lands, earning for himself much unpopularity
and much gain by this well-established cure by bleeding.[1]
Then in 1019 he presided over a synod at Goslar,
where a discussion took place concerning the marriage
of clerks, which had been forbidden by the decrees
of the council of Pavia, held under the presidency of
Benedict VIII. in the previous year.[2] In 1020 he
invites the Pope to Bamberg, renews and extends the
donations to the Roman Church made by Charles the
Great and Otto I. In 1023 he meets King Robert of
France, at Mouzon and Ivois, with a view to carrying
out a joint reform of the Church, and the two kings
decide that a great council shall be summoned at Pavia

<hr />

[1] Gies., *K.Z.*, 101, ii., pp. 78-90.   [2] Weiland, i., No. 34.

in their presence and in the presence of the pope to pluck out the abuses of the Church both north and south of the Alps. The German Church seems to have viewed these measures with distrust. We have no evidence that the decrees of the synod of Pavia were ever published in Germany, in spite of the close alliance between the emperor and the pope, and the conference between the German emperor and the King of France may have been caused by the emperor's consciousness that he was unable to carry his German prelates with him. It is at any rate significant that a synod of the suffragans of Mainz, held under Archbishop Aribo in 1023, attended by five bishops and ten abbots, and summoned at the very time when the sovereigns were engaged in conference at Ivois, passed several decrees with a view of strengthening the position of the bishop against the pope.[1] We cannot indeed conclude from this that the archbishop aimed at a complete breach with Rome, but it is clear that he desired a substantial measure of independence, and that he was jealous of the close union of pope and emperor. Benedict VIII. was a strong man. Under the pretext that Aribo had violated ecclesiastical law by attempting to divorce the Count from the Countess of Hammerstein, he refused Aribo the pallium, and the archbishop summoned a synod of German bishops at Höchst to protest against the high-handed proceeding of the pope. The letter of the suffragans of Mainz (present with one exception) to the pope has been regarded as "a glorious proof of the resolution of the German clergy to resist Romish pretensions." What it

---

[1] Harzheim, *Conc.* iii. 55, SS. v. 429 ; Hefele, *Concilieng*, iv. 639. The synod of Selingenstadt was held August 22, 1022. Aribo's name is, however, frequently found in imperial charters after that date, which shows that he cannot have broken off from the emperor (Will., *Reg.* i., p. 152, 35).

does prove is that the suffragans of Mainz made common cause with their archbishop,[1] and avowed their joint responsibility for his acts.

It may be regarded as a measure of the independence which a large section of the German clergy still preserved at the beginning of the eleventh century. Aribo was a rough, ambitious man, who would have died rather than relinquish any privilege which had been enjoyed by his predecessors.[2] He belonged to the secular rather than to the ecclesiastical type of churchman.[3] He wished to consolidate the various usages which existed within his diocese concerning ritual, and priestly discipline, and matrimonial law, but it would be extravagant to assert that he contemplated a wholesale ecclesiastical reformation to be carried out independently of emperor and pope. A limited reform which did not touch the two cardinal points in the papal programme, simony and Nicholaitism, was what he wanted, and he wished to carry out the reform by himself. And in this policy he was supported by his suffragans.[4] But he was no revolutionary. In 1031 he went on pilgrimage to Rome.

The work of Benedict VIII. and Henry II. was soon undone. The papacy relapsed into sin and impotence, and one of the worst popes who has ever disgraced the

---

[1] The letter is printed Jaffe, iii. 326, and Gies. ii⁵. 708. We do not know whether the council of Höchst ever really met, or whether Pope Benedict lived long enough to receive this letter.

[2] Aribo's undignified quarrel with Godehard of Hildesheim over the nunnery is narrated in Wolfher's *Vita Godehardi*, SS. xi. 167. For his attempt in 1026 to get the question decided in his favour during the absence of the emperor, cf. *Vita Meinw.*, SS. xi. 153.

[3] Aribo is the first Archbishop of Mainz of whom a denarius exists (Will., *Reg.* i., xlix.).

[4] For Giesebrecht's view, cf. *K.Z.* ii. 279 ; Bresslau, pp. 258, 68, 78 ; and Bayer's criticism on Bresslau's book in *Göttinger Gelehrte Anzeigen*, 1875, vol. ii., 1178.

tiara was not only the nephew of Benedict, but was
restored to power in 1038 by Conrad II.   Conrad
himself is one of the few purely secular and the
only illiterate emperor of the period.   The German
Church was, so far as Rome was concerned, left to its
devices.   In the north, Adalbert, Archbishop of Ham-
burg-Bremen (1045-72), was intent on founding a
patriarchate which should include Denmark, Sweden,
Norway, Iceland, Greenland and the Orkneys.   In the
centre, Archbishop Bardo of Mainz, whose eloquence and
piety and active zeal for ecclesiastical building have
been recorded,[1] is employed in uncongenial campaigns
in Bohemia (1040-1041).   In the south-east the Hungarian wars of Henry III., and the feuds of Duke
Conrad of Bavaria and the Bishop of Regensburg, left
little room for peaceful development.   Yet it is in
the reign of Henry III. that the first comprehensive
effort is made at clerical reform in Germany.   The
emperor's marriage with Agnes of Poitou had opened
Germany to Cluniac influences, and Henry was possessed
with a fine and constant enthusiasm.   In 1049 Leo IX.
came to Mainz, and held a synod before the emperor and
the princes of the empire, which was attended by forty-
two bishops.   The synod wholly condemned simony and
Nicholaitism, and the prelates were left to enforce the
decrees in their respective dioceses.[2]   Yet in spite of the
close alliance of Pope and emperor, the German prelates
were by no means inclined to sacrifice their interests or
the interests of Germany to the exigencies of the Curia.
When Leo IX., in 1052, came to Henry III. to beg for

---

[1] Will., *Regesta von Mainz*, vol. i., pp. 165-76 ; Vulculdi, *Vita Bardonis*,
SS. xi. 318.

[2] For the execution of the decrees in Adalbert's diocese, cf. Jocundi,
Trans. S. Serv., SS. xii. 90.

German swordsmen to deliver Apulia from the Normans,
the emperor ordered a large imperial army to attend the
Pope.   Bishop Gebhard of Eichstadt, who was a prudent
man, saw that there was more pressing work in Bavaria
and upon the Hungarian border.   He came to the emperor, when the army was already on its way, and
vehemently represented the folly of the undertaking.
Henry was persuaded, and the troops were recalled.
Only some seven hundred Swabians followed the Pope
to Italy, and of these many were *condottieri* in search of
loot, while many were cut-throats, outlaws and exiles.[1]
It was, no doubt, fortunate for the papacy that the great
German prelates, who commanded such large military
resources, did not join Leo in his Norman campaign.   A
German victory at Civitella opens a vista of possibilities,
upon which it would be idle to speculate ; but in any
case it would have weakened rather than fortified the
independence of the Pope.   But the main fact to notice is
that Leo IX., who was a Burgundian, and closely connected by ties of friendship and common purpose with
the Emperor Henry, was thoroughly defeated in one
of the decisive battles of history, because a German
bishop advised against sending an imperial army to his
assistance.   Another incident, far less important, illustrates the same point.   On December 26th, in 1053, Pope
Leo IX. and the emperor were at Worms.   The Pope
had asked the Archbishop Luitpold of Mainz to celebrate
the mass, and in the course of the service Humbert, one
of the archbishop's deacons, chanted the lesson.   Leo
sent for Humbert and degraded him for contumacy.

---

[1] William of Apulia, ii. 51, SS. ix. 256, mentions 700 Swabians.
Amatus, iii. 34, mentions only 300 Germans.   The character of the force
is described by Hermann of Reichenau, SS. v., p. 132.   The motives of
Bishop Gebhard are given in Steindorff, *Heinrich III.*, vol. ii., p. 218.

The archbishop sent to expostulate ; the Pope remained firm. When the gospel had been read and the offertory chanted, and the time came for the communion, the archbishop sat still in his seat and refused to complete the office unless the papal sentence were revoked. Leo ended by yielding to Luitpold, and the chronicler remarks approvingly upon the authority of the prelate who defended his dignity, and the humility of the pontiff who thought good to yield to the metropolitan in his own diocese.[1]

After the death of Henry III. the opposition of the German Church to the Gregorian reforms became obvious. The Antipope Cadalus was entirely supported by the Lombard and German clergy. There is indeed some reason for supposing that Archbishop Anno of Cologne represented Hildebrandine interests in Germany.[2] When by a daring *coup de main* he got possession of the person of the young emperor, he received the fervent congratulations of the papal party. It was thought that he had rescued Henry from the corrupt Camarilla of the empress, that he might rule Germany in the spirit of Henry's father. The expectation was indeed partially realized, for Anno summoned a council at Mantua and terminated the papal schism by transferring the allegiance of the German clergy from Cadalus to Alexander. Yet it is a remarkable fact that, although he was expressly ordered by Gregory to summon a council to put down Nicholaitism, there is no record of his ever having done so.[3] If he was all that

---

[1] Ekkeh., *Chron. Univ.*, SS. vi. 196, 197 ; Will., *Reg. von Mainz*, vol. i. p. 177, No. 8 ; Baxmann, *Politik der Päpste*, ii., p. 233.

[2] For Anno's ecclesiastical views, cf. Ennen, *Geschichte der Stadt Köln*, i., p. 312.

[3] Ennen, *Geschichte der Stadt Köln*, i., p. 317 ; Harzheim, *Concilia Germaniae*, iii. 177.

the ardent fancy of Peter Damiani pictured,[1] he was at
any rate more discreet in his ecclesiastical statesmanship
than the Italian party were prepared to be.   Instead of
engaging in a direct campaign against clerical marriage,
he offered additional inducements to clerical celibacy.
There was no monastery in Cologne which he did not
enrich.[2]

The demand for the celibacy of the clergy involved a
social revolution for which Germany was as little prepared as Lombardy itself.   The resistance to the
Gregorian decrees was general and vehement.   " When
the aforesaid statutes—and the same applies to almost
all the statutes—of the apostolic see were promulgated
through the churches either by letters or mandates,
they were opposed by almost everybody, and hence the
greatest hatred was stirred up against the Pope and the
very few who agreed with him, and very great schisms
were excited on all sides, but especially by the clerks."[3]
Siegfried of Mainz [1075] had practically to confess that
suspensions and excommunications had been totally
unavailing to put down concubinage.[4]   After the synod
of Erfurt two attempts were made upon his life, and he
wrote to the Pope to pray him to relax his vigour.   The
papal legate hardly escaped personal violence.[5]   The
bitterness of the strife was such as is stirred by great
social issues, and the ideal of the reformers was only
realized after the lapse of centuries.   Throughout this
period a steady practical resistance was offered by the
lower clergy to the Gregorian rules; it was a usual
practice of clerks to leave their prebends to concubines

---

[1] For Peter Damiani's letter, cf. Harzheim, *Concilia Germaniae*, iii. 197.
[2] *Lamberti Annales*, SS. v., p. 238.
[3] Berthold, *Chron. a.* 1075, SS. v., p. 278.
[4] Harzheim, iii. 176.   [5] *Ib.*, 186, 7.

and bastards, and a long series of conciliar decrees seems to have been unavailing to root out the mischief.[1]

It is only by taking into account the large demands which Gregory was making upon human nature that we can understand the attitude of the German prelates during the war of the Investitures. If the question had been merely one of Investiture, the Pope might have reckoned upon the support of the whole German Church. If the question had been merely one of simony, the prelates who were conscious of having purchased their promotion, and the patrons who were in the habit of selling their patronage, would doubtless have resisted him. There would have been the same kind of opposition as was offered in England to parliamentary reform. But the demand for the celibacy of the clergy struck far deeper. It broke up families, and called for a noble but inhuman abnegation. It was only attained by a succession of sacrifices after many centuries of organized and recognized hypocrisy, the injury of which is insufficiently atoned for by the few fine flowers of Catholic sainthood, or the single-hearted devotion of Catholic missionaries. German prelates knew that in their resistance to Gregory they would be supported by the mass of the secular clergy. In 1076 twenty-four bishops and several abbots signed the deposition of the Pope. In 1080 thirty bishops, many of them Germans, met at Brescia to elect an Antipope. In 1081 Gregory was forced, in response to the demands of his vicegerent in Germany, Altmann of Passau, to consent to temper the rigour of the canonical discipline, which was driving the Bavarian clergy into revolt.[2] In 1085, at a meeting held at Perststat in

---

[1] 1225 : Harz., iii. 274 ; 1246 : Harz., iii. 574 ; 1260 : Harz., iii. 589 ; 1261 : Harz., iii. 606, 7.

[2] Harz., *Conc. Germ.* iii. 197.

Thuringia, the Bishop of Utrecht maintained that Henry had been unjustly excommunicated, and the Archbishop of Mainz supplied a sophistical premise to support that conclusion. Although the balance of parties frequently wavered, and the weight of the Saxon prelates was consistently thrown into the papal scale, it is in the main true that the German Church supported Henry against Gregory. At the Council of Mainz, held in 1085, four archbishops and seventeen bishops stood by the emperor, while two archbishops and eleven bishops stood by the Pope, and of these thirteen papal prelates eight came from Saxon sees.[1]

Nor were the Popes satisfied with the condition of the German Church under Henry V.

" In your kingdom," wrote Pascal II. to Henry V. in 1110, " bishops and abbots are so occupied in secular cases that they are compelled to frequent the county courts, and to engage in soldiering. The ministers of the altar have become ministers of the court." [2] When Henry in 1110 proposed to Pascal that the question of the Investitures should be settled by asking the clergy to renounce their regalia, he must have known that he was proposing a solution which would alienate the

[1] Harzheim, *Conc.* iii., p. 201-3. The Henrician party was thus composed: *Archbishops*—Mainz, Trèves, Cologne, Bremen ; *Bishops*—Utrecht, Liège, Eichstadt, Freisingen, Regensburg, Hildesheim, Paderborn,* Toul, Strassburg, Basle, Minden,* Munster, Prague, Augsburg,* Constance,* Spires, Bamberg. The Gregorians as follows : *Archbishops*—Salzburg, Magdeburg ; *Bishops*—Augsburg,* Constance,* Paderborn,* Wurzburg, Halberstadt, Merseburg, Zeitz, Meissen, Verden, Metz, Minden.* The sees marked (*) were doubly represented.

[2] *Gesta Trevirorum*, i. 222. An interesting comment on this verdict is to be found in the *Vita S. Norberti* (*Acta*, SS. i. 826). The following objections are made against the saint : " Quare insuper habitum religionis pretenderet, cum in nullo religio et proprietas convenirent ? Et qua ratione pretiosas vestes abjecisset cum mos terrae id non habeat, et maxime apud nobiles qualis ipse erat, ut quam diu versantur in saeculo agninis seu caprinis vestibus utantur."

German Church from any Pope who was unwise enough to accept it, or from any emperor who was bold enough to enforce it. It was logical to say that if the Investiture was to be solely conferred by the spiritual authority, the objects conferred by Investiture should be solely spiritual. But to ask the Church to abandon its temporalities was to ask it to renounce one of the main instruments of its power, and Henry should have known that this renunciation would never be made. When Pascal II. was coerced to consent to his proposition, the Burgundian clergy, under the leadership of Guido of Vienne, rose against the Pope. The Privilegium was denounced as a Pravilegium, and through the whole of Germany the unlucky pontiff was branded as having betrayed the true interests of his order. The bitter allusions of Otto of Freisingen to the teaching of Arnold of Brescia, who preached the doctrine of apostolic poverty, are perhaps tinted by the recollection of the time in which that doctrine was actually accepted by a reigning Pope to the scandal of the orthodox.[1] The Church emphatically refused to renounce the regalia, and the Concordat of Worms recognized the fact.

Though St. Bernard was able to rouse Germany to a crusade, his pleading for apostolic simplicity fell upon idle ears. And when the struggle, which had only been suspended by the Concordat of 1122, broke out again at the accession of Frederick I., the German prelates, who had lost none of their secularity, and who were now consulted more continuously than ever upon imperial affairs, resolutely embraced the side of Barbarossa. When Hadrian's legates asserted that the emperor held his crown as a benefice from the Pope, the whole court of the emperor indignantly repudiated the claim. When,

[1] Otto Fris., *Gesta Frid.*, lib. ii., c. 20.

in 1165, the emperor summoned a court of princes to
Wurzburg, to extort from them an oath of fidelity to
Pascal III., the German Church did his bidding. It was
true that Pascal was the second of the imperial Anti-
popes, and that he had been irregularly appointed by
Rainald of Dassel, Frederick's warrior-bishop of Cologne,
in a small meeting attended by three cardinals, without
consultation with the emperor.   It was true also that
Rainald was not even in priest's orders, and that
Alexander III. had been accepted by the whole of the
French clergy.   Yet the German prelates took the oath.
They may have been persuaded by false misrepresenta-
tions; they may have been coerced.   A few refused to
swear except upon conditions.   One remarked that he
would sooner lose his regalia.   Salzburg and Mainz were
recalcitrant.   But the fact remains that Frederick carried
his clergy with him; that his Italian wars were waged
mainly with troops furnished by the ecclesiastical
principalities; that his chief generals and ambassadors
were the archbishops of his two most important sees;[1]
that a council composed mainly, if not exclusively, of
ecclesiastical princes gave to the emperor in 1183 the
right of nominating, with the advice of the princes, a
suitable person to the see of Trèves, if the electors should
not be agreed; and that, despite the protracted and
strenuous nature of the conflict, there is no trace of any
anti-imperial literature having been produced during his
reign in Germany.   The question, indeed, between

---

[1] Frederick I., like Henry V., claimed the right of nominating archbishops, bishops, and abbots in cases where the electors were divided.
The claim was based nominally, though quite unjustifiably, on the Concordat of Worms (Giesebrecht, *K.Z.*, vol. vi., p. 59, ed. Simpson).   The
Concordat gave the emperor the right of deciding in cases of disputed
episcopal elections, according to the counsel of the metropolitan, and
other bishops of the province.

Alexander and Frederick involved no direct issue which could be stated in abstract terms. The real issue was the Lombard revenue, which menaced the territorial independence of the Curia. It was for this that Frederick fought and that Milan fell, and it is not surprising if the ecclesiastical princes of Germany, whose troops had so large a share in proving this great victory, should have been blind to its true ecclesiastical implications.

The lesson of the Alexandrine conflict was not lost upon the proud and astute Milanese who ascended the papal chair in 1185 and assumed the title of Urban III. With a heart full of bitterness against the man who had once levelled his city to the ground and mutilated his relations, Urban was in no mood to drop the torch of quarrel which had been handed down to him by his predecessor, Lucius III. A disputed election at Tréves, the occupation of the Matildine lands and the county of Bertinoro, the restoration of a number of German clerks who had received their ordination at the hands of schismatics in the time of Alexander III., the coronation of Frederick's eldest son Henry as emperor during his father's lifetime, these were the questions in dispute between Lucius and the emperor. The balance of power in Italy was now decisively inclined against the Pope. The emperor had made peace with the Lombard league, was in open alliance with Milan, and had married his son to the heiress of Sicily. The Pope was an exile from Rome ; the decree of the Lateran Council in 1179 forbidding laymen to tax the churches without consent of the bishop was openly defied by the Lombard cities ; the finances of the papacy were crippled by the imperial occupation of the patrimony. Yet Urban did not despair of the situation. He saw that the clouds of discontent were massing themselves behind the Alpine barrier, and he determined to appeal to the German Church. He expostulated against the regalia and right of spoils, urging that these practices so impoverished a see that they drove a new bishop into extortion and rapine. He complained that the emperor under the specious pretext of reform had removed abbesses, appropriated their stipends, and by declining to appoint successors had caused the dispersion of several congregations. He objected to lay tithes and to lay advocates. He refused to crown the young Henry on the ground that two emperors could not co-exist, neglecting the precedent of Lothair and Lambert and Otto II. He cut the Gordian knot of the Trèves election by boldly appointing the candidate to whom Frederick was opposed.

The Pope had chosen his ground cleverly. The German bishops felt bitterly the injustice of the right of spoils which robbed them of the testamentary freedom which was accorded to the rest of the clergy, and which had been more than once expressly confirmed to the members of those collegiate foundations which were not immediately subject to the empire. The right to receive the regalia was less obnoxious, but it was against the canons of the Church, which ordered that the property of a see should be managed in trust by an oeconomus for the incoming bishop. The German Church too had long suffered from the oppressions of her advocates, and the appropriation of tithes to laymen entailed a double disadvantage. In the first place it sapped the revenues and impaired the utility of many ecclesiastical foundations. In the second place it perpetuated simony, for many candidates for preferment were only able to realize their desires by consenting to the appropriation by the patron of part of the tithe of

their benefice. The burden thrown upon the bishops
and abbots by the Italian wars of the empire, the
violence of the emperor's eldest son Henry, the prospect of
a hereditary empire which was disclosed by Frederick's
scheme for the coronation of his son, all these causes pre-
disposed the German clergy to side with Urban.   Philip,
Archbishop of Cologne, Conrad of Mainz, Volmar the
papal Archbishop of Tréves, and twelve other bishops
deserted Frederick.   The Pope made Philip of Cologne
his legate in Germany.

Frederick came over the Alps to stay the progress of
discontent.   In two years he had made peace with
Milan, subdued Cremona, occupied the Matildine lands,
conquered the papal patrimony, imprisoned the Pope in
Verona.   Master of Italy, he closed the Alpine passes
and forbade all communication with Urban.   Then, with
characteristic directness, he summoned the papal legate,
Philip of Cologne, to his presence.   " Lord," replied the
legate to the emperor, " there is no need that you should
doubt me, for you know that I always wish to stand for
justice ; for you have often proved my heart, and you
know that you may always trust me.   But if I may
speak with the mouth of all bishops, if you will deal
but a little more gently with us, and in your imperial
liberty lighten our burden, you would find us more
devoted to you and more available for every purpose.
But now it seems to us that we are overwhelmed by
certain expenses, albeit not unjustly, yet immoderately
And so the apostolic lord has thought it right to
object to the confiscation of churches on the death of a
bishop.   For all the moveables and revenues of the
current year are taken away, so that the new bishop,
when he enters his diocese, finds it empty and exhausted.
If, then, having regard to justice and our service, you

will spare us in this matter, through your imperial
clemency, we will humbly mediate between you and the
Pope, if not, we will on no account depart from the path
of truth." The emperor curtly refused the offer, reply-
ing that the bishops should be content with canonical
election, which had not been allowed to them by some
of his predecessors ; and as he saw that the legate was
still unmoved, he went on as follows : " Since I see that
you do not agree with me, I forbid you to come to the
court which is to be celebrated at Gelnhausen, where
there is to be an assembly of bishops." The archbishop
replied, "Let it be according to your pleasure."[1]

In November, 1186, the assembly met at Gelnhausen.
It was large and representative, and it included Philip
of Cologne, who must have made his peace with the
emperor. Frederick addressed the assembled prelates
and princes in a speech remarkable alike for its astute
omissions and for its frank avowals. He said nothing
of the regalia or the right of spoil, or the deprived
abbesses, or the patrimony of St. Peter ; but after professing his general devotion to the papacy, he enumerated his complaints against the Pope. It had never
before happened that a bishop of the German Empire
had received consecration before he had been invested
by the sceptre with the regalia, yet the Pope had
hurriedly and unconstitutionally consecrated Volmar of
Trèves, after a solemn promise, attested by three

[1] The story of the interview between Philip of Cologne and Frederick
(*Arnoldi Chron.*, iii. 18) has been doubted by Scheffer-Boichorst, *Der
letzter Streit*, pp. 112, 197, 198 ; and by Lappenberg, SS., xxi. 159, No.
14. Giesebrecht, *K.Z.* vi. 653 (ed. Simpson), would also reject so much of
the speech of Frederick at Gelnhausen as rests entirely on Arnold's
testimony, thus rejecting the passage concerning tithes and advocates.
Scheffer-Boichorst, p. 115, ff., and Prutz, *Friedrich I.*, vol. iii., p. 266 ff.,
do not go to this length. I cannot help thinking that Arnold's account
is substantially correct.

credible envoys, that he would do no such thing.
Further, Urban had retained the Archbishopric of
Milan after his appointment to the papacy, defraud-
ing the Church of a bishop and the empire of regalia.
Then the emperor went on to complain of the extraordinary burdens which the papal see had laid upon the
clergy of the empire, of the contributions in money and
in kind which the Pope's agents extorted from churches
and monasteries, which were scarcely rich enough to earn
their daily bread, and afterwards he turned to consider
two of Urban's proposals to the German Church—the
abolition of lay tithes and lay advocates. "We know,"
he said, "that tithes and offerings were originally
granted by God to priests and Levites. But when in
Christian times the churches were infested by foes,
powerful and noble men were given tithes as permanent
benefices that they might protect those churches which
were unable to protect themselves." He frankly confessed that the abolition of lay advocates would, on the
face of it, appear to benefit the prelates, but he could
not believe that a custom consecrated by such high
antiquity and confirmed by so just a tradition would be
readily abandoned.

Frederick was right in his belief. The adoption of
Urban's proposals might have freed the Church from
much tyranny and extortion, but it involved unaccept-
able consequences.

If a churchman were disabled from enfeoffing tithes
to laymen, he would be debarred from using a very
convenient fund for enlisting or rewarding military
retainers. Even if he were deprived of his official right
to impose charges on the see, the lay advocate would
still remain a formidable neighbour, and it was hardly
likely that he would relinquish his inherited privilege

without a struggle. Again, every ecclesiastical foundation by abolishing the lay advocate would lose a hold, slight indeed but not entirely ineffectual, over one noble family, and add to the sum of the enemies who were always willing to plunder the priests. It was better to keep a permanent official hereditary robber, to make treaties with him, to limit his eggs, and kine, and pigs, and wheat, and jurisdiction, and then to suffer such injuries as he and his servants might be pleased to inflict, than to lay oneself open to the unauthorized inroads of miscellaneous neighbours.[1] The papal bait was offered in vain.[2] The German Church rallied round the emperor as it had rallied round him in the days of Henry IV. Letters were sent from the bishops to persuade the Pope and the cardinals to concession and forgiveness, and to represent the evils which a quarrel between the empire and the papacy would bring upon the spiritual princes of Germany. The accusations which the Pope had levelled against Henry were met by the remark, more casuistical than true, that Henry occupied the papal states as a protector rather than a conqueror. The Pope was openly charged with having sent letters to the Lombard bishops, ordering them to refrain from helping Frederick in his campaign against Cremona. The consecration of the Archbishop of Trèves before investiture was denounced as an unprecedented insult to the empire. The exactions of the papal legates were condemned; while in an appeal *ad misericordiam* addressed to the cardinals, which was possibly judicious, probably sincere and certainly

---

[1] A *Sententia Principum* delivered in the time of Henry IV. decides that the Advocate of Tegernsee may not exact more than two measures of corn, two pigs, three casks of wine and meal, ten casks of beer, five measures of oats for thirty horses (*H.B.*, iii., p. 185).

[2] Scheffer-Boichorst, *Friedrichs I. letzter Streit mit der Kurie*, p. 15.

ignoble, it was represented that the princes, nobles, and vassals, who held fiefs of the Church and who were ever struggling to widen their possessions, would avail themselves of the first symptoms of ecclesiastical disloyalty to seize upon the property of the Church and confiscate it to their uses.   So inextricably interwoven were the interests of the Church and the empire.[1]

In the very darkest moments of the ninth and of the tenth centuries letters were written from the city of Rome by inconspicuous and sometimes even by corrupt and violent men claiming to have been summoned by the voice of God to preside over the Christian world. The tradition of the papal office was the same, whether its tenant was a statesman or a debauchee, and the official language of John XII. does not essentially differ from that of Nicolas I.   There was, indeed, no moment during the Middle Ages when the theoretical pretensions of the papacy were abated, and if except certain schemes for the abolition of the papal office doubtfully attributed to Frederick II. or to his minister, Peter de la Vigne, there is no sign that any German emperor desired to diminish the spiritual control of the vicar of Christ over the Catholic Church.[2]   The quarrel between the empire and the papacy in the eleventh and in the twelfth cen turies was not only a contest between emperors and popes, but also between popes and antipopes.   In the condition of belief at that time no emperor would have dared to fling down the gauntlet to the papal office,

---

[1] Weiland, vol. i., Nos. 315, 316, 317.

[2] The letter of Frederick I. to the Archbishop of Trèves (*Archiv. f. K. Oest. Geschichtsquellen*, xiv. 88) is probably a forgery, though it illustrates opinion : "Quid eius cis Alpes timemus excommunicationem cum trans Alpes ipsi vulgares parvipendunt?   Rome in sede sua vilipenditur sua excommunicatio et nobis tam gravis est sua indignatio?... Igitur quia vos primas estis cis Alpes et cor regni ... summam et misterialem tunicam Domini, id est ecclesiam, de manu illius Amorrei liberate."

and the imperialists who fought the battles of Henry IV. and Frederick I. were comforted by the reflection that, if they were fighting against one pope, they were also fighting on behalf of another. In the thirteenth century the case was different. Frederick II. had no antipope to oppose to Honorius III., Gregory IX., and Innocent IV.; the college of cardinals had escaped the control of the empire; there was no convenient informality attaching to the election of his adversaries. It was a source to him of serious weakness. Despite all the tragical eloquence with which his chancery advertised the fidelity of the emperor to the papal see, men doubted and wavered. The orthodox rallied together and crushed him as a new and unholy and revolutionary thing. Nor was there any wavering in the allegiance of the German Church to the papal see. The revival of the empire by Otto I. stimulated the connection of Germany with the Curia.[1] Papal confirmation was sought for ecclesiastical charters; the decisions of a German council were considered to be fortified by the presence of a papal legate, and the German canonists cheerfully subscribed to all the doctrines of papal absolutism enunciated in the false Decretals. The archbishops went to Rome for their pallia, and submitted their creed to the examination of the pontiff. The Pope's authority was required and demanded for the foundation and delimitation of new bishoprics, and during the reign of Otto I. two successive archbishops of Mainz were papal legates. Thus while Otto I. was drawing the German Church closer to the monarchy, he was also reviving and stimulating its communications with Rome.

[1] In the twenty-one years from Otto's assumption of the empire to the death of Otto II. thirty-eight papal letters go to Germany, while in the sixty-three years from Arnulf's to the revival of the empire we have only thirty-four letters (Hauck, p. 244).

Men were not clear thinkers in the Middle Ages, and it was long before the antinomy between the universal and the national character of the German Church was apprehended. The contemporaries of the Ottos were devout believers in the sacred pre-eminence and even in the infallibility of the popes, and there were doubts expressed in Germany as to the right of Otto I. to depose a vicar of Christ. When Burchard of Worms, in 1002, compiled a kind of canonical florilegium, he was, while recognizing the king's right to punish and correct clerks, concerned to point out that the Pope is a supreme judge, who may be asked to purge himself of an accusation, but who may not be judged by any mortal save himself. The contest between the papacy and the empire in the eleventh and twelfth centuries evoked a multitude of treatises upon the relations of the two powers.[1] Then first an attempt was made to settle the relations between the emperor and the Pope in the fantastic world of medieval theory. It is unnecessary here to describe the various analogical arguments which were used by these writers, but it is well to remember that while the papal ists vigorously contended that the emperor was subject to the Pope, the imperialists never averred that the Pope was subject to the emperor. There is perhaps no better illustration of the perplexities of the German mind upon this question than the writings of Gerhoh of Reichersberg, who, born in 1093, lived through all the later stages of the war of the Investitures into the heyday of Barbarossa's contest with Alexander.[2] After an education at Freising, Marburg, and Hildesheim, Gerhoh was appointed first of

---

[1] *Libelli de Lite Imperatorum et Pontificum* (M.G.).

[2] *Gerhohi Opera* (ed. Migne, *Patr. Lat.*, vols. cxciii., cxciv.) ; *De inven-tione Antichristi* (ed. Scheibelberger) ; *Libelli de Lite Imperatorum et Pontificum*, vol. iii. ; W. Ribbeck, *F.D.G.*, vol. xxiv., pp. 3-80 ; xxv., pp. 556-61.

all to a mastership of the High School at Augsburg, and
then to a canonry by the imperialist Bishop Hermann of
Augsburg. Following his patron, he began life upon
the imperial side, but as time went on his opinions
changed. He went to Rome, made his peace with the
Pope, embraced the monastic career, and spent the last
thirty-seven years of his life (1132-69) as prior of
Reichersberg. He writes against Henry IV. with the
passion of a combatant, the zeal of a convert, the
bitterness of a recluse. No charge is too foul, no
language too violent for the antagonist of Hildebrand,
and the tragic ending of the old king evokes nothing
but a frigid and vindictive comment. With equal
vigour Gerhoh throws himself into the long-standing
quarrel with the seculars and the simoniacs. He denies
the validity of sacraments administered by seculars, by
schismatics, by simoniacs. Outstripping in zeal the
current opinion of churchmen, he argues his point both
in Germany and Italy, rebukes St. Bernard for his
neutrality, and actually incurs the suspicion of heresy
by the very extravagance of his orthodox professions.
At one time it seemed likely that Gerhoh would become
the *enfant terrible* of the Curia. In 1125 he asked
Honorius II. why the weeds were not plucked up by
the roots, and the Pope drily but conclusively replied
that there were too many of them.[1] It is seldom
possible to instruct the fanatic, but Gerhoh was rescued
from the fanatic's doom by modesty, that finest gift of
the learner, and by a certain intellectual detachment
which is as rare as it is honourable. His views upon
the ecclesiastical and political questions of the day have
therefore the special interest, which attaches to the out-
pourings of an earnest, vigorous, and candid mind in no

[1] Migne, *Patr. Lat.*, cxciv., c. 1378.

way concerned to preserve its own logical consistency. In the bottom of his heart he is probably opposed to the temporal power of the Church. Laymen, he intimates, have no right to take tithes; churchmen have no right to take temporalities. The Pope is advised in one place to renounce his temporal power over Rome, or to share it with the emperor. The regalia of the Pope depend upon the emperor's consent, and even the vicar of Christ is not entitled to exercise criminal jurisdiction within the city of Rome. Yet Gerhoh recoils from a conclusion which would have subverted the whole organization of the Christian Church. He admits the force of that curiously assorted logical artillery with which the medieval Church repelled her adversaries. He defends the donation of Constantine against a Roman advocate who attacked it on the insufficient ground that the emperor was baptized by an Arian bishop.[1]

"Christ," he says, "wore a white robe before Herod, a purple robe before Pilate." It is a serious argument for the union of spiritual and temporal powers in the same hands. Temporal and spiritual possessions are now so intermixed that a bishop would seem to be despoiling the kingdom if he refuse to enfeoff church property to knights, and it is a well-known maxim that the Church cannot lose any possession which she has long held.[2] In one place it is suggested that a General Council should be summoned to decide how the Church contributions to the State should be paid. In another place it is suggested that the Church should conceal the temporalities, even as Rachel concealed the golden idols which she carried from the house of Laban. The

---

[1] Migne, *Patr. Lat.*, vol. cxciv., 19 ; cf. *De Invent. Antichristi*, c. 29.

[2] *Liber de Aedificio Dei*, c. v. and vi. ; Migne, *Patr. Lat.*, vol. cxciv. col. 1210 ; and *ib.*, cx., col. 1226.

temporalities are discreditable, yet on the whole they
must be retained. Still the Church is full of flagrant
abuses. The two swords have been confounded; prelates
exercise and delegate criminal jurisdiction ; tithes are
converted into lay benefices in order to provide prelates
with soldiery ; bishops go campaigning ; the cathedral
clergy have cast aside all restraints, and profligacy is even
more rife among clerks than among laymen. Nor are these
evils confined to Germany; they have their root in Rome
itself. Gerhoh inveighs against the papal city with all
the severity of a Bernard or a John of Salisbury. Since
Gregory was forced to hire soldiery to fight his battles,
the popes have become subservient to the avarice of
Rome. They buy their way to the chair by huge
donations to the Roman populace ; they are compelled
to take part in the civic feuds of Central Italy ; and to
maintain their position, they mulct Christendom. The
pomp and greed of the Roman legates have increased.
The appellate jurisdiction of the Pope has become an
open scandal. Its operations are corrupt, its assistance
is invoked to defeat the ends of justice. Appeals and
legations are already forbidden in Sicily, Apulia, and
Hungary. It is hinted that they should be forbidden in
Germany as well. Did not the Greek Church break off
from Rome because of its avarice ? Then there is the
corrupt transfer of parishes from one diocese to another,
of monasteries from the control of the bishop to the
control of the Pope. Concupiscence traffics in ecclesiastical frontiers. Monasteries which are exempt from
episcopal control are in an unnatural position. It is as
if a hand should hang direct from the ear, or a foot from
the thigh. Yet if the exemption be of long standing,
we tolerate the anomaly. But of recent years the
papacy has been extending these exemptions and

plucking old monasteries from their dioceses, to the destruction of discipline and the replenishment of the papal coffers. New oaths are exacted by the Pope from the prelates who receive their pallia, and, indeed, there is grave danger of papal omnipotence. When the Roman popes illustrate in speech, in writing, and in pictures the thesis that Caesar is bound to them by homage, when they prescribe how far he shall advance, where he shall stay, what cities he shall attack, what rebels he shall spare, are they not making themselves emperors and the lords of emperors, are they not making the emperors their vassals? If the Romans are able to subdue the emperor, and to deprive him of his crown and name, let them do so, and submit to the rule of a thousand masters. But if they allow him to bear the title and to wear the crown, why should they dishonour him in their words and in their paintings? The custom by which the emperor holds the bridle and the stirrup for the Pope should be discontinued, for it fosters pride in the Pope, hate in the emperor. The true relation between the temporal and the spiritual powers is exhibited in Constantinople, where the emperor and patriarch dismount when they pass each other in the street, and greet one another on equal terms. It is clearly insinuated that if the harmonious co-operation of Pope and emperor has been disturbed, it is the papacy, not the empire, which is at fault.

Gerhoh views the Alexandrine schism with many misgivings. On the whole he is on the side of Alexander, for Alexander has been elected by the majority of the cardinals, and has been accepted by the Churches of Jerusalem and Antioch. But, on the other hand, there are grave objections to him. He is openly charged with having procured his election by

entering into a conspiracy with the King of Sicily and
the Lombard towns, and if this accusation be indeed
true, then he cannot be accepted as Pope[1] He might
have dispelled the charge at the council of Pavia, but
he declined to appear, thus confirming the worst
suspicions. The Romans reply that the Roman see
is not bound to answer before any tribunal, and that
it owes its innocence to heaven alone. It is said that
the Pope alone can sit in judgment upon himself.
Gerhoh has not the fortitude to contradict this doctrine
in set terms, but he belongs to the middle party, who
desired a general council to put an end to the schism,
and to decide between the Victorines and their adversaries. The middle way is the safest.[2]

But if Gerhoh is a critic, he is no rebel. Like
John of Salisbury and Bernard, he speaks out candidly,
but the whole fabric of papal autocracy might be
built out of his, as it might be built out of their,
admissions. At one moment he will say that an
unrightful command of a pope may be disobeyed.
At another moment he will admit the propriety of
the decision of a synod in 502 that the Pope is
responsible to heaven alone, adding, however, by

[1] For this charge, cf. Otto Fris., *Gesta*, iv., 52, 69, 71, 72 ; SS. xx., pp. 473,
484, 487, 488 ; SS. v., p. 126.

[2] *Gerhohi opera, De Inventione Antichristi* [ed. Scheibelberger] ; "On
Criminal Jurisdiction," pp. 82-9 ; "On Secularity of Clergy," pp. 89, 90 ;
"On the Abuse of Appeals," 105, 106, 111, 161 ; "On the Pallium Oaths,"
166 ; "On Exempt Monasteries," pp. 172, 3 ; "On the Advance of the
Romans," pp. 106, 107, 108, 161, 171, 137 ; "On the Relations of Emperor
and Pope," pp. 174-177 ; "On the Simoniacal Transfer of Parishes," p. 149;
"On the Alexandrine Schism," p. 159 ff. For complaints as to the sub-
traction of benefices, canonries, and abbeys by the Popes, Ivo Carnot,
Ep., 133 ; Bern., *De Consid.*, iii. 1, 3 : *De Off. Episc.*, c. ix. ; Joannes
Sacerb., *Polycr.*, vii. 19, 21. "On the Abuse of Appeals," Hild. Tur., *Ep.*,
32 ; Bern., *De Consid.*, iii. 2 ; *Ep.*, 178, 189. "On Church Regalia," Otto
Fris., *Chron. Prol.*, i. iv. ; Plac. Non., *Lib. de Hon. Eccl.* [Pez. ii., 2, 75].

way of qualification, "in those causes which touch
his office or person." With characteristic subtlety
he ventures to suggest that the word "heaven" may
apply to a council of the Church, for he can see no end
to the schism unless Alexander submits himself to a
general council. After all, did not Christ show his
wounds to the young who doubted? Yet these passages of quaint and ingenious pleading only exhibit
the straits of the advocate looking about for some
orthodox buttress wherewith to support genuine con-
victions. The old familiar and sounding periods slip
in unobserved at rhetorical moments, and give the case
away. "Who may refute him, since he is as another
Jeremy, appointed not only over churches but also over
kingdoms, to pull up and destroy, to scatter and dis-
sipate, to build and plant?"[1] When institutions are
supported by literary authority, a familiar and resonant
text acts upon the mind with a force equal to one of
the recurrent phenomena of nature. It is possible for a
moment to ignore the experience, but the sound besieges
the memory as the sights of nature besiege the eye. As
the oft-quoted text or decretal rolled into the mind of
Gerhoh, his freer speculations must have seemed mere
idle phantasmagoria. With no genius for logical
symmetry he was content to allow contradictory pro-
positions to lie side by side in his writings, as they lie
side by side in the *Decretum* of Gratian, and it is
possible to excerpt from the pages of the keenest
German critic of papal abuses in the twelfth century
a cento of passages which might have issued from the
mouth of a Hildebrand or an Innocent III.[2]

---

[1] *De Invent. Antichristi*, p. 59.

[2] Thus he admits the papal right to depose sovereigns (*De Invent. Antichristi*, c. 32).

In 1198 the policy of the Hohenstauffen was put to the test. The throne was practically vacant, for Henry VI. had died, leaving but one infant son, Frederick, and he was far away at Palermo. At the same time Innocent III. ascended the papal chair. While Germany was kingless, the cardinals of the Roman Church had elected a king, who had the ability and the energy to pursue the high autocratic ideal which he so clearly conceived. Innocent resumed the policy of Hildebrand with equal ardour and determination, but with greater knowledge of men and of affairs, with greater tact and with a more complete legal equipment. Few men were more capable of extracting the greatest amount of profit from the situation in Germany. There were two objects which he set himself to pursue. In the first place, he wished to prevent the crown going to Philip of Swabia, the brother of Henry VI., who had been excommunicated for his government of Tuscany, and whose election would have carried with it the continued union of Germany and Sicily under the Hohenstauffen house. In the second place, he wished to bring the German Church under the more complete control of the papal see, by influencing the composition of the chapters; by excluding laymen from a share in elections; by reviving the rule that no translations could be made without his consent; by decreeing that candidates against whose election there was any canonical impediment must be postulated of the Pope, to whom alone belongs the right of according dispensation; by frankly providing to sees; by deposing prelates of whom he did not approve. The success of these measures would have involved the separation of the German Church from the empire, the dissolution of that national union which had existed since the time of Charles the Great, which Gregory had been able to shake but not permanently to disturb, and which, during the reign of Frederick Barbarossa, had victoriously resisted the onslaughts of five popes.

The German princes had no intention of tamely surrendering to Innocent III. or to the doctrines of the Third Lateran Council. A rumour went about the country that the Pope was aiming at the destruction or humiliation of the empire. On May 28th, 1198, the princes met at Spires and drew up a most memorable manifesto. They informed Innocent that they had chosen Philip to be Roman emperor after the death of Henry; that there was but little opposition to their choice, and that that opposition would be easily conquered. They asked the Pope to refrain from doing anything which might injure the rights of the empire, to show favour to their lord and to his true servant Markwald, Margrave of Ancona and Duke of Spoleto, since his Holiness must surely know that they would come without fail in all their power to demand the imperial crown for their lord. In other words they assume that the German king must necessarily be elected Roman emperor; that the Pope has no part or lot in the matter but to accept the choice of the German princes, even if the German princes should choose a man who was under the ban of the Church; and they hint to the Pope that the Italian conquests of the Hohenstauffen house are to be sacred, and that the German occupation is not to be disturbed. The document received the assent of the patriarch of Aglei, of four archbishops, twenty-three bishops and four abbots, that is to say of a majority of the German prelates.

The Pope would have preferred that the German princes should have entrusted him with mediatorial powers, but the note of revolt was too unmistakable to be questioned. The Archbishop of Cologne, actuated by purely temporal interests, had proceeded to elect Otto, the son of Henry the Lion, with the concurrence of eight princes.[1] On the 1st of March, 1201, Innocent III. formally recognized Otto as lawful king of the Germans, and declared himself ready to crown him with the imperial crown.[2] And he sent a papal legate to Germany to wage war against the house of Hohenstauffen.

The reports of the legate Guido illustrate the extreme resentment which was at this time felt in Germany against the papal chair. "When we had made our entry with Otto into Cologne, we only met a few princes at the appointed time. Some had not received our orders. Some had received them, but could not come. Others would not come. We infer that they would not come, because they shut their towns and houses in order not to receive our messengers, especially the men of Mainz and Spires and Worms." And again, "You may be convinced that if only the spiritual princes had from the beginning been true to King Otto, or if they would now give him the assistance of their counsel and their actions, there would be no difficulty, or but little difficulty, in discharging this mission, and the sunshine of success would soon smile upon our arduous beginning."[3] The cardinal had put his finger upon the right spot. It was the resistance of the German prelates which made the success of Philip the excommunicate a practical certainty. They were loyal to the house of Hohenstauffen; they resented the interference of the Pope in German affairs; they held to the ancient theory of the equipollence of the empire and the Papacy; they detested and defied and

[1] Weiland, ii., Nos. 18-22.   *Reg. de Neg. Imp.*, No. 32 ff.
[3] *Reg. de Neg. Imp.*, No. 51.

remonstrated against the Roman cardinal. "Where, they wrote to Innocent, "O ye popes have ye read; where, holy fathers, cardinals of the whole Church, have ye heard that your forefathers or their envoys have so interfered in the election of Roman kings as to assume the *rôle* of electors or of confirmers of elections? We do not believe that you can find an answer."[1] The Bishop of Spires seized two papal couriers, imprisoned one and ordered the other to be hanged.[2] The city of Mainz refused to receive Siegfried, whose election had been confirmed by the Pope, and persisted in its refusal, although Innocent threatened to transfer the archiepiscopal see to another place, and took the opportunity to free the kingdom of Bohemia from the province.[2] It was in vain that Innocent protested that he did not wish to humiliate the empire. The distrust of him was universal. In the spring of 1203 rumours were circulated to the effect that he was dead, and that his successor had been chosen. When Bishop Ludolf of Magdeburg, who had resisted all attempts to seduce him from the Philippians, received a letter, which he had good reason to suspect contained his excommunication, he gathered all his clergy round him and appealed beforehand against the document to Rome. Then he broke the seal. The Pope in fact was trying to introduce not only a political but an ecclesiastical revolution. A canon of the Third Lateran Council had forbidden offices or prebends to remain vacant over six months. If the nomination belonged to the bishop and he delayed to make it, then the chapter should make it, and *vice versa*. If neither chapter nor bishop did their

---

[1] *Reg. de Neg. Imp.*, No. 61.

Papal Letter, 3rd Oct., 1202; *Reg. de Neg. Imp.*, No. 72; Papal Letter 9th April, 1203; *Ep.*, vi. 39; Papal Letter, 20th and 21st April, 1204; *Ep.*, vii. 51, 53.

duty, then the metropolitan should make the appointment. There was nothing here said about the Pope, but
Innocent claimed that if the Metropolitan neglected his
duty, then the task of providing for the vacant prebend
devolved upon the Curia. The contingency on the first
blush seemed to be remote, but Innocent put a construction upon the term "vacancy," which made it a
common occurrence. He ruled that every prebend was
vacant which anyone should hold in addition to his
original prebend. The ruling was in accordance with a
canon of the Third Lateran Council against pluralities,
but it was in the sharpest antagonism to existing
German practice. The German bishops had long seen
in the accumulation of prebends a means of increasing
their influence, and there was probably not a chapter-
house in Germany which would have satisfied the papal
test. By cleverly uniting the canon against pluralities
with the canon on the right of devolution, Innocent
would be able to interfere with almost every nomination
to a prebend in Germany, so long as the archbishops,
bishops, and chapters remained unconverted on the
question of pluralities. We can prove that he did so
interfere in the dioceses of Bremen, Meissen, Wurzburg,
Cologne, and Magdeburg.

Again he decrees that no person against whom
there is any canonical impediment can be elected to a
bishopric. Any such person must be postulated from
the Pope, who alone can grant dispensation. This
sweeps into the papal net bastards, persons under
thirty years of age, persons whose character or knowledge are deficient, persons who are already bishops
of another see [1] What important limitations, how
revolutionary, how elastic! In the very first years of

[1] "Canon of the Third Lateran Council" (Mansi, *Conc. Coll.*, t. xxii., 217).

Innocent III.'s reign the stipulations of the Third Lateran Council had been most openly violated. There had been a series of translations, and the papal dispensation had not been asked for.[1] At Merseburg the illegitimate son of Margrave Dietrich was elected bishop in 1201, and the practice of nominating young men and unlearned men to important sees was often based upon considerations of dynastic and military expediency which could not lightly be disregarded. The Pope had made for himself a legal avenue by which he might approach and capture any see in Germany. If he could not object youth or bastardy, he might at any rate allege that character was tainted or learning insufficient. There was no legal bar to stop the enslavement of the whole German episcopacy. Yet there was one strong practical obstacle which Innocent recognized. As we have seen, the elections to bishoprics in Germany continued to excite general popular interest, for the bishops possessed political rights, ruled as temporal princes, kept small armies, and usually belonged to some prominent noble family. The participation of the lay nobles and *ministeriales* of the see in the election of a bishop tended to accentuate its secular as opposed to its ecclesiastical interests. When the Roman people shared in the election of the Pope, their favours had sometimes descended upon a boy, a ruffian, or a profligate, and until the Vatican Decree of 1059 confined the election to the College of Cardinals, the Popes had contributed almost as much to scandalous chronicle as to serious history. The principle of the Vatican Decree had never been applied to Germany, and an election to the see of Cologne or

---

[1] *Gesta Innocentii*, cap. 43 ff.; and cf. Schwemer, *Innocent III. und die deutsche Kurie*, p. 82.

of Mainz in the thirteenth century was rife with many
of those violent and corrupt influences from which
Nicholas II. had partially liberated the city of Rome.
Innocent III. saw in the continued existence of popular
election a barrier to the spread of hierarchical ideas.
He did not attempt a general manifesto against an
ancient usage, which there was no immediate chance
of suppressing, but he resisted it on particular occasions.
He prohibited the laymen of Mainz, under penalty of
excommunication, from giving more than "their due
assent" to an election.[1]   His nominee Bruno of Cologne
was mainly the choice of the chapter, and a curious
dialogue between a clerk and a layman exists to show
how bitterly the burghers of Cologne resented this invasion of their political liberties.[2]   The layman argues that
he has done homage and sworn fealty to one archbishop, and now the Pope and the clergy command
him to obey another.   He asks whether the Pope has
power to absolve him from an oath which he has lawfully and duly offered.   He contends that no election
can take place except in the presence of the nobles of
the land, the beneficed men of St. Peter, and the
chief officials of the bishop, and even conceding that
the bishop can be elected so far as he is an ecclesiastic
in the absence of the laymen, he asks how the clergy
has power without lay consent to appoint a duke who
exercises secular jurisdiction.   These considerations
really go to the root of the difference between the
Curia and the German Church.   Innocent wished for
a spiritual hierarchy sharply divided from the lay
world, strictly disciplined, strictly professional, wholly

[1] *Epist.*, ii. 24.
[2] " Dialogus Clerici et Laici contra persecutores ecclesiarum," ed. Waitz
(*Chron. Reg. Col.*, p. 316 ff.).

subordinate to himself. The German Church was none of these things. The prelates were secular princes, closely connected with the imperial government, but bent also on advancing their own territorial interests. If these interests should coincide with the policy of the Curia, well and good; but the coincidence was necessarily accidental, the tie necessarily fragile. We have only to study the career of the leader of the papal party in Germany, Adolph of Cologne, during the period of the disputed election to be assured of this. He embraced the cause of Otto in 1201 because the city of Cologne had long been connected by commercial ties with England, and because the Welf candidate was the nephew of the English king. He threatened to desert the cause of Otto in 1202, but was recalled by the firm attitude of the city, which made its allegiance to the archbishop dependent upon his fidelity to the papal king.[1] Finally he deserted Otto for Philip in 1204, braving excommunication and deposition as soon as he was convinced that Philip's was the winning side.[2]

We have dwelt at some length upon this episode of the contest between Philip and Otto, because it brings out into a clear light the real attitude of the German Church towards the greatest of the Popes. On two separate occasions the tranquil loyalty of the ecclesiastical princes had been seriously disturbed by the papacy. Gregory the Great deposed an emperor, and struck hard at the two most engrained abuses of

[1] Weiland, ii., No. 24. Cologne manifested its independence of the Papacy by remaining a year and five months under interdict, 1215 (*Chron. Reg. Col., Cont. III.*, 1215).

[2] *Chron. Reg. Col., Cont. III.*, 1204, p. 219, "Coloniensis vero Episcopus sacramentum quod dudum Ottoni fecerat parvipendens et perjurium et excommunicationem Apostolici non metuens ad eundem Philippum venit."

German clerical life, simony and marriage. National spirit and loyalty, natural affection and lust, avarice and ambition, and all the forces of sheer conservatism, as well as those which make for a low view of life, fought against him. He failed to spiritualize the German Church. Innocent III. renewed the attempt, and he also shot a double shaft, wounding the loyal susceptibilities of the princes by his interference in the election of the German king,[1] rousing their deep resentment and alarm by his legates, his counter candidates, his new-fangled application of the old doctrine of papal autocracy. He could no longer rely upon the prestige of excommunications. That weapon had been too often used to subserve private and family spite.[2] It had lost its magic and its terror. But in revenge he could play upon the ambitions of the ecclesiastical princes, some of whom were intent on building up small states, and might wish to escape the drain of the Italian wars of the empire. He was assisted too by a series of accidents. The murder of Philip in 1208 enabled Otto to mount the throne. The loyalty of the South Germans to the house of Hohenstauffen helped him to displace Otto for Frederick,[3] when Otto had shown himself to be an emperor after the old pattern of Barbarossa. But the decisive factor in these transactions is not the Pope but the German princes.

---

[1] For the protest against the popes concerning himself with the German election, cf. *Reg. de Neg. Imp.*, No. 61.

[2] There was conciliar legislation against this abuse in 1225 (Harzheim, iii. 521, and cf. Harzh., iii. 561). We are reminded of the way in which the Inquisition in Spain was made to serve the purpose of family vendetta (cf. Ranke, *Die Osmanen und die Spanische Monarchie*, p. 199).

[3] The formation of a Frederician party after the excommunication of Otto in 1211. Cf. Ficker, *Reg.*, 646 b.; *H.B.*, i. 195 ; *Ann. Col.*, Winckelmann, 499. If Frederick had been three hours later [Sept. 1212] the Bishop of Constance would have declared for Otto (Ficker, *Reg.*, 670 g).

It is true that both Otto and Frederick made ample
concessions to the Curia, but some of those concessions
they both could and did renounce without forfeiting
any considerable amount of support in Germany. What
did the German princes care for the states of the
Church? What would they endure to prevent the
personal union of Sicily and Germany, or to preserve the
papal suzerainty over the old Norman kingdom? In
part indeed the demands of the Curia coincide with
the interests of the German Church. The German
princes too wished for a renunciation of the right of
spoils and regalia, and for greater freedom of capitular
elections. But the princes were now strong enough to
make terms for themselves, and they saw that a compact between the king and the Curia was but a brittle
guarantee. It was not enough for them that the young
Frederick was the choice of Innocent III., and that
all the influence of the Curia was thrown upon his
side; they must treat with the man himself, and
Frederick knew it. He came to Germany prepared to
bribe. He bribed the princes to help him against
Otto; he bribed them again to put the king's crown
on his own head; he bribed them a third time to
recognize Henry as his successor. He bribed them in
money which had been supplied him by the king of
France, and never, as he afterwards confessed, was
money better spent. And he bribed them also by a
series of concessions. These concessions show whither
the wind was blowing. They tend to confirm the
territorial powers of the German prelates. To obtain
them the prelates were willing, if not openly to sacrifice at any rate to imperil the interests of the Curia.
They crowned Frederick's son Henry in 1220 in
manifest violation, so it seemed to Honorius III., of the

emperor's oath to the Pope,[1] and when the struggle
broke out between Frederick and the Papacy, the aim
of the German princes was to mediate between both
powers, and to extract the greatest amount of profit
from the conflict.

When Frederick was excommunicated by Gregory **IX.**
in 1239 the German spiritual princes wrote a letter to
the Pope, which proves how far removed they were from
blind acquiescence in the papal policy. They pointed
out that, as priests of the Church and at the same time
princes of the empire, they were specially bound to
mediate between the two powers; that at the outbreak
of the quarrel they had betaken themselves to the
emperor in order to move him to return to the Church;
that the emperor had laid before them the complaints
of the Pope and his answers, and had declared himself ready to repair any omissions according to the
judgment of the princes. They advised Gregory not
to embitter the emperor, which would bring religion
into great danger. However little they might believe
that the Vicar of Truth would protect the manifest
calumny of seditious rebels against the empire, they
were bound to confess that the general opinion
supported the emperor's contention that the Pope
had merely proceeded against him in the interests of
the Milanese and their allies. It was at any rate a
very serious matter that the papal legate at Milan,
Gregory of Montelongo, was seeking in every way to
seduce the loyal from their allegiance to the empire, as
the emperor had shown through letters and witnesses.

---

[1] Winckelmann, p. 20, denies that the ecclesiastical princes sold the
interests of the Curia in 1220 because they confirmed the old treaties of
the emperor and the Pope, and especially the partition between the two
kingdoms; but cf. Schirmmacher, ii. 452.

Although they were devoted to the Roman Church, they could not desert the emperor without breaking their troth to the empire. The Pope must not allow himself to be seduced by the false representations of a few princes who were merely seeking their own private advantage.[1] This was not merely the attitude of a few chosen adherents. The princes met together in Germany in the presence of the emperor's son Conrad, bound themselves by an oath to the emperor, and promised to reconcile him to the Pope.[2] In the course of April and May, 1240, an identical note was sent to Gregory from eight German bishops lamenting the discord which had broken out between Pope and emperor, pointing out that it was retarding the crusade, and producing enormous unheard-of evils.[3] While protesting their veneration of the Roman Church, the bishops remark that the emperor has promised to abide by the law, and that they are sending an envoy to the Pope to propose the basis of an agreement. The Archbishop of Mainz and the Archbishop of Augsburg joined in the prayer for peace in letters of substantially the same import. It was clear at any rate that in 1240 the German Church resented the high-handed proceedings of the Pope. Again the excommunication of the emperor was not published in Germany until two years after it had been issued by the Pope. It was then only published by the Arch-

---

[1] Ficker, *Reg.*, 2433 ; *H.B.*, v. 398. The princes who sign are probably the Archbishop of Salzburg, the Bishops of Passau and Freising, and the Abbot of Tegernsee. The allusion at the end is probably to the prelates. elect of Cologne and Liège, who were then at Rome.

[2] *Ann. Erph.*, SS. xvi. 33, 10.

[3] Weiland, ii., No. 225-232 ; Cologne, Worms, Munster, Osnabrück, Eichstadt, Strassburg, Spires, Wurzburg ; and cf. Ficker, *Mitt. d. Inst. für Oestr. G. Forsch.*, iii., 338 ff.

bishops of Cologne and of Mainz, both of whom had joined in the national protest against the Pope two years earlier, and whose change of attitude cannot be explained upon the hypothesis of any respectable motive.[1] The sentiment of the clergy in Bavaria was so markedly callous that the papal legate, Albert of Bohemia, had to report that they did "not care a bean" for sentences of suspension and excommunication,[2] and the proposal to elect the King of Denmark as King of the Romans was rejected by the steadfast loyalty of the German Church to Frederick. Time no doubt brought round some waverers to the Pope. Men tired of the struggle, and the papal legates busily fed their misgivings. When Albert said to the Duke of Bavaria that he and his fellow-electors had lost their right of electing a king because they had not exercised it within the lawful time, and that the Roman Church, which could not long go without a catholic advocate, might appoint a Gaul or a Lombard or some one else to be king, patrician or advocate, without consulting the Teutons, the duke answered, "Would that our Lord Pope had already done so. For this I would renounce both my votes and record the fact in a public instrument given to the Church on my own behalf and on behalf of my heirs."[3]

This sentiment was no doubt not peculiar. People began to wonder why Germany should endure so much for an absentee emperor. But, nevertheless, there

[1] *Reg. Konrad*, 4439 a.

[2] *H.B.*, v. 1032, " Dicunt enim canonici Bavarie omnesque alii praelati ex quo de suis beneficiis sunt securi posthac non timebunt tonitrua et fulmina Romanorum quia non darent pro ipsorum suspensionis et excommunicationis sententiis fabam."

[3] Höfler, *Albert von Behaim*, p. 16.

remained a strong resentment against the Pope.[1]   The
deposition of the emperor at the Council of Lyons in
1245 was met by a protest on the part of the princes,
the text of which has unfortunately not come down to
us[2]; but it is plain that the ecclesiastical princes of
Germany remained true to the doctrine which had
been so clearly stated by Frederick Barbarossa, " The
kingdom and the empire are held from God alone,
through the election of the princes." The Pope could
neither appoint nor could he depose the elected German
king. His *rôle* was passive. He was bound to confer
the imperial crown upon the choice of the princes.
The German king was necessarily destined for the
Roman empire.

By degrees, however, the machinations of the papal
agents wrought a change in the temper of the princes
of the Church. The Italian legates represented to the
Germans that the victory of Frederick would involve
the break-up of the elective and federal constitution;
they menaced the supporters of the "debauched heretic"
with every terror in the ecclesiastical armoury, and
they poured money into the scale. In 1246 the three
ecclesiastical electors, the Archbishop of Bremen and
the Bishops of Strassburg, Spires and Metz, met
together to elect a counter-king to champion the principles of election and of anarchy. Their choice fell
upon a Thuringian nobleman, Henry Raspe, who, after

---

[1] *H.B.*, v. p. 1131. Frederick tells the clergy and citizens of Worms to
resist the exaction of a fifth part of all ecclesiastical revenues. " Sustinere
non possimus ut ecclesie Germaniac libertas, que hactenus inconcussa
extitit, per sacerdotes sacrilegos inconsuetis angariis conculcetur."

[2] *Ann. Stad.*, SS. xiv. 369, 42, "Qua sententia (depositionis) per
mundum volante quidam principum cum multis aliis reclamabant
dicentes : ad papam non pertinere imperatorem eis vel instituere vel
destituere sed electum a principibus coronare."

an unexpected victory over Conrad, died in the following year. But the old Guelf cause survived his death,
and in the autumn of 1247 William of Holland, an
obscure squire, scarce twenty years of age, was elected
King of the Romans to continue the strife. The three
ecclesiastical electors again signalized their defection
from the Swabian house, and indeed by this time the
spirit of anarchy had so deeply engrained itself in the
political morals of Germany, that even the presence of
Frederick himself would have failed to exorcise it. But
the motives which guided the leaders of the German
Church at this crisis of European history were not
derived from the principles of the New Testament or
even from those of ultramontane theology. It is true
that the prelates were willing to co-operate with the
Papacy in a campaign against the right of spoils, the
exercise of which affected their dignity and their
pockets ; that they never dreamed of questioning the
spiritual authority of the Pope ; that they promoted the
Inquisition, which was even more savagely conducted
here than elsewhere ; and instigated a cruel and unnecessary crusade against the miserable and unimportant
tribe of the Stadingi. But while they would allow no
speck to rest upon the brightness of the armour of their
faith, they were mainly concerned in the consolidation
of their earthly principalities. Pride, self-interest, and
tradition fortified them in their resolution never to cede
their control over the imperial election. They had once
thought that it was menaced by the Pope ; they now
thought that it was menaced by the Swabians. A
federal constitution, headed by a weak or absentee
emperor, was the condition of their political independence. They had refused to make the throne hereditary
at the request of Henry VI. ; they had played Otto

against Philip, Frederick against Otto; they now played
Henry and William and Richard and Alphonse against
the cause of the autocrats. In the event they were
justified, for while the emperor's authority was attenu-
ated to a shadow, the substance of power remained
with the court of the princes, of whom some forty
were laymen, while more than sixty were clerks.[1]

[1] Ficker, *Vom Reichsfürstenstande*, pp. 264, 372 ff.

PART II.

CHAPTER XI.

IMPERIAL LEGISLATION IN ITALY.

MANY pages have been written upon the contrast between the genius of the Latin and Teutonic peoples. The spirit of order and discipline is generally attributed to the Latin, the spirit of romance and mysticism to the Teuton. While the Latins have given law to Europe, the Teutons have poured enthusiasm and vigour and individuality into the caldron. The one has been the regulative, the other the impulsive force in European progress. The one has written the prose, the other has dreamed the poetry of the west. Such contrasts are often drawn, but they must be accepted with reserve, for historical generalities never fit all cases or all ages. The Germans are at the present moment the most highly disciplined race in Europe, whereas in the tenth century they were perhaps the least obedient. The political genius of Rome has fled to London ; the Crusades, the most romantic of all enterprises, was the achievement of the Latin races ; the Divine Comedy, the most deeply felt vision of medieval Christianity, was the dream of a Latin poet. Still the history of the formation of the European

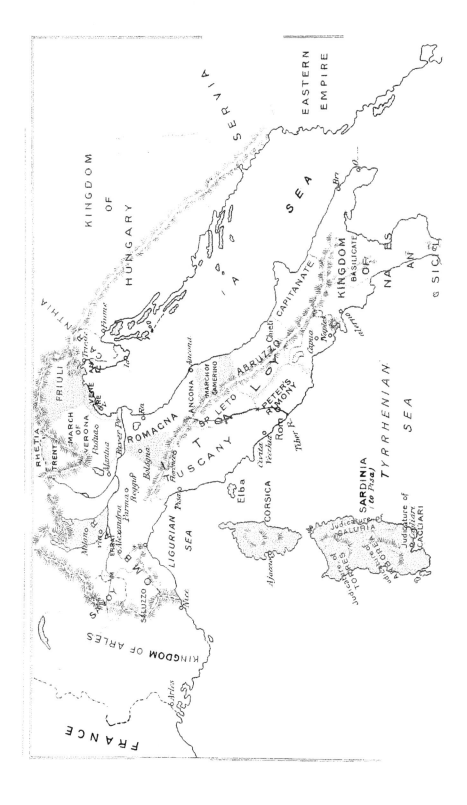

States may be regarded as the fusion of undisciplined Teuton force and enterprise into the civilized and ordered mould of a Latin church and a Latin empire. But by a curious turn of fortune, the Teuton found himself called upon to assume the political direction of a Latin country; to legislate for men who already possessed a body of laws which was far too good for them to realize, and far too elaborate for him to comprehend; to police with his rude but honourable vigour an old but demoralized civilization.

The Italy into which Otto I. descended was a land of ruins. The ninth century had been a lawless and a troubled age; and the first half of the tenth century had not been much better. In the seventy-five years preceding Otto's first campaign, four Italians, one Frenchman, three Germans, and four Burgundians had tried and failed to rule the country. The Saracens had, in the ninth century, cut the arteries of Italian civilization. They were settled in the south of Italy on the Garigliano; they held Narni, Rieti and Nepi, and for thirty years dominated Central Italy, leaving behind them traces in local nomenclature which last to this day. For one hundred years they occupied Fraxinetum and converted Provence and Piedmont into howling wildernesses.[1] Even John VIII., the most vigorous diplomatist and warrior of his time, the Julius II. of the ninth century, who rallies the south against the infidels, and beats them at sea, is forced to own their power and to pay them tribute. If the Saracens prey upon the peninsular in the ninth century, the Hungarians threaten to wreck it in the tenth. In 924 they burnt down Pavia, the Lombard capital, the centre of juristic studies in North

---

[1] Flach., *Origines de l'Ancienne France*, vol. ii., bk. iii., c. 3.

Italy, and the rude Latin hymn sung by the watchmen on the walls of Modena preserves the haunting memory of that hour.[1] In such an age the arts of peace were impossible. The only form of classical poetry in Rome had long been that of sepulchral inscriptions, and even these had ceased to be written with elegance after the end of the fourth century. The only form of pictorial effort was the mosaic, and the workers in this, the most conventional of arts, had long lost the richness of tone and the scope and freedom of composition which characterize the famous fifth-century frescoes at Ravenna. The race of architectural popes had died out almost as completely as the race of theologians. The Germanic portion of the population seems to have lost vigour, corrupted by climate, luxury, or incalculable misfortune. In the south the desperate struggles of Saracens, Greeks, and Lombards, fought over the wild Apulian hills or in the crowded cities of the coast, in the centre the strife between the Barons of the Campagna and the Papacy, put a stop to all intellectual and moral progress. With the single exception of Gregory of Tours, there are no medieval writers who portray a society so lost to every principle of morality, as do Erchempert, the chronicler of South Italy during the ninth, and Luitprand, the chronicler of North and Central Italy during the tenth century. The Church had not escaped the universal contagion. The picture of the Italian ecclesiastic of the tenth century, left to us by Ratherius of Verona, recalls the famous satire of St. Jerome, written some six centuries earlier. He is a luxurious feudal baron, treading soft carpets, living on delicate food, destitute of all moral

---

[1] Ozanam, *Documents inédits pour servir à l'histoire littéraire de l'Italie*, p. 64 ; Du Méril, *Poésies populaires antérieures au xii. siècle*, p. 264.

principle.[1] The annals of Farfa present the still
blacker picture of a monastery which for several
years averts reform by poisoning every one who is
sent to reform it. The land is utterly without
political direction. The Lombard duchy of Beneventum had split into three principalities. The Greeks
held a slice of its territory on the south-eastern coast.
Friuli, Spoleto, and Ivrea all struggled to obtain the
hegemony. Four Germans since the death of Lewis II.
[875], Charles the Bald, Carloman, Charles the Fat, and
Arnulf, intervened in Italian politics, exercising ephemeral
half-acknowledged authority. The political force of the
Papacy died with John VIII., and for thirty years of the
tenth century the Pope became the sport of licentious
women or the underling of a municipal tyrant. The
caustic Bishop of Cremona, generalizing from the uncon-
tradicted experience of many generations, summed up
the situation in the famous saying, " The Italians wish
to have two lords, in order that they may coerce the
one by the terror of the other."[2]

The "iron age" of Italian history was no time for
legislation. A few brief capitularies of the Spoletine
dukes, Wido and Lambert, have survived from the
wreck, and if others were issued, they were unknown
to the diligent Pavian lawyer, who made his collection of capitularies some time between 1000 and
1014. There had been indeed no lack of capitularies

---

[1] Ratherius, *De Cont.*, *Can.* ii., 2 (opp. 367), "Quaerat et aliquis, cur
prae ceteris gentibus baptismo renatis contemptores canonicae legis et
vilipensores clericorum sint magis Italici.... Quoniam quidem libidino-
siores eos et pigmentorum venerem nutrientium frequentior usus et vini
continua potatio et negligentior disciplina facit doctorum." For modern
accounts of the state of ecclesiastical morals in Italy during this period,
cf. Giesebrecht, *De litterarum studiis apud Italos primis medii aevi saeculis*,
and Dresdner, *Die Italienische Geistlichkeit des* 10 *und* 11 *Jahrhunderts.*

[2] *Luitprandi Antapodosis*, i., c. 37.

in the days of the early Carolings. Several of them were
specially applicable to Italy, and in theory it would seem
that all the general capitularies made for the Frankish
realm were intended to hold good in Italy as well.
But if they were applicable, they were not applied.
How could edicts framed in Francia for a Frankish
society, saturated with Frankish ideas and Frankish
terms—*trustis, mitium, fredus*—really affect Italian
practice? They might be recorded in collections of
Italian law, they might be commented on by schoolmasters and jurisconsults, but their interest was academic
rather than actual. Before the eleventh century there is
no trace of them in Italian charters and documents.
The other capitularies, those made for Italy, or in Italy,
especially the capitularies of Pippin and Lothair, have
a different fortune. These accord more closely with the
spirit and vocabulary of the Lombard law—a body of
customs first codified by Rotharis in 640, and progres-
sively improved and expanded by his more enlightened
successors. But the scope of these edicts is not restricted
to Lombardy. They never form part of the Lombard
edict. They are intended to be valid over all Italy.
They are part of an imperial scheme of legislation. But
in the political chaos of the ninth and tenth centuries,
there was little care bestowed upon this precious deposit,
and the anarchy of the times is reflected in the disordered
texts of the manuscripts. All the early collections of
capitularies made in Italy are private compilations.
There is the greatest variety of text and arrangement.
Omissions are frequent, and are dictated by the taste of
the copyist. Canons of councils, statutes of abbots,
chapters of canonical law, scraps from the Salian, the
Ripuarian, the Bavarian and Lombard codes, constitutions
of emperors, glosses of jurisconsults, passages from St.

Augustine, judgments of judges, private notes—all this miscellaneous farrago finds its way among the capitularies. In those days anything or everything written may be held to be law in Italy. There are, however, four manuscripts written in Italy, and of the eleventh century, which contain a collection of capitularies free from the confusion of the earliest manuscripts, and presenting the material in practically the same chronological order. This collection was probably made by a master of Pavia for the use of schools somewhere in the first fourteen years of the eleventh century. It is known as the *Capitulare* or the *Liber Papiensis*.[1]

This book—the famous product of the Pavian School of Jurisprudence—is the first sign of revived interest in legal matters after the long agony of the iron age. It is not the collection which would have been made by a practising lawyer. It is not the collection which might have been made by an exact historian. There is much repetition, there is much contradiction, there is much that is incomplete, there is much that is antiquated, there are several mistakes. The capitularies of Lewis II. are attributed to Lothair, and so are the Worms capitularies of Lewis the Pious. The compiler does not always understand the words of the Caroling period; he does not always know what a capitulary is, for some canons of the Church and some fragments of Italian custom find their way into his collection. Still the formation of this collection marks an epoch. The *Capitulare* was bound up with the Lombard edict, and the two collections together formed a *Corpus Juris Italici*, a collection of all the written

---

[1] Merkel, *Geschichte des Langobardenrechts*; Boretius, *Die Capitularien im Langobardenreich*, and *Praefatio ad Librum Papiensem*; *L.L.* iv., p. xlvi. ff.

laws, Lombard and Frankish, which had been given
to Italy by her barbarian invaders. They were the
subject of much learned and acute dissertation, which
has been preserved to us in a glossed collection made
for the use of the Pavian schools between 1019 and
1037. But how meagre and obscure is the text, how
ample and ingenious the comment! We feel that
these Pavian jurists were struggling not so much with
a living body of law as with a collection of legal
scraps belonging to various times, stages, and civilizations extending over a period of more than three
hundred years, inadequate to express the needs of a
society which had passed through the caldron of social
dissolution. To interpret and harmonize these scattered
texts, and to fill up the lacunae, was a task which might
be performed in one of two ways. You might seek light
from Lombard and Germanic custom, or you might
seek light from Roman law. The judges of the Sacred
Palace at Pavia, whose comments upon the *Liber
Papiensis* have come down to us, appear to have been
divided into two schools. There were the Romanists,
who held that the Roman law had a general supple-
mentary force, and that Rotharis himself had intended that the curt definitions of his edict should
be interpreted by the principles of Roman jurisprudence.[1]
There were the Lombardists, who maintained that the
Lombard law was self-sufficient and self-explanatory.
The Romanists won the day. They were, it is true,
extravagantly unhistorical. They accredited to poor
Rotharis an acquaintance with the Novels; they in-

---

[1] *Lib. Pap. Exp. ad Roth.*, 1, sect. 2 ; *Grim.*, 4, sect. 3 ; *Wid.*, 5, sect. 4,
"Antiqui dicebant quod haec lex nihil inde preciperet, ideoque juxta
Romanam legem, quae omnium est generalis, hoc esse definiendum cense-
bant." Cf. Pertile, *Storia del diritto Italiano*, i., pp. 401, 402 ; *Exp. ad
Roth.*, 359, sect. 3.

vested Lombard law with Roman forms; they interpreted
it by Roman analogies; at times they threw it overboard
with every circumstance of disrespect.   But the future
of Italian law lay rather in the application of Roman
principles to a society which. although in origin partially Germanic, had become practically Latin, than
in any adaptation of early Germanic custom.   The
process was accelerated by the fact that a large part
of Italy was actually in the tenth century dominated
by Roman law.   In Venice, in Istria, in the Exarchate,
there are only a few isolated traces of persons professing to live Lombard law.   In Rome, Roman law
was practically triumphant, though Lombardists still
made their protest.   And it should be remembered
also that all the forces which made for the territoriali-
zation of law, the introduction of the Scabinate, the
growth of city life, the multiplication of human
relations by commerce, the spread of education, the
intermarriage of Lombard and Latin families, made
also for Romanism.   In Bergamo, where there was a
strong Germanic colony, in the south of Italy, where
the mixture of races was great, where life was wilder
and more primitive, the territoriality of law came late.
In the south it had not been accomplished even at
the opening of the fifteenth century.[1]   But by the
end of the twelfth century the personality of law had
practically, in Northern Italy at least, become a thing
of the past.   Men lived according to "the right and
the good usage and the custom of their city."   The
great noble families, who have special legal traditions,
possibly guaranteed by ancient Lombard or Frankish
privilege, and here and there a stray Lombard in a

---

[1] There are people living Frank and Lombard law as late as 1418
(Pertile, *Storia del diritto Italiano*, i., p. 384).

rural castle, make profession of Lombard law. Everywhere else the territorial principle has won the day.[1]

How far was this growth of territorial law the result
of imperial influence? We have seen that the capitu
laries were intended to apply to the whole of Italy, that
the *Liber Papiensis* of the eleventh century formed a
nucleus of Italian law, which was in theory applicable
alike to those who professed the Lombard and to those
who professed the Roman system. An ample stream of
imperial legislation in Italy during the tenth, eleventh,
twelfth and thirteenth centuries might have created
something like a uniform body of Italian law. But
instead of a stream we have a rivulet both tiny and
intermittent. In the two centuries and a half which
elapsed from the first intervention of Otto the Great to
the accession of Frederick II., there are only fifteen
general imperial pronouncements upon law made in the
country, one of which is made in a papal synod, and
two of which are doubtfully authentic. There are long
periods of absolute drought during the reign of Henry
IV. and his son, when the War of the Investitures was
raging, and again during the struggle between Frederick
I. and the Papacy.

Yet these imperial edicts have their importance.
Although some apply only to special towns or districts
or classes,[2] others are either expressly or implicitly valid
for all Italy. " By whatever law," says Otto I. in 967,
introducing the procedure of trial by battle into the
determination of certain cases, " a man shall live in the
whole kingdom of Italy, even if it be the Roman law,

---

[1] In penal matters, in the capacity of individuals for civil acts, in
matters relating to religious belief, matrimony and oaths, the personal
principle is preserved (Pertile, i. 386).

[2] Thus Henry III. issues a decree for Lombardy, 1052. Weiland, i.,
No. 52.

we order him to observe all these decrees, as we have decreed them in these chapters concerning battle."[1]   The archbishops, bishops, abbots, marquises, counts and all judges in Italy, these are the recipients of Otto III.'s decree against the alienation of Church lands.   The feudal constitutions of Conrad II., of Lothair, of Frederick I., are clearly valid for all Italy.   Many edicts too of Frederick II. are imperial, though there are many which have sole reference to the kingdom of Sicily, and thus a small but not unimportant *corpus* of edicts was formed, which was valid for the whole of Italy, and which served to maintain the conception of a law common to all parts of the peninsular.   As under Frederick L, Henry VI. and Frederick II. the residence of the emperor in the country became more and more continuous, and the imperial control over the administrative and judicial machinery more and more complete, an increasing degree of unity must have been introduced into judicial method.   We must remember too that the emperors were Roman emperors, and that in Roman law they found a welcome justification for absolutism.   Conrad II., in 1038, had decided that Roman law was to rule the Roman territory. Frederick I. appealed to Bologna, the home of Roman legal studies, when he wished for a careful statement of his regal claims in Italy.   And Frederick II. in one place appears to legislate against personal law in the kingdom of Sicily.   "We do not wish," he says "to have any distinction of persons before the law, but whether a man be Frank or Roman or Lombard,

---

[1] Weiland, i., No. 13, sect. 9; *ib.*, No. 23; *ib.*, Nos. 45, 120, 148, 149, 177. Cf. also *M.G. Dipl.*, vol. i., ed. Sickel, p. 509, where on April 18th, 969, Otto gives "laws and precepts" to the Calabrians, Italians, Franks and Germans.

plaintiff or defendant, we wish to administer equal justice to him." [1]　Thus by issuing edicts valid for all Italy, by encouraging the study and practice of the Roman law, which was the law of the predominant portion of the population of Italy, by constructing something like a common administrative system, by unifying the law of procedure in the Sicilian kingdom, where the territorial principle was weakest, these later Hohenstauffen emperors aid the formation of a common Italian law, part written, part unwritten, a *Consuetudo Regni*.　Behind all the varieties of local customs was the "common law of all the emperors." [2]

If the emperor contributed little or nothing by express edict to mould the German feudal law, leaving it rather to form itself out of the decisions given from time to time upon feudal questions by his court, his interference in the feudal law in Italy is more easily marked and more decisive.　Italy expected legislation of the emperor.　It was a land of written law, of juristic studies, of legal curiosity, whetted by the antagonism of rival codes.　The appearance of the emperor upon the field of Roncaglia was the signal, not only for an extended series of legal decisions, but also for the publication of edicts. [3]　He was called upon not only to mitigate long-standing rancours and to decide all kinds of disputes, but to give general decisions upon unsettled points of law, to improve procedure, to modify the existing law itself.　And there was a sufficient

---

[1] *Const. Regn. Sic.*, 2. 17.　　　　　　[2] Ariprand, tit. lvi.

[3] *Gesta de Federigo I.*, ed. Monaci.　Wherever the emperor was present in person he had concurrent jurisdiction with the ordinary local judges. Otto Fris., *Gesta Frid.*, i. 2, c. 13, "Alia itidem ex antiqua consuetudine manasse traditur justitia, ut principe Italiam intrante cunctae vacare debeant dignitates et magistratus ac ad ipsius nutum secundum scita legum jurisque peritorum judicium universa tractari."　Cf. Ficker, *Forsch.*, vol. i., pp. 275-6.

divergence between the social and legal condition of
Germany and Italy to stimulate legislation, for it
always seems easier to legislate for foreigners than
for ourselves. Thus Otto I. re-introduces the Germanic
procedure of trial by battle, although it had been
carefully limited by the enlightened efforts of the
earlier Lombard kings, and Otto III. extends the
application of this barbaric remedy.[1] But procedure
was not the most suggestive theme for the German
legislator upon one of his flying visits over the Brenner.
When he had pronounced the magic word " duellum,"
he had practically said his say.[2] Roman law again
stood in no need of his assistance, and the development
of municipal life had created conditions which made
most of the Germanic legal ideas inapplicable to by
far the largest portion of the Lombard population.
But the law relating to fiefs stood on a different plat-
form. Here there was every reason why the emperor
should wish to have his " say," there was every reason
why his "say" should be anxiously elicited. Fiefs
were a Germanic institution, and the German emperors
appear largely to have depended for their influence
south of the Alps upon certain great feudatories of
Germanic origin. When the time came for the Roman
march, a certain quantum of military service was
demanded by the Lombard king, and this, so it would
seem, had been originally fixed by contracts made
between the emperor and the tenants-in-chief. The

---

[1] Grimoald, c. 4 ; Luitprand, c. 71, 118. Luitprand's remarks [A.D.
731] are significant : " Quia incerti sumus de judicio Dei et multos
audivimus per pugnam sine justitia causam suam perdere, sed propter
consuitutinem gentis nostrae Langobardorum legem ipsam vetare non
possumus" (*L.L.*, iv., p. 156).

[2] The emperor, however, was occasionally asked to lay down a rule of
procedure. Cf. the *Constitutio Auximana* of 1177 ; Weiland, i., No. 273.

maintenance of these feudal obligations was thus a vital matter to the German ruler. It was one of the main pillars of his trans-Alpine rule.

Again, there were two special points of contrast between the condition of the fief-holding nobility in Germany and the condition of the fief-holding nobility in Italy. In Germany there was little town life ; there was a large rural nobility holding fiefs directly or indirectly of the crown. In Italy the towns were everything, the rural nobility comparatively insignificant in numbers and importance.[1] We know the names of the great North Italian nobles who attend the courts of Frederick Barbarossa, whose signatures are upon his charters. They are most of them from the north-west, and they can be numbered upon the fingers of both hands. It is doubtful whether any of them were very wealthy, or from a military point of view very important. There was in fact a constant drift of the nobility, even of the higher nobility, into the towns, and many who possessed estates in the country also had their town houses. The paucity of great feudatories, the absence of a continuous royal court attended by the greater nobles, and deciding points of feudal law in the interests of the higher rank of the aristocracy, the continuous and abundant drift into the towns, where feudal considerations were at a discount, the influence of Roman law, the precocious development of Italian commerce—these forces tend to relax the strictness of feudal law in Italy, to favour the vassal at the expense of the lord, to promote the free treatment of the vassal's fief. Whereas in Germany the vassal can only dispose of the fruits of his benefice

---

[1] For the absorption of Italian feudatories in the towns, cf. Pertile, *Storia del diritto Italiano*, pp. 277, 313, n. 47.

without the consent of the lord, in Italy he can alienate half, and in many districts, for instance in Milan, the whole of his fief without the lord's consent. The German rule, giving to the lord the right of transferring the lordship of his vassal's fief to another without the vassal's consent, holds good only among the Milanese and Cremonese, and then with the qualification that the vassal must, during his lifetime, receive no damage from the change. In all other parts of Italy the man's consent is required. Again, whereas in Germany the fief descends only to the actual descendants of the last possessor, in Italy ascendants and collaterals are included under the category of potential heirs.[1] While in Germany the lord enters on the fief during a minority, in Italy the fruits of the fief and the representation of a fief during a minority belong to the guardian of the minor's allodial property. The German law is more favourable to the lord, the Lombard law more favourable to the vassal.[2]

The prevailing disposition of the German emperors was to favour the bishops and the higher Italian nobility, and to apply to Italy those strict feudal principles which were popular north of the Alps. The bishops and the higher nobility—these were in truth the German garrison. We may trace in the marriages contracted from time to time between the Italian and the German noble houses the constant preoccupation of

---

[1] The right of succession, which was probably originally restricted to brothers, was extended first to the third, then to the fourth, then as far as the seventh degree, and then even that limit disappeared. But the fief could only go to the descendants of the first feoffee (*Libri Feudorum*, i. 5 ; viii. 1 ; ii. 50). In the south of Italy Frederick II. admitted the succession of collaterals only up to the third degree.

[2] This was especially the case according to the custom of Milan. Cf. *Libri Feudorum*, ii. 28. 1, 37. 1, 24 n., 40. 2, 34. 3 ; Pertile, *Storia del diritto Italiano*, vol. iv., sect. 131.

the emperors to maintain the Germanic character of this small but invaluable force. The marriage of the Margrave Azzo II. with the Welf heiress Cuniza; the marriage of Hermann of Swabia with Adelheid, eldest daughter of the Margrave Olderich—Manfred II. of Turin; the marriage of Otto of Schweinfurt with his second daughter Immula; the marriage of Boniface of Tuscany with the daughter of Duke Frederick of Upper Lorraine—all these alliances belong to the reign of Conrad II., and may be taken as samples of a continuous principle of imperial policy. The natural tendency of every German emperor would be to favour the great man against the small man, the lord against the vassal, the bishop nominated by himself, holding his office for life, bound to receive him and to entertain him and to furnish him with troops, against the bishop's man.

But there was a distinction to be drawn between the lay and the clerical portion of the German garrison in Italy. The German bishops held their office for life, the German nobility became rooted in the soil, and with every generation became less Germanic and more Italian. In the reign of Henry II. all the more prominent noble families in North Italy had thrown themselves on the side opposed to the empire. They had supported Arduin of Ivrea as a candidate for the Lombard throne, they had been vanquished by the force of German arms, and many of them were despatched north of the Alps to languish in German prisons.[1] Nor was the resistance of the Anti-German

---

[1] Pabst, *Heinrich II.*, ii., p. 354 ff. The five great North Italian families in Conrad's reign were: (1) the Margraves of Turin; (2) the Aledramides of Acqui and Savona; (3) the Otbertiner with county rights in Genoa, Luni, Tortona, Milan; (4) the house of Este with their five

party entirely vanquished by the vigour of Henry II. On the death of that monarch the envoys of the Italian princes offer the Lombard crown to King Robert of France for himself and for his son, and, rejected at Paris, they proceed to Poitou to sound William V., the learned, orthodox and powerful Duke of Aquitaine. The story of these negotiations need not be told in all its fulness. The facts, however, are clear. William was ready to accept the Lombard crown, not indeed for himself, but for his son, provided that he could be secure of adequate support in Italy. But the North Italian prelates remained true to the German connection, and William was too pious a prince to accept the suggestion of his more unscrupulous adherents, that he should depose all the bishops in Italy and appoint his own personal adherents in their place.[1] Other circumstances—troubles in Aquitaine, the lukewarmness of the Margrave of Turin, the failure of diplomatic combinations in France—may have contributed to bring about William's "great refusal." But the central fact in the situation was that the bishops of North Italy could not be seduced from their German allegiance. Conrad drew the appropriate moral. He saw the value of the episcopate ; he determined to maintain, to increase, its German character. He saw the danger of the Italian nobility ; he determined to marry them into German houses. He would have a German aristocracy, lay and clerical, ruling both north and south of the Alps. And opportunity favoured him. Two cyphers and a dissolute boy suc-

counties of Modena, Reggio, Mantua, Brescia, and Ferrara ; (5) the Margraves of Tuscany, who have also the Duchy of Spoleto and the Margraviate of Camerino in their family. Bresslau, i., pp. 69-71, pp. 365-443.

[1] Cf. the remarkable letter of William to Leo of Vercelli [Bouquet, x., p. 484].

ceeded one another in the papal chair. There would
be no pontifical expostulation against simony or alien
influence or secularism. He packed the Italian sees
systematically with Germans and personal adherents.[1]
He forwarded intermarriages between the Italian and
German nobility so successfully that by 1036 three out
of the five great North Italian families had married
into German houses.[2] To bind the great feudatories
to the German interest was the first object of Conrad's
policy.

It happened, however, that the first pronouncement
of a German emperor upon feudal law in Italy was made,
not in favour of the tenant-in-chief, but in favour of the
vassal.[3] The circumstances which led to Conrad II.'s
famous edict of 1037 cannot be very perfectly dis-
entangled, but certain facts are clear, and they are
sufficient to explain the emperor's action. Aribert, the
Archbishop of Milan, had become practical ruler of North
Italy. "He disposed of the whole kingdom of Italy at
his pleasure."[4] It is possible that, encouraged by the
independent traditions of the Milanese Church, he may
have aimed at constructing an ecclesiastical state for
Milan in the north, as the Popes aimed at building up
an ecclesiastical state for Rome in the centre of Italy.
It seems certain that he was opposed to the spread of
German influence in his own province,[5] and that his
tyranny and oppression roused an insurrection of the

---

[1] Bresslau, *Konrad II.*, ii., pp. 175-87.   [2] *Ib.*, ii., pp. 188-191.

[3] Sigonius, *De Regno Italico*, t. iv., attributes feudal legislation to
Lothair in 825, "Proditum etiam est memoriae Lotharium pro foribus
Basilicae Vaticauae de feodis statuisse consilio sapientum Mediolani
Papiae, Cremonae, etc."

[4] Giesebrecht, ii. 5, 314.

[5] Bresslau, vol. ii., p. 187, points out only two cases—Henry of Ivrea
and Richer, Abbot of Leno—of imperial adherents of Germany appointed
duriug this reign to ecclesiastical office in the province of Milan.

valvassores of Milan, which then widened out into a general rising of all the valvassores and lower knights of Italy against their lords. The defeat of the archiepiscopal and aristocratic party at Campo Malo in 1035 determined Aribert to invoke the emperor. The imperial influence would surely, he reflected, be thrown into its wonted scale. But, whatever may have been Conrad's original intentions when he entered Italy, circumstances rapidly threw him into the arms of the valvassores. On the second day of his visit to Milan, the emperor was disturbed by a serious tumult of the Milanese, which he attributed to Aribert. Dissembling his indignation he left the city and summoned a parliament at Pavia. Here the general indignation caused by Aribert's misrule flamed out clearly. The emperor accused the archbishop of disloyalty (he may have been referring to the Milanese riot or to earlier deeds, the particulars of which have been lost), and the Count of Milan and several other Italians brought up manifold charges of oppression, and specially it would seem of property wrongfully seized. Conrad, who does not seem to have desired to push the case too hardly against the archbishop, merely admonished him to restore the property which he had embezzled. But the archbishop, after consultation with his friends, boldly denied the jurisdiction of the imperial court, and was handed over to the custody of the Patriarch of Aquileia as guilty of treason. One night at Piacenza the archbishop fled from his prison, rode to Milan and raised the city against the emperor. The citizens who hated their count, now connected by marriage with the German nobility, rallied round the archbishop. The emperor summoned reinforcements from Germany, and called upon the Italian princes to join him before the walls of Milan. It was during the siege of Milan, on May 28th, 1037, that the edict concerning the benefices of the kingdom of Italy was issued.

We would fain know more of this revolution in Italy. That the main discontent came from the third order of feudatories, the *milites secundi* or *valvassores minores*; that their chief grievance was insecurity of tenure, and the liability to be deprived of their fiefs at the arbitrary discretion of their overlords; that Conrad's edict pacified the country and satisfied the claims of a large and important military class—these things seem established. But we cannot tell whether Aribert and his fellows were revolutionaries, attempting to enforce upon their vassals the doctrine of the revocability of the fief, which may have been held in theory by some feudists north of the Alps, though it had certainly been abandoned in practice. We do not even know whether they pretended to justify their violence by legal technicalities. We can only tentatively reconstruct the advice which a subservient Lombard lawyer would have given on the one side, or an independent Lombard lawyer on the other. That the princes had secured the heredity of their fiefs is certain; that the captains had also secured the same privilege is highly probable. As early as 883 the annals of Fulda relate that Charles the Fat caused a revolution among the great Italians, by depriving them of benefices which had remained for three generations in their families.[1] But it is conceivable that the heritability of the fief, though long recognized among the two superior orders of the

---

[1] *Ann. Fuld.*, SS. i., p. 398, "Imperator ... animos optimatum ... contra se concitavit. Namque Witonem aliosque nonnullos exauctoravit, et beneficia quae illi et patres et avi et atavi illorum tenuerant vilioribus dedit personis."

nobility, had not been so completely guaranteed in respect of the benefices of the valvassores.[1]   We must remember too that the original revocability of the fief had never been lost sight of, and that it is solemnly stated in the opening chapter of the first book of the *Libri Feudorum*.   Still we cannot help thinking that the valvassores were defending and their superiors attacking the established custom of North Italy.   Not only does one of the chroniclers expressly say that Conrad merely confirmed the law of earlier days,[2] but in the commentary of Ariprand, a judge of the Marquis of Este's, who certainly wrote before these events, it is assumed that fiefs are hereditary.[3]   They may be forfeited indeed for certain special causes, but only after a judgment of a vassal's peers, and from this sentence there is an appeal to the overlord.   If the lord alienate or lease or exchange a fief without just cause, he is to pay a hundred pounds of gold, half to the king, half to the damaged person.   Neither here nor in the *Libri Feudorum*, nor in the Milanese custom, is there any exception made to the general rule of heritability, to the detriment of the valvassores.   The law of Conrad appears to be very little more than an amplification of the views which appear to have prevailed in the court of the Margrave of Este.[4]

If Conrad was forced to conciliate the vassals, he was not debarred at the same time from providing a gateway through which imperial influence might flow into Italy. He decrees that no knight of bishop, abbot, abbess, marquis or count, who holds an imperial or ecclesiastical

---

[1] Bresslau, ii., p. 201.   [2] *Herim Aug. Chron.*, 1037, SS. v., p. 122.

[3] Anschütz, *Lombarda-Commentare des Ariprand und Albertus*, lib. iii., tit. 8, "Sed si decesserit qui feodum quaesivit, filii ejus succedunt et per filium descendentes mares."

[4] Anschütz, *Die Lombarda-Commentare des Ariprand und Albertus.*

fief, shall lose it except for some certain and proved
fault, "according to the constitution of our ancestors
and by the judgment of his peers." Again, upon the
death of any knight, be he greater or less, his son
succeeds to the benefice ; and if he have no son living,
but only grandsons by a son, then the grandsons are to
succeed, after paying the usual heriots to their seniors.
And if he have no grandsons, but have a brother lawfully begotten by his father, then, if that brother wish
to become the knight of the senior and to do satisfaction to him, let him have his father's benefice. No
senior is to exchange, lease, or convey any benefice
belonging to his knights without their consent. And
no one is unjustly to divest them of their properties or
leases. The knight is thus secured both in that which
he holds by a beneficiary and that which he holds by
a non-beneficiary title.[1]

The emperor has cast his protection over feudal
possessions. If a dispute arise concerning a benefice
between one of the greater valvassores and his senior,
then the question is decided by the peers of the sub-
tenant. But even if the peers have decided against him,
he may hold his benefice until plaintiff and defendant
and the defendant's peers come into the emperor's presence, that the case may be decided there. But if peers
be lacking to the defendant when judgment is given in
the first instance, then the defendant shall hold his
benefice until he and his seniors and his peers come into

---

[1] In the *Libri Feudorum* [Bk. i., sect. 2], the legislation of Conrad is thus
described : "Cum vero Conradus Romam proficisceretur petitum est a
fidelibus qui in ejus erant servitio, ut, lege ab eo promulgata, hoc etiam
ad nepotes ex filio producere dignaretur et ut gratis fratri sine legitimo
herede defuncto in beneficio, quod corum fratris fuit, succedat. Cui autem
unus ex fratribus a domino feodum acceperit, eo defuncto sine legitimo
herede, frater eius in feudum non succedit, nisi hoc nominatim dictum sit."

the presence of the emperor.   A notice of such appeal on the part either of senior or knight must be sent in to the other litigant six weeks before the journey be begun. But if the dispute concern not the greater but the lesser valvassor, it shall be brought to a termination either before the seniors or before an imperial *missus*.   Conrad here affirms a great principle, one which, had it been worked out by an adequate and continuously active staff of imperial judges, might have brought all the judicial business of Northern Italy into the imperial court.   He affirms the principle that no one need be dispossessed of his fee without a decision of the emperor or of his agent. He affirms the principle that no one should be divested of his property or of his leasehold unjustly, by which we may perhaps understand, " without judgment of his peers." He imposes a fine of a hundred pounds of gold upon whomsoever shall infringe the edict.   If he had given the right of appeal in the second case as he had given it in the first, his edict would have covered the whole ground occupied by the proprietary and possessory assizes of Henry II. of England.   These assizes definitely gave to the royal court of England its supremacy among competing jurisdictions.   They were not, as was the edict of Conrad, issued *en bloc* as a public royal act of legislation.   They were, it would seem, informal in-structions of a technical kind issued to the king's judges when they went upon circuit.   We do not even know when they were first given.[1]   But they were infinitely more effective than was Conrad's edict.   They form in fact a turning point in English legal history.   They were more effective because they did not merely apply to military tenures ; because they did not merely concern a given district or a given class of men ; because, above

[1] *H.E.L.*, vol. i., c. v.

all, they were administered in the provinces by the king's itinerant justices, who thus purveyed cheap legal remedies to the litigant's own home. How many a Lombard valvassor would have tramped over the Alpine snows with his recalcitrant peers and his angry senior to hunt the restless German court on its irregular untimed rounds through that lawless, sparsely peopled, inclement land? What imperial agent could have wrung that crushing fine from an Archbishop of Milan for instance, who, despite six weeks' notice, should decline to face the incommodities of Switzerland, on the invitation of a sub-tenant who had not been able to get his peers to take the same view as himself? The right of appeal must have been seldom exercised. It can have little profited the emperor to cast his palladium over beneficiary possession, in the absence of a permanent imperial staff of judges in Italy. The opportunity which Henry II. of England made, coming as the reintroducer of law and order after a period of anarchic feuds, that opportunity Conrad II. of Germany, descending into Italy after a period of social strife, managed to miss. The edict had the effect of making the fiefs of the valvassores hereditary. But it did nothing permanently to increase the imperial authority south of the Alps.

Not a single legislative act affecting the tenure and succession of fiefs has come down to us from the three Henries. But the Saxon Lothair promulgated an edict, which is in fact a reversal of Conrad's policy, and an application of the stricter rules of German feudal law to Italy. It was issued at the diet of Roncaglia in 1136, the traditional place at which the emperors took stock of their rights and privileges, and issued ordinances for the administration of justice and the preservation of peace in Northern Italy. The great nobles of North

Italy had come to the diet with a very scanty following of knights; the Roman expedition would be an unusually and scandalously thin one. The empire was in danger of losing a large part of its Italian military service, and the great nobles were called on to explain the situation. They said that their knights had alienated their benefices recklessly and piecemeal, and that being now destitute of fiefs, refused to undertake the military service, which was attached to the alienated property. A somewhat similar situation in England provoked Edward I.'s statute of *Quia Emptores*, which on the one hand facilitated alienation, but on the other hand forbade subinfeudation, thus conciliating royal and feudal with economic necessity. The assembly of Roncaglia devised another . remedy. No one could alienate a benefice which he had received from his seniors without the senior's consent; or enter into any contract which should be prejudicial to the interests of the empire or of his superior lords. Any person violating this law shall lose both the price he is paid upon the contract and the benefice as well, and any notary composing such an instrument shall lose his office and sustain the danger of *infamia*. This constitution was received into the Lombard law and into the *Libri Feudorum*.[1] It was a law issued in Lombardy, and issued for Lombardy. It was by no means so clever a solution as Edward's statute; it put a considerable impediment in the way of the free economic treatment of the knightly fee. But it was undoubtedly popular with the great lords, and it can scarcely have ever been allowed to become a dead letter.

---

[1] Weiland's edition is partially based upon an edition of a twelfth century MS. belonging to the Register of the Archiepiscopal Court of Genoa. Boretius, *LL.* iv., p. 639; Stumpf, 3339.

It was the fate of the medieval empire that it could only advance by antiquarianism, by the resurrection of ancient rights and privileges and memories. This is the destiny of all institutions whose glory lives in the past, and the glory of the medieval empire had expired with Charles the Great. After centuries of foiled and broken effort to recover the vanished power of Constantine or of Charles, a man comes to take up the imperial task with more passionate insight, more resolute will, and with, above all, a larger opportunity than had been accorded to his predecessors. Frederick I. felt and understood the peculiar nature of his inheritance. We find him everywhere insisting on traditional rights, stereotyping privilege, reviving and consecrating afresh the past. He declares that the princes of the kingdom of Arles are imperial vassals; he invests and receives the oath of homage from the archbishops of Lyons, Vienna, Arles, Tarantaise and Aix, or their suffragans; in 1162 invests Count Raimund Berengar II. with Provence; in 1178 he gets himself, his wife and son crowned in the cathedral of the Burgundian capital.[1] The canonization of Charles the Great is typical of his aims. As he says in his encyclical to the Teutons and Latins, issued in 1162, after the destruction of Milan, "We will turn our army and our victorious eagles to effect the complete restoration of the empire—*ad plenariam imperii reformationem.*" He feels that the service of the empire cannot be properly performed if fiefs are alienated indefinitely, if the strict rules of feudal law as understood in Germany are not observed, if great ecclesiastical principalities are impoverished by the profligate expenditure of ecclesiastical princes. He is aware that in Italy

[1] Ficker, *Reichfürstenstand*, pp. 296-308.

there is much obscurity as to the extent of the imperial rights, for the visits of his predecessors had been brief and intermittent.[1] Accordingly, no sooner does he cross the Brenner than he begins to scrutinize, to revise, to restate the regalia, speaking at his first diet of Roncaglia in the following fashion : " The vassal who does not go the Rome-journey with the king pays his lord host-money ; the Lombard twelve pence a bushel ; the German a third part of the fruits of the year." And in 1158 he sets the four famous doctors of Bologna to inquire into the regalia of the Lombard kings. It is in accordance with this spirit that he approaches the feudal law, again and again affirming the principle which is the essential condition of effective medieval rule, "No imperial fief can be alienated without the emperor's consent." In all his dealings with cities he respects the rights of feudal overlords. All persons who happen to have been in Crema during the siege are to lose their fiefs and allods, but the fiefs are to return to the lords, who are to have full power to deal with them subject to the imperial authority.[2] As in Germany, so in Italy, he brings his bishops into the feudal pen. "I do not want their homage," he says, "if they do not want their regalia," and he finds Italian friends to refer him now to a passage of St. Augustine condemning ecclesiastical opulence, and now to a passage in Roman law supporting the thesis that a bishop's palace is one of the royal rights.[3]

Frederick then comes to Italy, determined to enforce feudal obligations. At his first diet of Roncaglia, he not

---

[1] Weiland, i., No. 440.

[2] *Scripta de expugnatione Cremae*, 1159-60 ; Weiland, i., Nos. 191-3.

[3] Toeche, *Heinrich VI.*, pp. 14, 15, remarks, "The idea which lay at the bottom of the feudal system is first developed in his [Frederick I.'s] reign."

only confirms Lothair's edict, "Fiefs may not be alienated without the lord's leave," but he adds, "All alienations hitherto so made, however ancient, are null and void." He applies too to Italy a doctrine which had long been recognized in Germany, "Whoever does not help his king or lord, either in person or in purse, paying according to the quantity of his fief, when a public expedition has been announced to take up the imperial crown, if such an one can be convicted by his lord, let him lose his fief." And four years later, at a still more famous diet of Roncaglia, Frederick recurs to the same theme, issuing the *Constitutio de Jure Feudorum*.

This famous document is a summary of Frederick's feudal policy, and is one of the many engines which were forged in the year 1158 to further the great project of recovering the imperial rights. The first four clauses are in the main repetitions of the constitution of 1154, but there are some technical improvements, some further definitions. An action is given to a *bona-fide* buyer against the vendor of a fief; the neglect to seek investiture for a year and a day is only to involve forfeiture in the case of those who are more than fourteen years of age; service on the Roman journey may be done either by sending another who shall be acceptable to the lord, or by paying one year's revenue. The other clauses are more important. (1) No duchy, marquisate or county is in future to be divided.[1] Any other fief—if those who have a share in it should wish—may be divided, but all those who take a share in such a fief must do fealty to the

---

[1] The charters of Bergamo show how in the eleventh century the office and title of count was divided among several members of the same family. In 1082 three counts of Bergamo appear before Henry IV. (*Sull' antichissima origine dei governi municipii Italiani*, Antonio Pagnoncelli, Bergamo, 1823, t. i., c. 8).

lord either before or after the partition.   But the vassal
cannot be bound to more than one lord for one fief ; and
the lord cannot transfer the fief to another without the
consent of his vassals.   (2) If the son of a vassal offend
the lord, the father must, upon the request of the lord,
either bring the son to give satisfaction to the lord or
else he must separate the son from himself.   Otherwise
he must lose his fief.   If the son refuse to obey his
father or to do satisfaction to the lord, then on the
father's death he is not to succeed to the fief unless
he first do satisfaction.   And the vassal is similarly
responsible for all in his family.   (3) If B, a vassal
holding of A, have a sub-tenant C, and C offend A, then
unless C did it in service of B, let him (C) lose his fief,
and let the fief revert to B unless, on the requisition of
B, C is prepared to satisfy A.   And if B refuse to make
this requisition, then let B lose his fief.   (4) If a controversy about a fief arise between two vassals, let the lord
terminate the controversy.   If between lord and vassal,
let the quarrel be settled by the peers of the court.   (5)
To every oath of fealty the emperor is to be excepted by
name.

It was a gallant but a forlorn attempt to revive the
official idea which once actually underlay the system of
fiefs, and which was destined to persist, in a state of
reverent interment in the historical introduction to the
Libri Feudorum.   To declare the indivisibility of the
great official fiefs was easy, to secure it impossible,[1] and
this clause in Frederick's ordinance, like so many other

---

[1] Also in 1255 the partition of Peter of Savoy was resisted on the
ground "quod comitatus non debet dividi nec ducatus juxta legem
Frederici quondam imperatoris."   It appears, however, to have been
easy to get a dispensation from Frederick's rule [Ficker, *Forsch.*, i. 246].
Frederick restores to the Counts of Prato the alienated parts of the
county [Ficker, i., pp. 245-6].

imperial edicts, survived rather as an aspiration than as
a rule, sharing the fate of that clause in the Mirror of
Swabia, which, while permitting the partition of principalities, marquisates and counties, declares that none of
the co-partners shall style themselves prince, marquis or
count.[1] In 1192 we hear of a sixteenth part of a county.
The clause in the *Constitutio Feudorum*, " Qui allodium
suum vendiderit, districtum et jurisdictionem imperatoris
vendere non praesumat," was a dead letter from the first.
It was impossible that property and jurisdiction should
so be severed. So the county went the way of all private
property.[2] The law of Frederick could be evaded by
express dispensation, or by legal fictions, by joint and
several partnerships.[3] Custom decided that jurisdictions
and castles could be bought and sold, and though the
law was on the other side, custom won the day. The
Italian lawyers confessed to its victory.[4]

There is a collection of the feudal laws and customs of
Northern Italy which goes under the name of the *Libri
Feudorum*.[5] It is a miscellaneous mass of decisions in
doubtful cases, casual commentaries on or statements of
municipal custom, of imperial rescripts either in full or
in excerpts. Critics are divided as to the exact date and
origin of the different component parts of this collection.

[1] Pertile, *Storia del diritto Italiano*, i. 270, n. 60.
[2] In 1215 the Lords of Robbio sell to the Commune of Vercelli 11/32 of
the castle, 13/32 of the villa of Robbio, 17/32 of Rivoltella, 1/3 of the
castle tower, villa and court of Palestro, and 1/37 of the court of Meleto
with all public authority and jurisdiction [Pertile, i. 270, n. 59].
[3] Gregori, *Stat. di Corsica*, Introd., 123.
[4] Fabianus de Monte, *De Empt. et Vendit*, Tract. vi., i. 45, n. 11, " Sed
de consuetudine contrarium usurpatum est : nam toto die videmus vendi
castra cum jurisdictione et mero et mixto imperio, quae consuetudo vincit
legem " [Pertile, i., p. 268, n. 49].
[5] Laspeyres, *Ueber die Entstehung und aelterste Bearbeitung der Libri
Feudorum* ; Dieck, *Litterargeschichte des Langobardischen Lehnrechts* ;
Viollet, *Précis de l'histoire du droit Français*, pp. 140-142.

But on all hands it is agreed that it was complete before the death of Frederick Barbarossa. A new recension was made of it by Jacobus de Ardizone, a Veronese lawyer, who studied at Bologna under Azo, and whose *Summa Feudorum* was written between 1234 and 1250, and this recension became the *corpus vile* of a long row of commentators from Joannes Blancus of Marseilles, the contemporary of Joinville, to Petrus Ravennas, the contemporary of Shakespeare, who taught in the Protestant University of Wittenberg. The skeleton of this body of feudal law is formed by the edicts of the three emperors, Conrad, Lothair, Frederick, but the skeleton is clothed with a mass of custom and gloss and judge-made law.[1] Nothing indeed can more clearly illustrate the difference between German and Italian civilization than the transmutation undergone by German feudalism in the legal climate of Milan. The corner-stone of Frederick's feudal system was the obligation on the part of the vassal to seek investiture. The Milanese custom declares that the vassal does not lose his fief, though a year and a day have passed without his seeking investiture, unless he has been specially required to receive investiture or to do fealty by his lord, or has been summoned three times by the peers of the court.[2] It is a general rule of feudal law, that if a man desert his lord in the field he loses his benefice. But the Milanese lawyers, whose rules are adapted to the exigencies of inter-municipal warfare, rank civil before

---

[1] Lehmann, *Das Langobardische Lehnrecht*, p. 80, "So sind es die drei Kaiser, Konrad II., Lothair III. und Friedrich Barbarossa zu denen die Feudisten aufblicken.... Aus den gesetzen dieser drei Kaiser, und aus der praxis der Mailänder Kurie hat die Jurisprudenz von Pavia und Mailand die *Consuetudines Feudorum* geschaffen.

[2] Cf. a decision given at Trent in 1220, "Si quis vassallus per annum et diem non solverit hostaticum ... dominus se in feodum intromittat" (Pertile, i. 270, n. 57).

feudal ties. "Not if his lord has war with our city
and he does not aid him, but stands by the city
against him, and this because he is not compelled in
respect of any fief to serve against his country [*patria*],
for which he is bound to fight by the law of nations."[1]
According to the conceptions of Frederick the essence
of a benefice was feudal service. The municipal law of
Milan says that a vassal does not lose his fief however
long a time may have elapsed since he has exhibited
service to his master. The German emperor attempts
to prevent free commercial dealings with a fief. The
Milanese custom encourages the transfer of part of
the fief without the consent of the lord.

One law is suited for a rural aristocracy, another for a
community of merchants.[2] The emperor saw in the
feudal service the means of securing an army and a
revenue, and he attempted to define and strengthen
feudal obligations. The town saw in the feudal tie
between the burgher and the castle outside the walls a
danger to municipal independence, and it attempted to
whittle the tie away. For the Milanese and the Florentine the true "patria" was his city ; for him the political
essence of feudalism rapidly evaporated, leaving a body
of rules concerning a form of real property, many of
which were interpreted and transformed by alien principles drawn from the alien jurisprudence of Rome.[3]

---

[1] It is curious to compare the thirteenth century Italian collection of
Cato's distiches, which give the whole duty of man, "Adora a Domenideu,
ama to pare, e toa mare ... *obedis a lo mercato* ... tempra a dal vino, *conbate
per lo to paese.*" Cf. Monaci, *Crestomazia*, vol. i., No. 51.

[2] Pertile observes that most of the imperial fiefs given to Italian lords,
the *diplomata* of which are preserved in Laing's *Cod. Dip. Ital.*, are made
descendable to females (*Storia del diritto Italiano*, vol. iv., p. 142).

[3] Cf. Obertus de Orto on the causes of losing a fief, *Libri Feudorum*, ii.,
x. 8 : "Natural and civil reason shows that a benefice may be lost in the
aforesaid ways. This can be collected by any one who reads Novell, 115,

But if the attempt to revive the strict official feudalism was forlorn, it was not one of those failures which mean disaster.   The feudal class in Italy was now a small class, for most of the nobles had allowed their rights to be bought up by the cities, and it was therefore with the cities rather than with the nobles that a monarch desiring to rule Italy must deal.   By a series of contracts with the great cities of the north, results could be achieved of a far more brilliant and permanent character than could possibly be derived by the application of strict feudal theory to a society which had abandoned the rural castle for the town.   In dealing with a *Communitas* the emperor was dealing with an overlord more powerful, more wealthy, more capable of rendering him constant and effective assistance than was any marquis of Montferrat or of Este.   And Frederick I. perceived the fact.   A series of compacts were made between the emperor and several important cities of the north, creating or defining the military and financial obligations of the contracting cities to the empire.[1] But the resistance of the Lombard league prevented this system of special treaties from being widely extended, and the Peace of Constance in 1183, by giving an exclusively binding force to the laws and customs of the several cities of the league, shows clearly that the time had gone by for imperial legislation on a large scale in Italy.

Of all the medieval emperors Frederick II. alone seems to have the true temper of the legislator.   Brought up amid the motley population of Palermo, amid Greeks and

---

on the lawful causes of disturbance, and other ancient constitutions concerning divorce, the dissolution of matrimony and the lawful revocation of gifts."

[1] *E.g.* in 1162 with Genoa, Ravenna, Cremona, Lucca.   Weiland, i., Nos. 211, 212, 213, 214.

Lombards, Franks and Normans, he was familiar with the clash of personal laws.[1] As king of Sicily he succeeded a race of legislator kings, and could command the services of trained legists and officials. As emperor he felt himself to be one of the descendants of the great legislators of antiquity, of Constantine, Justinian, Theodosius, Charles the Great. We cannot unfortunately tell how much of the language and thought of Frederick's constitutions and charters is due to the emperor himself, and how much to his advisers and to the traditional style of the Sicilian chancery. Gregory IX. attributed the constitutions to James, Archbishop of Capua, while a general tradition ascribes their compilation to Peter de la Vigne.[2] The rules of the chancery inform us that much of the work of the Sicilian government was carried on without the personal intervention of the sovereign.[3] But it is impossible to read the laws and charters of the reign without coming to the conclusion that they are pervaded by the same spirit. The deep impression made upon his contemporaries by Frederick's personality, his undoubted energy and high intelligence, his singular detachment from most of the current superstitions of his day, his zeal for detail, his domineering will, his passionate belief in the imperial prerogatives, force us to

---

[1] For the legal condition of the south of Italy, cf. Brandileone, *Il diritto Romano nelle legge Normanne e sveve del regno di Sicilia* ; Perla, *Del diritto romano giustiniano nelle provincie meridionale d'Italia prima delle Assize Normanne*, in the *Archivio Storico Napolitano*, vol. x. ; Brandileone, *Il diritto Greco-Romano nell' Italia meridionale sotto la dominazione Normanna* [*Archivio Juridico*, vol. xxxvi.].

[2] There is a clause at the end of the constitutions which attributes the compilation to Peter de la Vigne. As it is not to be found in the Greek text or in the oldest MSS., it is judged to be an interpolation. Conrad IV., however, in 1252 speaks of the *Constitutio Petri de Vinea*. For the whole subject, cf. *H.B.*, Intr., p. cxxviii.

[3] *Statuta Officiorum*, Winkelmann, *Acta imperii*, No. 988, vol. i, pp. 733-7.

believe that the main initiative lay with him.[1] The man who struck the first gold coin which might have come from a mint of ancient Rome or Greece, who made the first reasonable treaty with the Saracens in Palestine, and who insisted upon knowing how every penny was spent by his treasury,[2] is just the man to have inspired the constitutions of the kingdom of Sicily, and the administrative work which was carried out there. There are also many personal notes struck in the charters of the time, which reveal Frederick's active interest in the work of government, and though his life was spent in almost constant warfare, the chancery followed the army, and the kingdom of Sicily was often governed from the camp. It is his prerogative, he repeats over and over again, to issue laws and to adjust the legal system to the changing needs of society.[3] The constitutions of the kingdom of Sicily are full of conceptions, partly derived from Roman jurisprudence, partly derived from a cool and reasonable outlook on the world. The legislator measures institutions by the law of nature, by his own high standard of reasonableness. Trial by battle he considers to be barbarous: he makes no scruple to abolish it, or to contract its use within the narrowest limits.[4] Ordeals are superstitious and unjust. They are

---

[1] A characteristically passionate outburst is detailed in the *Annales Placentini Ghibellini*, 1236 [SS. xviii., p. 474], "Ascendens in equo elevata voce coram principibus conquestus fuit, dicens quoniam peregrini et viatores ambulant ubique, ego autem non sum ausus agredi per terras imperii." Then he seizes the eagle and dashes across the stream.

[2] *Statuta Officiorum*, Winkelmann, *Acta*, No. 988, vol. i., pp. 733-7.

[3] *H.B.*, v., 958, "Imperialis excellentia cui datum est leges condere," and *H.B.*, vi. 156-61, "Nil veterum principum auctoritati detrahimus si juxta novorum temporum qualitatem ... nova jura producimus."

[4] He allows its use in the case of the trial of a poisoner, homicide, or traitor, when all other modes of proof have been exhausted. Elaborate and curious provisions are inserted for ensuring a fair fight; cf. Kington, *Life of Frederick II.*, vol. i., pp. 384-6.

to cease forthwith.   The use of love philtres is absurd.
The people must be educated to see it.   It is against
the law of nature that daughters should not succeed to
their father's inheritance, in case there are no sons.[1]
The law of nature must prevail.   " The authority of the
Jus gentium supported by natural reason, permits anyone to have a guardian for his person." [2]   Rules are
accordingly laid down determining the conditions of
tutelage.   It is in such a spirit that Frederick II.
approaches the task of legislation.[3]

If any government could have laid the basis for a
common Italian law it was the government of Frederick, for the instinct of codification was strong within
it.   But the obstacles in Frederick's path were too
great to be overcome by any one life, however full and
impressive.   His constitutional position was one thing
in the kingdom of Sicily, another thing in Central and
Northern Italy, and a third thing in Germany.   In his
own Sicilian kingdom he could legislate as the Norman
kings had legislated, he could prolong the great high-
road which they had already begun to engineer, which
was to lead from the confusion of personal laws to a
territorial common law for the *Regno*.   But outside the
Regno conditions were different.   Here there were a
mass of cities, all of them possessing " good and approved customs," many of them active laboratories of
statute law.[4]   How could a Roman emperor legislate for
Bologna or for Venice or for Milan ?   How could he

---

[1] *Const. Regn. Sic.*, iii. 26.   [2] *Const. Regn. Sic.*, iii. 16.
[3] For Frederick's rationalism, cf. *H.B.*, v. 491, 493; *Constitutiones Regni
Siciliae*, iii. 73 ; ii. 31 ; ii. 32 ; *Novae Constitutiones Regni Siciliae*, iii. 28.
[4] The oldest town statutes are: Genoa, 1056; Verona, 1100-1228; Mantua,
1116 ; Pistora, 1117 ; Genoa, 1143 ; Campagna, 1161 ; Pisa, 1162 ; Brescia,
1200-80 ; Milan, 1216 ; Ferrara, 1208 ; Modena, before 1213 ; Parma
before 1226 ; Bergamo, before 1237.

control the public law which regulated the constitutional machinery of these cities? How could he control the treaties which bound together a Tuscan or a Lombard league? Still weaker was his position in Germany. In Italy written law was the rule, and imperial constitutions, though they might excite contempt, would never arouse surprise; but in Germany the place of written was taken by unwritten custom; the place of legislation by the unrecorded decisions of the royal court. The towns who possessed their customs, the nations who clung to their traditional and archaic law, the princes who had received special legal privileges, and who legislated in their own courts, these elements of society were not receptive of external legal influence. When the emperor legislated it was either to confirm or to concede.

Sicily was Frederick's delight[1]; Germany, with its inclement skies, its unwritten law, its turbulent nobility, was distasteful to him. He visited it three times only, he complained of the hardships of the journey, he left the country to be governed by his sons, he sanctioned the usurpations of the German princes, and legalized the dissidence of the German political system. Yet he never intended to relinquish any particle of the empire. It was no part of his programme to become a mere Italian or Sicilian king. The city of Aix was in his eyes still the second imperial capital,[2] and no emperor since Otto I. showed such an intelligent appreciation

---

[1] *Novae Constitutiones Regni Siciliae*, iii. 14., "Qualiter peculiaris regni nostri Sicilie populus cujus specialiter nos cura sollicitat, cujus nobis est hereditas omni possessione preclarior"; and i. 95, "Regnum ipsum pre ceteris velut electum quoddam viriduarium inter agros cura precipua colere disponemus." It is to be the "invidia principum et norma reg_norum."

[2] *H.B.*, ii. 649, "Quae sedes et caput regni familiari prerogativa inter Cisalpinas resplendens ecclesias regali et imperiali triumphat fiducia."

of Germany's mission in the Slavonic East.[1] Careful
that the Sicilian in him shall not obliterate the Roman,
he quits his "peculiar people, his inheritance more
brilliant than any possession, his chosen spot of green
among the fields," to labour and fight under the
hot Italian sun in the month of August, that he
may preserve the empire from being broken to pieces.
When the Tartars were threatening Europe in 1240,
he wrote to the Senate of Rome to point out that
throughout his life he had spurned delights, that he
had crossed the rough sea and the rugged mountains
of Germany for one object only—to consolidate and
unify the forces of the empire.[2] The encyclicals of the
emperor are full of this imperial language. He felt
that it was not without a purpose that Providence
had united in one hand the sceptres of Jerusalem, of
Sicily and of Germany. The star which ruled the
destiny of the emperor was plainly pointing to the
monarchy of the world.[3]

The conflict of facts with ideals has seldom been
more tragically illustrated. For all his imperial sentiment and enlightened zeal for legislation, Frederick
added scarcely anything to imperial law in Italy. His

---

[1] Cf. *H.B.*, ii., pp. 423, 424, for Frederick's interesting letter on the
races of Livonia in 1224 ; *H.B.*, ii., pp. 549-552, for Frederick's privilege
to Hermann, master of the German Order, 1226 ; *H.B.*, iii. 497, for
Frederick's letter to the Stadingi, 1230 ; and cf. *H.B.*, ii., p. 625 ; iv., pp.
822-824, 940, 941.

[2] *H.B.*, v., p. 1140.

[3] Cf. the remarkable encyclical of 1236 [*H.B.*, iv., pp. 847-852]. Cf. also
H.B., v., p. 161 ["Qui fere totius orbis habenas universaliter mode-
ramur"], and Eccelin da Romano's letter to Frederick [*H.B.*, v., p. 267],
and Frederick's letter to the Senator, Senate, and people of Rome in 1236
[*H.B.*, iv., p. 901], in which, after reminding them of their former glory
and taunting them for having allowed Milan to insult them, he continues, "Ecce quod legem habetis et Caesarem qui pro exaltatione
Romani Imperii personam exposuit, thesauros aperuit, laboribus non
pepercit.

ecclesiastical edicts against heretics, his solemn confirmation of all the old Roman provisions on *laesa*
majestas, his edict against clerks refusing the sacraments or omitting the mass, against monks moving
from place to place—all these are to be inscribed
among municipal charters. "That all and every corporation [*universitas*]," so runs the tenth clause of
the *Edictum contra infideles imperii Italicos*, "which
is recognized to have received the privileges of jurisdiction or certain honours from us and the empire,
may answer worthily, we order all universities and
communes, under penalty of the loss of our favour
and the privation of their jurisdictional privileges, that
the present edict of our Serenity should be literally
and openly transcribed in the books of their statutes,
and that the transcript should be inviolably preserved ;
that their podestats, consuls and rectors should be
bound at the beginning of their office to swear to
observe the statute ; and that a proviso be added
that no license or leave to transgress it can on
any account be granted. . . . The corporation or
commune transgressing these statutes is to be deprived
of all jurisdictions, privileges and regalia. The podestat, consul or rector who does not swear the oath on
taking office is to be deprived of all his goods, henceforth to be considered a private person, and to incur
the penalties of infamy."[1] These were brave words,
and Frederick, legislating with ecclesiastical sentiment
and Roman law on his side, could afford to use them.
There would be no great objection to making heresy
a matter of high treason. And ecclesiastical law was
necessarily of universal application. It would have
been more difficult to ask the towns to incorporate

[1] Weiland, ii., No. 213 ; and cf. *H.B.*, i., p. 881 ; iii., p. 4.

into their statutes new rules as to procedure or as to private law.   As a matter of fact, Frederick never appears to have taken such a step.[1]   The Popes and the Lombard towns gave him an absorbing occupation of a different character.   He was driven to adopt a policy, to which probably in an age of peace he would not have consented.   He was forced to buy municipal support, wherever it could be purchased, by confirming "the good uses and approved customs" of the Ghibelline towns.[2]   But in reality he conceived himself to be the sole fountain of right.   "They have offended against our majesty, which is the living law upon earth, and the source from which civil laws arise," he remarked in 1232 of the Alexandrines and the Milanese.[3] Holding that no intermunicipal treaty or league was valid unless the emperor had consented to it,[4] he aimed at reducing the Lombards to such a state of subservience as existed among the towns of the Sicilian kingdom.   When he negotiates with the Milanese after Cortenuova in 1237, he speaks of "the jurisdiction which we wish to have simply as any king in his land."[5]   He looks behind the liberties guaranteed by the Peace of Constance, and sweeps them away.   When the Lombard towns did not appear on June 24, 1226,

---

[1] Sentences passed by municipal courts in the north of Italy must have sometimes come up for the emperor to review.   In 1230 he writes to the Chapter of Lucca, telling it to carry out a sentence given by the Vicar of Rainald of Spoleto in favour of a citizen of Pisa, "Quia singulis imperil nostri fidelibus in suis judiciis tenemur adesse." *H.B.*, iii., p. 200.

[2] *H.B.*, v. 116, 117, 155-177 ; vi. 21, 64, 164.

[3] Böhmer-Ficker, *Reg.*, 1959.

[4] *H.B.*, v., p. 197, "Cum etiam sine assensu nostro et imperii contracta fuerit societas supradicta." Cf. also *H.B.*, v. 204, and ii. 614, 615, where Frederick annuls the boundary treaty between Modena and Bologna ; *H.B.*, v. 265, vi. 339, where he absolves Chieri from all special pacts with cities, churches, nobles, colleges.

[5] Böhmer-Ficker, *Reg.*, 2297 d.

to atone for their misdemeanours, they were solemnly excommunicated, and put to the ban of the empire after due legal proceeding. The Patriarch of Jerusalem, the princes and great men, the judges and lawyers of the imperial court, declared them to have forfeited all their rights and franchises, even those contained in the Peace of Constance, and to be outlaws and enemies of the Reich. Thirteen cities—Milan, Brescia, Mantua, Verona, Piacenza, Vercelli, Alexandria, Lodi, Treviso, Padua, Vicenza, Bologna, Faenza—were involved in this sentence, which was as impracticable as it was magnificent.

A year later the sentence was recalled,[1] but Frederick never lost sight of his ultimate aim—the destruction of the municipal autonomy guaranteed at Constance. So in the negotiations of 1236 he demanded the surrender of these liberties, and refused to have the Peace submitted to arbitration, declaring that it was injurious to the empire and to ecclesiastical liberty, and that a decision of the princes of the empire had laid down that he was under no obligation "to observe a peace which was made in evident prejudice of law and of the empire."[2] What wonder if the Milanese, distrusting the prospects of a stable peace, replied in 1237, "We know your cruelty, for we have learnt by experience. We would rather die under our shields by the sword, the lance or the arrow, than by the rope, famine and fire."[3] So also he makes light of setting aside the authority of podestats, consuls and communes, of granting a privilege *non obstante* some recognized local custom or law,

---

[1] Böhmer-Ficker, *Reg.*, 1693 ; Winkelmann, *Acta*, 263.

[2] Böhmer-Ficker, *Reg.*, 1638ᵇ, 1658, 2197ᵉ, 2289ᵇ, 2374ᵃ; Ficker, *Forsch.*, ii. 895 ; *Vita Greg.*, *ap. Muratori*, iii. 589.

[3] Matt. Paris, iii. 496.

of appointing municipal magistrates.[1] His vicars try
civil and criminal cases, name judges and notaries, tutors,
curators and guardians, grant franchises, make natural
sons legitimate, and exercise all the functions of supreme
power, "saving in all things our imperial justice."[2] A
system of government was applied to the north and
centre of Italy, which was more complete and defined
than any which had been devised by Frederick's predecessors.

A general legate [*Legatus totius Italiae*] represented
the imperial power from the Alps to the confines of the
kingdom of Naples. Under him were five general
vicars, each governing a defined district. And under
the vicars there were captains nominated by the emperor
in the principal towns. The system of government did
not begin to act regularly until 1237, when Frederick
broke finally with the Lombard league, and it was dissolved at Frederick's death in 1250. But it contained
in it the seeds of a national system. Almost all the
imperial agents whose names have come down to us
were Italians; they exercised full authority—administrative, military, judicial. They were assisted by trained
Italian judges, drawn from the chief towns of Northern
Italy, from Parma and Reggio, Milan and Bologna, Pisa
and Florence.[3] With time and with tranquillity such a
staff might have done much to promote a common
Italian jurisprudence. But the Lombard league and the
Papacy rendered this consummation impossible. As

---

[1] *H.B.*, i., p. 34, where Frederick grants to the Ugolini full power to
build and rebuild in their lands in the cities of Florence and Bologna,
"Nulla unquam propria potestate consule consulibus vel communi collegio
vel universitate...contradicente"; and cf. *H.B.*, ii. 309-11, iv. 498;
Böhmer-Ficker, 2314, 2314 a; Ficker, *Forsch.*, ii. 531.

[2] *H.B.*, ii. 41-2. Powers of the imperial vicar in Tuscany.

[3] Ficker, iii. 174.

the Guelph resistance organized itself, the emperor was
forced to abjure pacific appointments.   The rule of
warriors succeeded the rule of prelates.   From 1239 to
1249 Frederick's young son Enzio is legate of the sacred
empire of the whole of Italy, and his military talents
justified the selection.   From 1232 to 1259 the real
imperial vicar in the Trevisan March is Eccelin da
Romano, one of the monsters of Italian history, whose
legend lives still in the minds of the Trevisan peasantry
after a lapse of more than six hundred years.   The
division of Lombardy into two vicariates, divided at the
important strategical centre at Pavia, was probably dictated by military reasons ; and the appointment of local
Ghibelline lords to the vicariates is possibly due to the
same necessity, for it was a violation of one of Frederick's
cherished administrative principles.[1]   Stern fate forced
the emperor more and more into the position of the
mere party leader.   In the impassioned conflict which
rent the north of Italy from 1237 to 1250 the machinery
of his government assumes a military and despotic
character.   Yet even in the later years of Frederick's
reign it is noticeable that some of his vicars were chosen
to fill the office of podestat in important Ghibelline
towns, which affords at least some presumption that
they were men of character.[2]   Whatever happened
Frederick never lost sight of the great administrative
task which he had set before him.   It was characteristic of the man who had gone out of his way to warn
the German nobles against foolish expenditure at a
court festival, that during the autumn of 1239, when he
was besieging Milan, he sent despatch after despatch to
his agents in the kingdom of Sicily regulating even
the minutest details of forest or of household manage-

---

[1] *H.B.*, v., pp. 786, 914.   [2] *H.B.*, i., p. cdlxxvii.

ment.[1]   It was characteristic of him too that in spite of the war he made in 1240 a most important reform in the judicial organization of Italy.

During the earlier years of his reign Frederick resided mainly in the kingdom of Sicily, and there is no sign that any of his Sicilian judges exercised jurisdiction in Italy or Germany.   The great court of Sicily, presided over by the great justiciar, which was certainly established under the later Norman kings, and which during Frederick's absence in Germany in 1216 appears to have sat at Palermo, did indeed extend its functions after Frederick's return.   We hear no more of the great justiciar of Apulia, who under the later Norman kings seems to have been the chief ruler of the continental portion of the *Regno*.   His functions are absorbed in those of the Sicilian court, which establishes itself in Apulia, is fixed there and does not follow the emperor outside the *Regno* or even to Sicily.   From this court there is an appeal to the personal justice of the emperor, and when the emperor goes to Sicily he is accompanied by many of the judges of his Curia, who assist him in the exercise of his appellate and his immediate jurisdiction.   But the great justiciar remains behind, not only as president of the great court, but as permanent viceroy of Apulia.   There can be little doubt that in course of time Frederick established a supreme court and a master justiciar of Sicily, for he quitted the island in 1227 never to return again.   But the most important court remained the Apulian court, which until 1240 did not follow the king.   But in

---

[1] The series is most remarkable [*H.B.*, v., pp. 409-63].   The ordinances for the *Studium generale* of Naples appear to have been issued about the same time [*ib.*, pp. 493-7].   Napoleon's famous Moscow memorandum on the French theatre suggests itself as a parallel.

1240 Frederick made another arrangement.   He had been absent in Germany in 1235, and hardly had he returned when the troubles of a Lombard war came upon him.   Circumstances were compelling him to spend a far larger share of his time outside the *Regno* than he either contemplated or desired, and where the emperor came, there litigation was gathered together.   Judges must follow his court, and some of these judges must be drawn from the highly trained legal circle of the *Regno*.   Already in 1239 Roffrid of San Germano, the famous south Italian legist, and Laurence of Parma are hearing a case in the royal camp at Padua, and in the spring of 1240 Frederick comes to the conclusion that the master justiciar and four judges must follow his court whithersoever it might go.[1]

While other officials, two captains, and great justiciars are created to fill the gap in the *Regno*, henceforward a strong Sicilian court travels with the king.

Under happier circumstances this court might have done much to fix a common standard of legal practice and procedure in Italy.[2]   The master justiciar was to receive "all petitions, both of justice and of grace, both from the *Regno* and from the empire.   His court was to be at once a supreme court of equity, a supreme court of appeal, and a court of first instance for the determination of certain classes of litigation, such as cases concerning fiefs entered on the royal rolls, high treason, litigation between courtiers, the complaints of the destitute.   It was also to act as a

---

[1] *Novae Constitutiones de officio Magistri Justitiarii*;   H.B., vi., pp. 156-161.

[2] " Et ut secundum ordinem singula tractaremus Curie nostre providimus ordinare justitiam a qua velut a fonte rivuli per regnum undique norma justitie derivetur."

court of reference, to give advice, that is to say, to the inferior judges upon perplexed points of law and to supervise them ; and a written record was to be kept of its decisions. It was the first attempt to establish a supreme professional court for the Italian portions of the empire. Had the dynasty survived, this court would assuredly have run a brilliant course. It was not to be expected that a court manned by Sicilian judges would have had much weight in Germany. There were already signs of a feeling that the Curia Alemannie could not be held anywhere but in Germany itself, and, if a court of princes, most of them German,[1] sitting with the emperor at Naples or Palermo appeared an inconvenient and improper tribunal to a Flemish litigant, how much more inconvenient, how much more improper this innovation of a purely Italian and professional bench ? For as a matter of fact the justiciar and his staff are Sicilians without exception. But in Italy this objection would not be felt. Although there was a great diversity of municipal law in Italy, yet there appears to have been less of strict provincial or aristocratic sentiment in legal matters than in Germany.[2] While a Saxon would have rebelled against a Swabian judge, and a Swabian against a Saxon judge, a Bolognese would be invited to Rome as senator, a Lombard into a Tuscan town as podestat. Indeed the internecine strife of the Italian cities had long familiarized them with the advantage of appointing some stranger to exercise the office of magistrate, and the habit of resorting to arbitration

---

[1] Ficker, *Forsch.*, iii., pp. 346-7. Generally German magnates alone are among the judgment-finders when a German case has to be decided in Italy. But there are exceptions.

[2] Ficker, ii., pp. 270, 271. Ficker observes [iii. 344-57] that the principle of *Judicium parium* was only applied in Italy (*a*) in feudal cases, (*b*) in cases involving the infliction of penalties on a crown vassal or a town.

both in private concerns and in intermunicipal politics, which is sufficiently well marked in Italian history, must have helped to divest Frederick's new Sicilian court of any air of unfamiliarity. It was merely an improved professional version of that fortuitous concourse of nobles and clergy which had helped the emperor to do justice at the diet of Roncaglia and elsewhere on his travels through Italy.

We know little of the history of this experiment. It would appear, however, that there were no limits set to the competence of this travelling court. When Civita-nova petitions for the confirmation of its ancient law, the emperor orders the general vicar of the march to make a report upon that law and to send it on to the imperial judges, who will see what parts are to be confirmed and what parts are not to be confirmed.[1] If municipal customs are to be unified, here clearly is a powerful engine ready to Frederick's hands for the purpose. The court will try a case in first instance between the Abbot of S. Salvator and two citizens of Sienna.[2] It will hear fiscal appeals from the general captains and general vicars.[3] It will try cases of high treason. When Frederick makes confirmation of judicial immunity to a town, as for instance to Fano in 1243, he stipulates that the citizens shall be amenable to " our great court or the court of our vicars in the march, if the magnitude or character of the cases demand "[4] He intends his court to be a great fountain of law, a great leveller of inequality.

The services which the Hohenstauffen dynasty might have rendered to Italian civilization may be conjectured from what Frederick was actually able to perform within

[1] *H.B.*, vi. 242.   [2] *Ib.*, vi. 252, 4.
[3] Ficker, i., p. 371.   [4] *H.B.*, vi. 67, 83.

the limits of the *Regno*. When in 1220 the emperor
returned to his kingdom, a full-grown man of twenty-
six, he found all in disorder. Thirty-four years of
anarchy, intrigue, and bloodshed had passed over the
land since the death of William the Good.[1] German
adventurers and Norman nobles warred on one another
without restraint and oppressed the commons. Saracen
tribes ruled the western parts of the island and rushed
down on every occasion from the mountains to pillage
the Christians of the plain. The nobles had ceased to
render the customary services to the crown, and charters,
which had been easily enough procured from a usurper
like Tancred, an absentee like Otto, or a condottiere like
Markwald, were exhibited as evidence of their political
independence. The greater part of the royal domain
had been occupied by the towns or the nobles. The
famous Sicilian navy had gone utterly to decay, and the
central organization which had been so powerfully
constructed by the great Roger, was now broken in
pieces.

In the work of reconstruction Frederick was assisted
by the impressive tradition of a strong and wealthy
government, which had created institutions and issued
laws, by the comparative smallness of the kingdom,
by the number of antagonistic creeds and races and
societies into which it was divided, by the survival of
Roman law, by the intelligence of a few highly-trained
jurists in South Italy who knew what the good government of the Norman kings had meant, and by what
means it might be restored, and above all by the
atmosphere of refinement and luxury which prevailed

---

[1] All traces of Henry VI.'s Sicilian legislation have perished. It may,
however, have been merely administrative. Cf. *Otton. Fris. Cont. S. Blas*,
SS. xx. 328.

manners, customs, and laws of his subjects except in so far as they conflicted with his own edicts.[1] His code is brief, severe, autocratic, Roman. In some places he even literally reproduces passages from the Pandects and the code of Justinian, and the same remark applies to his successors, William I. and William II.[2] There are too in Roger's code penalties which appear to come from Byzantium, such as flogging and the mutilation of the nose. Frederick follows in the same line. His constitutions deal but little with private law, for that was a sphere which might safely be left to municipal legislation.[3] Yet a difficult subject— the law of *protimesis* or pre-emption, is cleared up in a luminous constitution copied from a novel of the Byzantine Emperor Romanus Senior Lacapenus.[4] The rules as to the succession of fiefs are revised, for that was a matter which touched the fisc, and a custom prevailing in some parts of the kingdom which excluded women from succeeding to the property of counts, barons, or knights, was abolished as contrary to right reason or natural law. The law of prescription was also dealt with, and this appears to be the chief point of private law in which the constitutions of the kingdom of Sicily

---

[1] Merkel, *Commentatio*, p. 16 (1), p. 33, " Leges a nostra majestate noviter promulgatas generaliter ab omnibus precipimus observari : moribus, consuetudinibus, legibus non cassatis pro varietate populorum nostro regno subjectorum ... nisi forte nostris his sanctionibus adversari quid in eis manifesti juris videatur." So in 1150 he issues an instruction [in Greek] to the judges in Calabria and the Val de Grace as to the custom of succession (Brünneck, *Siciliens mittelatterliche Stadtrechte*, pp. 240-6).

[2] Brünneck, p. xxii.

[3] Yet the Constitutiones override all municipal law (*H.B.*, iv. 24, 72). The only exception is Palermo in virtue of a privilege of 1233 (*H.B.*, iv. 454).

[4] *Jus Graeco-Rom.* ed. Zachariae a Lingenthal, iii., *Col.* iii., *Nov.* ii., p. 234. Cf. Brünneck, pp. xxix., xxx.; *Zeitschrift fur Rechtsgeschichte*, xiv., p. 129.

affect the practice of the Sicilian towns.[1]   But the main
subjects of Frederick's legislation are the penal code,
procedure, and the construction of the necessary organs
of government.

Frederick starts by unifying the penal law.   There
had been one tariff of compensation for the Lombards,
another for the Normans, while the penal code had been
different for those who lived Roman law.   But fixed
tariffs were clearly irrational and multiple penal standards inconvenient.   Henceforth the criminal law is to
be one and it is also to be administered by royal judges
in royal courts, and three towns alone are allowed the
privilege of retaining their independent criminal jurisdiction. Again, while in the main following the Roman penal
law, Frederick and his advisers stop to discriminate and
improve.   The *aestimatio* or penal composition went, according to Roman law, to the injured party, but according
to the custom of some provinces in the *Regno* entirely to
the fisc.   Frederick steers a middle course, and assigns
one third to the injured party and two thirds to the
fisc.[2]   Again, he steers a middle course between the
Roman and Lombard law on the protection of immovable
property.   The Roman had held that if one person
violently deprived another of possession before judgment, he was not only bound to restore possession,
but he lost whatever proprietary rights might have
belonged to him, or else if he had no such rights he was
compelled to pay their equivalent in money.   The Lombard, on the other hand, had assigned a paltry fine of six
shillings to the offence.   Frederick saw that the Lombard

---

[1] Brünneck, p. xxvii.

[2] *Const. Regn. Sic.*, iii., 42 ; *Inst. Just.*, iv. 4, 7. I am indebted for my
references to Roman law to F. Brandileone, *Il diritto Romano nelle legge
Normanne e Sveve.*

was too lenient, the Roman too stern. He ordered the intruder to restore possession, and he fixed the penalty at half the value of the immovables.[1] He removes the Roman laws against calumny with an explanatory comment that the calumny must not merely be unproven, but must be evident.[2] He tempers some of the severe ordinances of his Norman predecessors.[3]

On procedure Frederick is equally sweeping. Here too he begins by unifying. "We wish to have," he says, "no distinction of persons; but whether it be a Frank or a Roman or a Lombard who is plaintiff or defendant, we will administer justice to him equally."[4] Then he goes on to cast out the irrational elements from procedure. He abolishes the ordeal, not for the reason on account of which Innocent III. had denounced it, that it was a tempting of God, but because it did not regard the nature of things or respect truth.[5] He abolishes trial by battle except in the case of secret homicides, traitors, and poisoners, because it cannot be called a true proof so much as a kind of divination.[6] In the cases in which the duel is admissible, its practice is discouraged and its inequalities diminished. No duel can be fought except with the leave of the supreme

[1] *Const. Regn. Sic.*, i. 25 ; Liutp., 148 ; *Cod. Just.*, viii. 4, 7.

[2] *Const. Regn. Sic.*, ii. 14.; *Cod. Just.* ii., 7. 1 ; ix. 46. 3.

[3] *Const. Regn. Sic.*, iii. 88-89.

[4] *Const. Regn. Sic.*, ii. 17.

[5] Cf. *Const. Regn. Sic.*, ii. 31. "Leges que a quibusdam simplicibus sunt dicti paribiles, que nec rerum naturam respiciunt nec veritatem attendunt, nos qui veram legum scientiam perscrutamur, et aspernamur errores, a nostris judiciis separamus." Cf. also the remarkable language on love-philtres, iii. 73 ; Bohmer, *Reg.*, No. 310.

[6] The municipal law of Messina [c. 44] somewhat differs from the constitution, extending the Duel to all cases which involve loss of life or limb as their penalty. As the clause expressly refers to a royal ordinance, it is possible that Frederick's constitution may have been expanded in this sense, and that we have lost the revised version.

court. The lord of the beaten champion is executed. In place of these barbaric practices procedure and proof must be as far as possible in writing. Instead of the verbal *proclamatio* which was current, at anyrate in all parts of Apulia, save in the city of Benevento, the indictment was to be delivered in a written document, the *libellus* of Roman law. The proofs were to be mainly in writing,[1] and the sentences of the court were to be recorded not upon the fragile papyrus in use at Naples and Salerno and Amalfi, but upon enduring parchment.

Another feature of Frederick's legislation upon procedure is his desire for speed. Judges are to cut down the perorations of the advocates, and the advocate whose dilatory eloquence is fatal to his client is condemned to pay the costs. The defendant is to be summoned to court by a peremptory summons, which is to be delivered, in case of his absence, at the house in which his wife or his daughter or his family may be staying. As soon as the *libellus* or indictment is presented, the trial must proceed. The interval of deliberation allowed to the defendant by the Roman law is abolished. After the minutes of the evidence have been taken, the advocates have only two days to dispute about the law. Dilatory exceptions are carefully scrutinized and limited. The rules laid down by the Roman law as to contumacy in civil cases are substantially preserved, but all the processes are quickened.[2]

The royal courts are not merely to be business-like,

---

[1] *Const. Regn. Sic.*, ii. 32.

[2] *Const. Regn. Sic.*, i., 44, 92, 97, 100, 102 ; ii., 18, 19, 23. 21, 24 ; *Cod. Just.*, iii. 1, 13. 3 and 4 ; vii. 72. 9, 39. 8. 3, 43. 9 ; *Novell.*, liii. 3 ; *Cod. Just.*, iii. 19. 2 ; vii. 50. 2 ; viii. 36. 12, 13 ; ix. 1. 9 ; ix. 1. 1; iii. 8. 4 ; iii. 8. 1 ; Bethmann-Hollweg, *Civilprozess*, iii. 300-311.

they are also to have full control over the conduct of a case. It is one of Frederick's principles that processes should be as little as possible dependent upon the will of the parties. If for instance the plaintiff and defendant agree to prorogue a trial without leave of the court they must pay a fine of a hundred *augustales*.[1] The machinations of individuals must not be allowed to make litigation immoral. The plaintiff in a criminal case who has been induced by a bribe to desist from his accusation without leave of the court must pay double the sum which he has received. After the parties have once appeared in court, no composition can be made without leave of the judge, nor can the two parties by mutual consent agree to abandon a case after once a citation has been issued, except in a civil action, and then only with permission of the court. Recourse is no longer to be had to arbitrators voluntarily chosen by the parties—a habit which apparently throve in Naples, Amalfi and Sorrento—but all causes were to be heard by the royal judges.[2]

There were other important innovations in the law of procedure. The defendant in a criminal trial was permitted to be represented by counsel. A powerful instrument for the detection of crime and heresy was found in the inquisition, which had been long effectively employed by the Norman kings of England, and which in Sicily as well as in England was a specially royal method of procedure. The Roman law of contumacy in criminal cases was modified according to the dictates of reason and humanity. The Code and the

---

[1] The *augustalis* was equal to a fourth of a gold ounce, that is to say it amounted to about twenty shillings of our money. *Const. Regni. Sic.,* i. 104. 5; *Just. Inst.,* iv. 16. 1; *Nov.,* cxii., c. 2.

[2] *Const. Regn. Sic.,* i. 81-3, ii. 15, 16.

Digest condemned the man, who, having been accused of a capital charge, remained contumacious for a year, to lose his property, whether he possessed sons or not, without any further right of defence. Frederick had no desire to encourage contumacy, but he saw that the rule fell with unjust severity upon the innocent. The Sicilian constitution declares that as soon as the contumacy is verified the offender is to lose one-third of his moveables ; that after a year of contumacy the rest of his property is to go to the fisc, provided that he should have no sons, and that he should be condemned to the awful penalties of outlawry, to live, that is to say, as an outcast, who may be injured or slain with impunity by no matter whom.[1]

Frederick does not pretend to issue an all-inclusive code. His constitutions are, however, to be the primary authority upon the subjects with which they deal. When a count or baron is brought to trial, the counts or barons who are called upon to give sentence, are to declare the law according to the sacred constitutions, or, failing them, according to the approved customs of the realm, and, lastly, according to the common law, that is to say, the Lombard and the Roman Law, according as the quality of the litigants shall demand.[2] In later times there appears to have been much doubt as to what the common law of the kingdom of Sicily really was, and historians are at the present day unable to decide what value a Sicilian or Apulian judge at the end of the thirteenth century would have assigned to the Roman and the Lombard law

[1] *Const. Regn. Sic.*, ii. 1 ; Ficker, *Forsch.*, i. 29 ff. ; *Cod. Just.*, ix. 2-6; ix. 40 ; *Dig.*, xlvii. 17. 1-4.
[2] *Const. Regn. Sic.*, i. 47 ; Savigny, *Geschichte des Römischen Rechts*, ii., p. 203.

respectively. It is clear, however, that great legal diversity continued to exist in Sicily in spite of Frederick's legislation, which, as we have seen, hardly dealt with private law at all.[1] Yet in two directions his influence was decisive. It moulded procedure and the penal code. The Beneventine Romanist Roffrid, who was one of Frederick's judges, still respects the Lombard penal law. The Sicilian lawyer, Andrea of Isernia, who wrote in the fourteenth century, and who acknowledges that the Lombard law is in some parts of the country actually preferred to the Roman, was able to say, "We make no use of the Lombard laws in criminal cases."[2] It seems then that Frederick had effectively expelled the ancient compositions for crime.[3]

In some respects Frederick's legislation was not clearly in advance of his age. No medieval legislator could have afforded to ignore the deep ravines which divided class from class, the noble from the burgess, the burgess from the peasant, and still less could these distinctions be ignored in a kingdom which was stocked

---

[1] Savigny, *Geschichte des Romischen Rechts*, vi., p. 447 ; Lamantia, *Storia della legislazione Siciliana* ; Capasso, *Sulla storia esterna delle Costituzione del regno di Sicilia promulgate da Frederico II.*, p. 22 ff., and Intr. xxi. ; and the *Proemium* of the customs of Palermo (ed. Brünneck), "Cumque felicis urbis jam dictae incolae Romanorum lege viventes in quibusdam causis et casibus jure non scripto municipali (quod consuetudinarium dicitur) uti vellent, ad instar ex orbis gentibus aliquarum, ut tam ex eis, quam ex veteribus legibus Romanorum inter eos vigeret pacis et justitiae plenitudo, nova jura quodammodo de naturae gremio producentes quasdam sibi fecerunt consuetudines . . . quibus consuetudinibus ipsi ac successores eorum postmodum usi et gavisi sunt ex consensu regnantium dominorum."

[2] *Lectura ad Const. Sic.*, i. 65.

[3] There is scarcely any penal law at all in the Sicilian municipal codes. Palermo and Messina are the exceptions, and Palermo was autonomous in virtue of the privilege of 1233. We have therefore really no statutory evidence as to the operation of Frederick's laws in this respect (Brünneck, p. 355).

with Norman families, proud of their aristocratic origin.
Frederick observes them. The count and the baron
are to be tried indeed before the royal judges, who
are not counts or barons, but the judgment is to be
found by the peers of the accused, unless the judges
receive a special commission from the nobility to conduct the case themselves. No villeins are allowed to
bear witness, even against mere knights, and the value
of judicial testimony is gauged by a scale based upon
the social hierarchy. A count can be convicted by
the testimony of two counts, or of four barons, or of
eight knights, or of sixteen burgesses. Two barons
or four knights or eight burgesses will suffice to convict
a baron, except in the case of high treason, where these
rules do not apply.[1] Again a special penal tariff is
arranged for injuries done to noble persons by their
inferiors or their equals. Yet, although the constitutions of Sicily do not provide for perfect equality before
the law, they go as far in that direction as was possible.
The nobles preserve certain privileges, but they lose
the substance of their power. Criminal jurisdiction
has been taken from them. They are debarred from
appointing judges.[2] When they sit in judgment upon
their peers they are compelled to take an oath to give
judgment according to the evidence and their good
conscience, and the evidence is presented to them by
a professional judge. No count, baron, or knight,
or any other who holds barony, castle, capital fief
or registered fief, can marry a wife, or can give
daughter, sister, niece, or son in marriage without

[1] *Const. Regn. Sic.*, ii., 32.

[2] The counts and barons in the region of Conversano were subsequently
given the right to appoint annual judges (Winkelmann, *Acta Imperii*,
vol. i., No. 942, p. 716).

the king's permission.[1]   The sons of a deceased count or baron cannot receive the oaths or the reliefs of their men until they have obtained royal license. If a noble strike a noble, he loses his knighthood ; he is prevented from sitting as a judge upon his peers; he is banished from the kingdom for the space of a year.   The *collecta* or general subsidy hits baron and noble, clerk and commoner alike, for there is no leveller of persons like enlightened finance.   So, too, the Jews and the Saracens were taken under royal protection. "Hateful though they be, through their divergence from the Christian sect, and destitute of all other help, yet we cannot allow them to be defrauded of the power of our protection."   Frederick was intolerant enough against the Patarines, who were numerous in the Lombard cities, and he may cynically have reflected that a profession of Catholic orthodoxy might be usefully combined with a crusade against his political enemies, but the Jews and Saracens stood in a different position, for the Jews lent him their money, the Saracens their arms, and Frederick, who was naturally indifferent to religion, recognized the substantial value of their friendship.   The trouble which the emperor took to dispel the fable of the Jewish custom of infanticide, and the zeal with which he overcame the prejudices of the German princes, is one of the most remarkable passages in his life.   Through all the harsh, cynical, and superstitious elements in Frederick's character, there was a real ardour for enlightenment, a passionate desire for

---

[1] This provision seems to have been originally due to William I. (*Ugo Falcando*, ed. Siragusa, pp. 64, 78).   It was extremely unpopular both in William I.'s time and under Frederick II., who relaxed the rule in favour of the smaller tenants in 1231, and in favour of the smaller tenants in chief and all mesne tenants in 1241.   Cf. Winkelmann, *Acta Imperii*, No. 803, p. 625 ; and No. 850, p. 654 ; No. 858, p. 659.

culture and ordered rule, a romantic zeal for the wel-
fare of his Sicilian home.

The constitutional organization of Sicily was even
more important than the penal and procedural reform.
Frederick's object was first of all to obtain control of the
whole administration, and, secondly, to secure that
the administration should be efficient and impartial.
No prelate, count, baron, or knight was to act as justice
in his own lands. No podestats, consuls, or rectors were
to be appointed in the towns without his consent. Only
three towns were allowed, in accordance with ancient
privileges, to preserve independent rights of criminal
jurisdiction. Every care was taken to avert official
malversation. All the higher offices were remunerated
with fixed salaries ; all offices were annual, and every
official was bound to render an account of his office at
the end of the year, and to wait fifty days after the end
of his appointment to answer any charges which might
be brought against him. No man could be a justice in
any district in which he had house, land, or relations.
The judge or notary who forged or tampered with public
documents was condemned to death, and no judges were
permitted to enter into a contract during their term of
office. Any official who could be proved to have used
his office to injure others must first restore the sum which
he had embezzled, and then pay a penalty equal to four-
fold that sum. In 1234 four representatives from every
large town, and two representatives from every small
town, were ordered to hold a court of inquiry into the
conduct of officials twice a year, and the court was to
last fourteen days.[1] A special court for the verification
of official accounts [*curia ratiocinii*] was established at
Barletta, and afterwards [1247-48] departmental courts

---

[1] *Const. Regn. Sic.*, i. 41-49, 50-5, 57-62 ; *H.B.*, iv. 460.

were added for the same purpose at Monopoli, Caiazzo and Melfi.[1]   The precautions appear to have been partly vain, and the principles upon which they were framed were occasionally violated even by the emperor himself. The complaints of an indifferent poet may possibly be discounted by the hypothesis that he was also an un-successful litigant,[2] but it is likely enough that the wars of Frederick, which necessitated a military, judicial, and financial reorganization of the kingdom in 1240, and a concentration of the highest military and judicial authority in lower Italy, may have led to a dislocation of justice and to a decline in the standard of administrative probity.   At any rate, there is evidence of financial malversation and judicial misconduct.   But the strict control of the Chancery must have reduced this mis-conduct and malversation to a minimum.[3]

This connected body of rational and explicit pre-cautions against administrative and judicial abuses is by no means a unique feature in the Italian legislation of the Middle Ages, although there was nothing ana-logous to it in Germany.   Among all the benefits which the survival of Roman law secured to Italian civilization, none perhaps was greater than the mass of securities against official misconduct which had been accumulated during the days of vigorous Roman provin-cial administration.   The Italian Republic of the twelfth and thirteenth centuries, susceptible to every solicitation of jealousy and suspicion, was just the kind of society to

[1] The *Constitutiones super scholas ratiocinii*, 1248 ; Winkelmann, *Acta Imperii inedita*, No. 922, p. 700.

[2] Cf. the curious poem printed by Winkelmann, *Friedrich II.*, vol. i., Appendix.

[3] Cf. the Articles of inquiry into the conduct of G. de Montefuscolo, the Justiciar of Calabria.   Winkelmann, *Acta Imperii inedita*, No. 879, p. 670, and No. 856, p. 658, " Contra solitam impositorum et collectorum nequiciam."

appreciate this legacy. It revelled in creating checks and limitations upon the power of its officers. The twelfth century municipal statutes are full of them. The consul in general holds office for one year only, receives either a fixed salary or an assignment on certain taxes, is forbidden to accept gifts, to be re-elected within five years, and neither father, brother, or son may succeed him in his office. The outgoing consul must within a stated time give an account of his office and of the moneys which have passed through his hands, and all important affairs must be submitted to the community.[1] Frederick and his advisers legislate in the same sense not for a city, but for a kingdom, not for a republic, but for a despotism, and nowhere, save possibly in England under Henry II., had there been such a connected system of central control over a whole country since the Barbaric invasions broke up the administrative fabric of Diocletian in Western Europe.

Frederick's rule in Sicily was the rule of a strong enlightened bureaucracy, tempered occasionally by an assembly of notables. It was unlike anything which any other part of the medieval empire had experienced, or was likely to tolerate. Of the towns in the *Regno*, Palermo alone retained its autonomy, but it was the official capital and the royal residence, and likely to be specially influenced by the court. Messina, which was more important commercially, and which gave its town law to Gergenti and Lipari, Trepano, and Patri, was allowed no such liberty. The life of the feudal lord must have been scarcely tolerable, for at every point it was controlled by the crown. His arms, accoutrements, and horses were viewed by inspectors three times a year, and the annual

---

[1] Pertile, *Storia del diritto Italiano*, vol. i., p. 43-54. The rules, of course, differ in detail from city to city.

value of his fief in victuals, wine, money, and revenues
was estimated at the same time.[1]   If he deteriorated his
fief, he was put upon an allowance like a child, unless he
had an heir or relation who could be substituted for
him.[2]   Royal license must be obtained to levy a relief,
to knight a son or a brother, to marry, to receive the
oath of a vassal, to sell or divide or transfer a fief, to
receive a foreign resident.   The rules of wardship
are so strictly interpreted, that as soon as it is notified
that a feudatory has died leaving no heir of full
age, the Magister Camerarius enters into possession,
and the sons of the house must "labour after the
court" to get the royal license to be provided with
the necessaries of life.[3]   The country is kept down by
royal castles filled with carefully supervised garrisons,
each of them supported by special lands and vineyards
told off for their maintenance.[4]   As the Italian war goes
on, the taxation becomes more and more crushing.   In
1231 the government acquires the monopoly of salt, silk,
iron, and dyeing.   The import duties and export duties,
the excise, the feudal dues, the farming of offices, the
judicial fines, the taxes upon Jews are no longer
sufficient.   Throughout the whole reign it appears that
a land commission is at work, the *redintegratores
feudorum*, examining titles; resuming the alienated
portions of the royal domain; recalling fugitive villeins
and men who have commended themselves to other
lords, or who have fled to church lands, which owe no
service to the crown; claiming foreigners as the king's
men.   No title is safe from disturbance which cannot
be shown to have existed a year before the death of

---

[1] Winkelmann, *Acta Imperii*, No. 803, p. 625.   [2] *Ib.*, No. 927, p. 705.
[3] This arrangement was modified in 1247-8.
[4] Winkelmann, *Acta Imperii*, No. 764, p. 607.

King William II., that is to say in 1188.[1] When we
reflect upon the time over which this *quo warranto* inquiry extended, upon the mass of difficult litigation, the
disturbance of vested interests, and the forced transplan-
tation of human beings from one locality to another and
from one master to another, to which it must have
given rise, when we consider the energy and persistency
with which the inquiry was pursued into every detail,
we are amazed at the docility of the country which
acquiesced in these proceedings. Nor was this all.
The Norman kings had been in the habit of collecting
a general subsidy when they were levying an army
for the defence of their kingdom, or upon the occasion
of their coronation, or of the knighting of their son,
or of the marriage of their daughter. Frederick on
his return from crusade first levied one of these aids,
which in principle represented the equivalent for the
burghers and the peasants of the personal military
service which the feudatories were bound to perform.
But these aids, levied first exceptionally, soon became
annual, and were styled *collectae ordinariae.*[2] The
sums raised were enormous: in 1238, 102,000 gold
ounces; in 1242, 60,800 gold ounces; in 1248, 130,000
gold ounces.[3] The tax was an *impôt de repartition*,
a certain quantum being required from each of the

---

[1] Winkelmann, *Acta Imperii*, No. 920, vol. i., p. 695; No. 806, p. 627.
There is much extremely interesting information about this Domainial
Commission in the *Excerpta Massiliensia* published in the first volume of
Winkelmann's *Acta Imperii*. Cf. No. 777, p. 611; No. 781, p. 612; No.
783, p. 613; No. 806, p. 627; No. 807, p. 628; No. 876, p. 668-9; No. 924,
p. 701; No. 927, p. 704.

[2] Letter of Martin IV., 1284, in *Raynaldi Ann. Eccl.*, iii., p. 563;
Cadier, *Essai sur l'administration du royaume de Sicile sous Charles I.
et Charles II. d'Anjou.*

[3] Winkelmann, *Acta Imperii*, No. 936, p. 712; No. 873, p. 665; No.
811, p. 631.

provinces of the kingdom. According to the regu-
lations of 1241 all the justices meet at Foggia, and
swear to impose the tax. They then summon two
or four of the better men from each city or castle,
by whose indication all the collectors of subsidies from
the time of the coronation are summoned. Of these
two are sworn in from each neighbourhood or con-
stabulary, and these two point out the richest men in
their district. The richest men are then taxed first,
and after them the next richest, and so the tax
descends. When the subsidy is collected, it is compared with the register of past subsidies, and if it should
be found that any person has paid less than he should
have paid, the deficiency is exacted not only from the
defaulter but from the collector himself.[1]

The task of collecting Frederick's subsidies must have
been as invidious and as onerous as the task which fell
upon the *élus* of the *ancien régime*. In one year many
of the collectors fled out of the kingdom rather than face
their liabilities, and the royal chancery made efforts
to coax them back.[2] What an ironical inversion of
Frederick's hopes! He wished to make the *Regno* a
paradise upon earth. He tempted strangers to settle
there by offering them exemption from all taxation for
ten years.[3] But circumstances forced him to drain the
country of its wealth in order to sustain his war against
the Papacy and the Lombard towns, and in his hands the
instrument of government which had been forged by the
Norman kings became a thing of penetrating tyranny.[4]

---

[1] Winkelmann, *Acta Imperii*, No. 811, vol. 1., p. 631.

[2] *Ib.*, No. 854, vol. i, p. 656.   [3] *Ib.*, No. 799, p. 622.

[4] Frederick recognizes the fact in his will, "Item statuimus ut
homines regni nostri sint liberi et exempti ab omnibus generalibus
collectis, sicut consueverunt esse tempore regis Guglielmi secundi"
(*H.B.*, Intr., p. cdxix.).

But he still remains the only member of his house who founded durable institutions. When the brief period of French rule was passed, the Sicilian constitution as it had been shaped by Frederick II. emerged in all its main features. The Arragon kings indeed enlarged the liberties of the towns, which had helped to drive the French from the island and to plant the Spanish dynasty upon the Sicilian throne, but the constitutions of Frederick remained the code of Sicily, and the registers of Charles of Anjou illustrate the continuity of that fiscal and administrative system which was founded by Roger the Great and so firmly compacted by the wisest and the ablest of the medieval emperors.[1]

[1] *Les Archives Angevines de Naples*, par Paul Durrieu ; *Essai sur l'administration du royaume de Sicile sous Charles I. et Charles II. d'Anjou*, par Léon Cadier [*Bibliothèque des Écoles Françaises d'Athènes et de Rome*, Fasc. xlvi. et lix.]

CHAPTER XII.

THE EMPERORS AND THE CITY OF ROME.

WHEN the emissaries of Otto the Great arrived in the city of Rome to prepare the way for his coming, the Pope prescribed an oath in the following form, which the Saxon was to take as a preliminary condition to his reception within the walls : "To the Pope John, I king Otto promise and swear by the Father, the Son, and the Holy Spirit, and by this wood of the living cross, and by these relics of the saints that if by the permission of God I shall come to Rome, I will exalt the Holy Roman Church and thee its ruler according to my power. And thou shalt never by my will, consent, counsel or exhortation, lose life or limb or the honour which thou now hast and wilt have through me. And in Rome I will hold no plea, and make no ordinance concerning all those matters which pertain to thee or thy Romans without thy consent. And whatever part of the land of St. Peter shall come into our power, I will restore to thee. And to whomsoever I shall commit the kingdom of Italy, I will cause him to swear to help thee to defend the land of St. Peter according to his power." The suspicions of the Pope were reasonable enough, and Otto took the oath only to break it. In the famous privilege of 962, in which he confirmed the donations of previous emperors to the Papacy, he also repeated a clause, according to which an annual report was to be made to the emperor or his son concerning the administration of justice within the city, and which gave to the Pope the power of referring cases to be decided by special commissioners from the imperial court.[1] The antagonism between the oath and the privilege epitomizes the relations between the emperors and the city of Rome. While the popes were anxious to safeguard their patrimony and their temporal jurisdiction both within and without the city, the emperors would content themselves with no measure of control less than that which had been exercised under the emperor Lothair [824]. Otto I. sternly crushed the family of the Crescentii, who styled themselves patricians and represented the cause of municipal independence. The widow of Otto II., Theophano, went to Rome, subdued the surrounding region, styled herself emperor, sent her agents through the patrimony of St. Peter and held court days within the city itself. Her son, Otto III., schooled alike in classical learning and monastic abnegation, scourges himself secretly in the cave of Subiaco, while nourishing the most exorbitant imperial schemes. This passionate young visionary, half Greek, half Saxon, the plaything of scholars and of monks, meant to make Rome again the capital of the empire. Violating the Teutonic sentiment of equality, he sat apart from his nobles at a table raised upon a dais. He lived in an ancient palace on the Aventine, surrounded himself with Roman companions, and introduced the ceremonial of the Byzantine court, with its stiff etiquette and its official nomenclature. But his only reward was the bitterest disillusion. The Germans disliked the Greek, who made no secret of his abhorrence of " Saxon

---

[1] Weiland, i., No. 12.

rusticity," and the stern justice of the emperor outraged the turbulent populace of Rome.   In 1001 the emperor was closely besieged for three days in his palace on the Aventine by the citizens of his favourite city.   " Are you," said the poor lad, speaking to the crowd below from the top of a tower, "my Romans? For you I have left my country and my friends.   For love of you I have sacrificed my Saxons and all the Germans, my blood.   I have adopted you as my sons, I have preferred you to all.   For you I have stirred up against me the envy and the hatred of all.   And now you have rejected your father, you have destroyed my friends by a cruel death, you have excluded me whom you should not exclude, because I will never suffer those to be exiled from my affections whom I embrace with paternal love."   The Duke of Bavaria and Hugh, the Marquis of Italy, rescued Otto from his danger. The emperor escaped with a handful of attendants from the city to meet with his death in the following year.   " All regions which belong to the Romans and the Lombards he had faithfully subdued to his dominion save Rome alone, which he ever loved and affected before all other cities."

Otto's dream of a restoration of the Roman Empire in the antique sense perished with him at Paterno.   The German emperors were never able to acquire even the most fleeting authority in that barbarous and turbulent city, whose ancient buildings gave shelter to the bandit nobles of the Campagna, and whose debased but arrogant populace continued to cherish a tradition of republican liberty.   Received with hymns and litanies and processions of senators and priests, the royal guest was generally driven from the city after the ceremony of the coronation was over, by a Roman rising against

his German troops.   There was hardly an imperial
coronation which did not finish with some such bloody
and humiliating epilogue.   An insurrection eight days
after his coronation drove Henry II. from the city.   A
dispute between a Roman and a German concerning an
ox-hide evoked a wild scene of carnage which dimmed
the splendour of the coronation of Conrad II.

The disgust of the Roman nobility at the vices and
incompetence of the Tusculan popes induced them to
invite the intervention of Henry III. and to lay at
his feet the patriciate, an office said to have been first
created by the Byzantine exarchs, but which, owing
to the use made of it by the family of the Crescentii,
was now held specially to confer the right of the
election and investiture of the Pope.   But the authority
which Henry III. was able to exercise in Rome was
not more long-lived than the momentary exhaustion
of party-spirit.   The emperor was crowned in 1046,
after deposing three popes, and nominating a German
to the papal chair under the title of Clement II. ;
but in 1047 Clement died, and the anti-German party,
supported by Boniface of Tuscany, then the most powerful prince in Italy, raised its head anew.   Benedict IX.,
a debauched Tusculan noble, who had been elected
Pope at the age of twelve, and had been deposed by the
emperor at the Synod of Sutri in 1046, bribed his way
back into Rome, and managed to maintain himself in
the papal chair for eight months and nine days ; and
Henry, who, at the request of the larger part of the
Romans, had caused the election of another German,
Poppo of Brixen, found some difficulty in negotiating
the entry of his candidate into the city.   The submission of Boniface to the emperor, and perhaps also
the exhaustion of Benedict's purse, paved the way for

the reception of Damasus II. The Roman populace seem for a time to have been genuinely weary of papal scandals, and the imperial patrician, who had begun by deposing three popes, nominated no less than four in succession to the Roman see—Clement II., Damasus II., Leo. IX., and Victor II. Yet this signal achievement weakened rather than fortified the hold of the emperors upon the city. The genius, the zeal and the courage of the son of a Tuscan peasant—Hildebrand of Soana—restored the damaged finances of the holy see, and directed the policy of Leo and of Victor ; and the revived Papacy, guided by this fiery subdeacon, who had made his monkish profession in the strict Cluniac house of St. Mary's on the Aventine, disputed the very foundations upon which the emperors rested their power of ecclesiastical patronage in Rome.

The immediate successor of Victor II. was Frederick of Lorraine, the brother of Duke Godfrey of Lorraine, who had been one of the most formidable antagonists of the emperor in Germany, and who had married Beatrice of Tuscany, the widow of that Count Boniface who had led the opposition to the emperor in Italy. Frederick himself had been persecuted by Henry, and the nobles, clergy and people of Rome who proclaimed him Pope under the title of Stephen IX., on August 2, 1057, were at once gratifying their traditional hatred of German domination, and resuming those electoral rights which ten years earlier they had ceded to the emperor.[1]

---

[1] The emperor's consent was afterwards obtained. *Ann. Alt.*, "Rege ignorante postea tamen electionem ejus comprobante." The Pope was consecrated on August 3rd, but it was not until December that Hildebrand and Anselm of Lucca started for Germany to obtain the consent of the court. Bonitho's statement that Henry III. was persuaded by Hildebrand to lay down the patriciate, and to restore to the Roman clergy and people their ancient privileges, is clearly false. Cf. Martens, *Gregor. VII.*, i., p. 73.

The new Pope would have changed the morals of the Church and the political map of Italy. He convoked the clergy and people of the city in frequent synods, and laid down the rule that no one, from a subdeacon to a bishop, should be allowed to marry. He designed to expel the Germans, to conquer the Normans, to found an Italian kingdom under his brother Godfrey, and to extend the territories of St. Peter.[1] But he died on March 29, 1058, with these mighty schemes all unrealized ; and the Tusculan party, aided by all the antagonists of reform in the city, and scouting the injunction which the deceased Pope had laid upon them to wait till the return of Hildebrand, who was absent in Germany, paraded the city with armed bands, conciliated the mob with liberal doles, and in the dead of night raised a Tusculan noble, John, Bishop of Velletri, to the Papacy under the title of Benedict X.

Germany was now governed by the empress Agnes during the minority of Henry IV., and Agnes was a friend to the reformers. The cardinal Hildebrand came to Florence as her plenipotentiary ; the services of Godfrey and Matilda were enlisted on his side, and a party of the Roman nobility, who were opposed to the Tusculans, were induced by Hildebrand to send an embassy to the German court to obtain its consent to the choice of Gebhard of Florence. At a synod of Sienna the Florentine bishop was elected Pope, under the title of Nicolas II. ; but although the empress had favoured his election and had directed Godfrey to escort him

---

[1] Leo Ost., ii. 94-7 [SS., vii., pp. 690-695], "Disponebat ... fratri suo duci Gotfrido apud Tusciam in colloquium jungi eique ut ferebatur imperialem coronam largiri : demum vero ad Normannos Italia expellendos, qui maximo illi odio erant, una cum eo reverti."

to Rome, the German influence was not powerful enough
either to mould or to assist the policy of his party.   It
was only by dint of hard blows and lavish bribes that
Hildebrand had driven the Tusculan from the Lateran,
and he realized that the empire was an insufficient
shelter against electoral scandals, and that the turbu-
lence of Roman factions could only be quelled by a
nearer and more available ally.   His first act was to
pass that famous Vatican decree of 1059, which transferred the election to the Papacy to the college of
cardinals, and thus deprived both the nobility of Rome
and the Roman emperor of the influence which they had
in turn exercised over papal elections.[1]   His second
act was to ally himself with the Normans, who in
defiance of the empire had settled in the south of Italy,
to invest them with all their conquests, saving only
Benevento, as fiefs of the Roman see, together with
Sicily, then occupied by the Moors, and afterwards to
win his way into Rome with an army of Norman
mercenaries at his heels.[2]

The parts were now reversed.   The party of ecclesi-
astical reform, which had been given a footing in
Rome by Henry III., had turned against the empire.
The Papacy, which, thanks to Henry, was no longer the

---

[1] For the text, cf. Hugo of Flavigny, [SS., viii. 408]. The decree bears
every sign of compromise. The consent of the clergy and people of Rome to
the election of the college is stipulated for. There is a vague clause safe-
guarding the *debitus honor* of the emperor, which, however, is significantly
omitted in the Pope's letter (1061) publishing the decrees to Christianity
at large.

[2] Bon. ii., 642, "Pontifex Apuliam tendens Normannos vinculo absolu-
tionis absolvit tradensque eis per investituram omnem Apuliam et Calabriam
et terras b. Petri ab eis olim invasas, excepto Benevento, omnes in
deditionem accepit et eos sibi jurare coegit." Leo Ost., iii. 15 [SS., vii.
706], mentions the inclusion of Sicily in the grant to Robert Guiscard, and
the tribute of 12 pence for every pair of oxen. The oath of fealty ["Sancte
R. Ecclesiae et domino meo Nicolao Papae"] is given in Watterich, i., 234.

appanage of a Tusculan or Roman family, now found itself obliged to seek the support of foreign troops. On the other hand the city nobility, the counts of Tusculum and Galeria, and Segni, and Ceccano, all who were jealous of the Pope's dominion over the city, all who were opposed to ecclesiastical reform, the very party which had brewed trouble for the Ottos and created the situation which Henry III. came down to amend, now turned round to the imperial side, and on the death of Nicolas II., in 1061, sent the symbols of the patriciate to the young Henry—the green cloak, the mitre, the ring and the diadem—and invited him to name a Pope in Rome.[1]

Hildebrand had thought it worth while during the lifetime of Nicolas to keep in touch with the German court, and had sent the cardinal Stephen to propitiate the regent ; but the cardinal was refused admittance, Nicolas II. was deposed at a German synod, and Hildebrand cut the last cable which bound him to the imperial party. So in 1061, when Nicolas died, Hildebrand pulled the strings of the papal election. Anselm of Lucca was elected Pope, under the title of Alexander II., in accordance with the provisions of the Vatican decree, while the king's confirmation was not even asked, and Richard of Capua, hired, says a hostile witness, by the bribe of a thousand pounds, after a hard day's fighting with the Roman citizens, enthroned "the new antichrist" in the Lateran, and did him fealty.

The pontificate of Alexander II. was a flagrant defiance of imperial rights. The German party could not look with equanimity upon a step which deprived it of all control over the appointment to the greatest

---

[1] Leo Ost., iii., 19 [SS., vii. 711] ; Benzo, vii, 2 [SS., xi. 672]; Martens i., p. 297.

spiritual office in the western world, and of the most important political office in the city of Rome. At an assembly of German and Lombard bishops held at Basle, the Romans crowned the young Herny as Patrician ; the council annulled the Vatican decree and the election of Anselm ; and a Veronese bishop of Parma, Cadalus, was elected Pope under the title of Honorius II.[1] The city of Rome was the scene of the most dramatic and violent episodes in the contest between the two rival popes. But in these struggles the empire was little more than a makeweight. Cadalus opened with a great victory over the Hildebrandines in the Neronian field [April 14, 1062], but he was not strong enough to force his way across the bridge of Hadrian, and upon the failure of supplies he was constrained to break up his camp and to retire upon Tusculum, and in the end to accept the terms imposed upon him by Count Godfrey.

In the autumn of 1062 there was a revolution in Germany ; the government was seized by Archbishop Anno of Cologne, who kidnapped the young Henry, recognized the election of Nicolas II., and declared Alexander II. to be the legally elected Pope. But there was an inexpugnable element in the Roman nobility which Germans and Normans and Tuscans were unable to subdue. The adherents of Cadalus still victoriously held the Leonina, and the antipope gained possession of St. Peter's and the castle of St. Angelo. For more than a year the Pope at St. Peter's held his own against the Pope at the Lateran; the city was given

---

[1] There was, as Richter points out [*Annalen*, vol. iii., p. 23], an antagonism between the Roman nobility and the Lombard bishops, who united to promote the election of Cadalus. The Romans wished to regain their influence over the papal elections, the Lombards to put the matter in the hands of the king.

over to street fighting, in which the Norman mercenaries
of Alexander were sometimes beaten, and it was not
until 1064 that the Leonine party agreed to acquiesce
in the nominee of Hildebrand.   But the acquiescence of
the party of Cadalus was but momentary, for Rome was
divided between two families whose enmities were too
deep to be easily assuaged.   Each party was equally
ready to invoke aid from outside, but neither party
would have conceded to its ally any permanent power
in the city of Rome.   From this long contest Henry IV.
reaped no advantage whatsoever.   The majority of the
Romans were faithful to Hildebrand, whom in a frenzy
of enthusiasm they had proclaimed Pope by the open
grave of his predecessor.   It was in vain that in 1076
Henry appealed to the Roman clergy and people to rise
up against "that invader and oppressor of the Church,
that plotter against the Roman republic and our
realm," and to depose him.   When the emperor's
letters were read in the Lateran, and Roland his
ambassador, turning to the clergy, coolly informed
them that they were expected to present themselves
before Henry before Whitsuntide, and to receive from
his hands a father and a pope, the Bishop of Porto
cried out in a loud voice, "Take him," and the
prefect, rushing forward sword in hand with the
judges, knights and nobles of Rome, would have
assuredly slain the envoy there and then but for the
personal offices of the Pope.[1]

Three times did Henry besiege Rome—in 1081, in
1082 and 1083—and on each occasion the resistance
was obstinate.   At last, in June 1083, his troops forced
an entrance into the Leonine city, and from this position

---

[1] Bern., *Chron.*, SS. v. 433 ; Hugo Flav., *Chron.*, SS. viii. 435; Bruno,
c. 8 ; Paul Bern., c. 69 ; Lambert, 1076.

of advantage he was able to induce the Pope and the Romans to negotiate.

A treaty was indeed made with the Pope, who promised to summon a council in November to decide on the king's cause, but it was waste paper from the first. The Pope would only summon his own adherents, and Henry, violating his oath, intercepted their journey. But the Roman populace were at last weary of famine and the hardship of a siege; they had made in June a secret compact[1] with the king that they would aid him in obtaining his coronation within fifteen days of his return, whether Gregory was alive or dead, whether he consented or declined; in case of Gregory's flight or death, they had given hostages to Henry as a guarantee of their good faith; and they now urged the Pope to give him the crown. They were still, however, faithful to their master; they suggested that a solemn unction and coronation was unnecessary, and that the Pope might merely offer the crown; but Hildebrand scorned all subterfuges, and at last the Romans deserted him and invited Henry to return to the city. "On the day of St. Benedict," wrote the emperor after his coronation to Dietrich, Bishop of Verdun, "we entered Rome; this fact seems a dream to me; I may say that God has effected for us with ten men what our ancestors could not have accomplished with ten thousand. Despairing of taking Rome I was ready to return to Germany when Roman

---

[1] For the oath, cf. SS. viii. 461, "Tibi dicimus, Rex H., quia nos infra terminum illum quam tecum ponemus ad xv. dies postquam Romam veneris, faciemus te coronare papam Gregorium si vivus est vel si forte de Roma non fugerit. Si autem mortuus fuerit, vel si fugerit et reverti noluerit ad nostrum consilium ... nos papam eligemus cum tuo consilio secundum canones, et ipsum papam studebimus ... ut te coronet et, ut Romani tibi faciant fidelitatem."

messengers recalled us to the city, which received us
with rejoicings."

It was a brief triumph. Henry indeed received the
coveted symbols of power—the imperial crown and the
patriciate. Wibert was consecrated Pope under the
title of Clement III., but Gregory was still in the castle
of St. Angelo. His nephew Rusticus held the Caelian
and the Palatine; the Corsi were on the Capitol; the
Pierleoni on the island of the Tiber. A war of sieges
ensued, in which the colonnades of the Septizonium on
the Palatine, one of the finest monuments of the city,
were destroyed, in which the palaces of the Corsi were
burnt on the Capitol, and the Pope beset in the castle
of St. Angelo. Again the mighty architectural relics of
ancient Rome were too much for the feeble strength of
a medieval emperor. Thirty-six thousand Norman
lancers were visible in the Campagna, before the garrison
of St. Angelo had shown signs of distress, and Henry
and Clement hurriedly left the city, leaving in the ruins
of the Leonine town a savage valediction.[1]

Twenty-seven years elapsed before another German
sovereign set foot in Rome—years of gloom, tumult and
disaster—during which half the city was burnt by the
Normans, and popes were alternately exiled and recalled.
In 1111 Henry V. appeared before the Leonine walls to
demand the imperial crown. He had already made a
treaty with Pope Pascal II., according to which the
king was to renounce the investiture and the clergy the
fiefs of the crown, and had sworn that he would never
connive either at the deposition or death or mutilation

---

[1] *Vita Gregorii*, ap. Watterich, i. 306, " Ipse vero ad ecclesiam S. Petri
cum Guiberto veniens civitatem S. Petri quam Leo IV. edificaverat
funditus destruxit. Sicque valefaciens Romanis una cum Guiberto re-
cessit."

or imprisonment of the Pontiff. While the German army was still waiting outside the walls, envoys from the Roman people required Henry to confirm the laws of Rome, and it was only after this had been done that the emperor was admitted to St. Peter's.

The scene in the cathedral on February 12, when the German prelates blazed out in indignation at a pact which would have reduced them to apostolic poverty ; when the Pope called upon the emperor to renounce the right of investiture ; when the king demanded corona-tion, and the Pope refused ; when the German knights, tired of the altercation, drew their swords, surrounded the high altar, and carried off the Pope and his court to prison ; when priests were robbed and slain, and the ornaments of the Church pillaged by the greedy foreigners, is one of the most dramatic in the history of the city. The scene on the morning of the next day was equally typical of the visits of Roman emperors to their Italian capital. The populace of Rome, wild with indignation at the capture of the Pope, stormed into the Leonine city, and fought desperately with their German enemies. But though the battle resulted in the repulse of the Romans, Henry had won but a Cadmeian victory. The imperialist losses were so great that he was forced to leave the Leonina, and two days later, since the Romans were still undaunted and menacing, to march away from the city altogether, carrying with him the captive Pope, sixteen cardinals, and several consuls and citizens. It is significant of the temper of the Roman populace that Henry was unable to bribe or to bully them into submission. The city refused to admit him unless he released the prisoners, and Henry declined to take this step unless the Pope would crown him and formally concede to him the right of investiture. The unfortunate Pascal, threatened with the death of all his fellow-prisoners, at last consented to these bitter terms. On April 13 Henry entered the Leonine town and received the imperial and the patrician crowns, but the gates of Rome were closed against him, and he never set foot within the city itself.

Henry twice revisited the scene of his *coup-d'état* and hurried coronation. In 1117 the fickle Roman populace, led by the nobility who had resolved to free the prefecture of the city from papal influence, put Pascal II. to flight, and the emperor was received in triumph by the victorious faction. He married his illegitimate daughter Bertha to Ptolemy of Tusculum, the most powerful of the nobles of the Campagna, whose lands extended from Tusculum to the sea, and made him a tenant-in-chief of the empire. He distributed bribes, and confirmed the popular candidate Peter, a nephew of Ptolemy's, in the prefecture, and then he retired. A year later he returned, summoned by the inordinate jealousy of the papal power, which has always been a potent lever in Roman politics. The Frangipani had rushed into the conclave, which had just elected Gelasius II. [January 24, 1118], bound the Pope with chains, and imprisoned him in a tower. But the populace of Rome rose in revolt, and Cencius Frangipani was forced to release his captive, and demand absolution. But though this brutal imitation of the *coup-d'état* of 1111 had failed, the Frangipani were not at the end of their resources. They pointed out to Henry that here in Rome a Pope had been elected by the College of Cardinals, and that the rights of the Roman patrician had been clearly violated. Henry hastily marched on Rome, and the old Pope as hastily retreated, pursued in his flight down the Tiber by the arrows and curses of the

Germans. The emperor would have preferred to come
to terms with Gelasius, as he had come to terms with
Pascal, but the Pope had escaped from his clutches, and
would hear of no compromise. There was nothing for it
but to elect an antipope. An assembly of nobles was
collected in St. Peter's; the election of Gelasius was
quashed, and Burdinus, Archbishop of Braga in Portugal,
was proclaimed Pope, led to the Lateran, and on the
next day consecrated in St. Peter's as Gregory VIII. It
is a commentary upon the stability of the imperial power
in Rome that in 1121 this same Burdinus rode through
the streets of the city in the triumph of Calixtus II.,
seated amidst culinary utensils upon a camel with his
face to the tail, clad in a rough goat-skin, and assailed
with the stones and gibes of the populace, which had
greeted him with enthusiasm three years before.

In truth it mattered not what side the emperor took
in the ecclesiastical controversy, Rome was always his
secret or declared foe. Lothair was induced to espouse
the cause of Innocent II., who had fled from his Roman
enemies to France, and who was supported by the whole
weight of St. Bernard and of the French Church. But
though the king of the Romans conducted the Pope
back to the Lateran, and received from his hands the
imperial crown, he was never master of more than that
fraction of the city which lay between his palace on the
Aventine and the Lateran Church. Anacletus II., the
representative of a wealthy Jewish family, the Pierleoni, which had obtained great weight in civic politics,
was housed in the inexpugnable fortress of St. Angelo,
and acknowledged in Rome, in the Campagna and among
the Normans of the south, and soon after the departure
of the German troops Innocent was obliged to take
flight for Pisa.

The tenacity with which the Roman emperors maintained an intermittent simulacrum of power within the
walls of Rome is only less remarkable than the opposition which they encountered. Not a right but was
vigorously contested and obstinately maintained. The
Vatican decree of 1059 had degraded the patriciate,
but emperors still received the symbols of the office,
and occasionally nominated an antipope in virtue of it.
The control of the highest civil office in Rome, the
prefecture, was contested between the Pope and the
emperor, and according to the opinion of an orthodox
writer, the prefect was expected to do homage to the
Pope, while he received the sword or the insignia of
temporal authority from the emperor. The emperor
Frederick I. guardedly abandoned his claims to the
praefectura urbis at Anagni and at Venice, but it is
probable that in so doing he meant to relinquish not
the right to invest the prefect, but the civil control
over the papal patrimony which his officers had been
exercising. In 1244 a prefect of the city was signing
an imperial charter at Acquapendente, and in the
same year Frederick II. complained that the Pope
had seduced the prefect, " who had always belonged
to the empire and received his dignity from the
empire, and as to whom there was never a question
raised by the Church." [1]

That the emperor was able for so long to keep alive
these prerogatives was due less to any active exhibition
of power on his part than to the balance of parties
and to the prestige of the imperial crown. No German
garrison was ever lodged for more than a month or
so at a time within the city walls. No German Deceleia

[1] Gerloh von Reichersberg, *Expositio in psalmum* lxiv.; Migne, *Patr.
Lat.*, cxciii.; *H.B.*, vi. 166, 219; Ficker, *Forschungen*, ii., pp. 307-8.

menaced the capital from the Campagna, no permanent and salaried representative of the empire maintained a court or a party among its half-ruined palaces. Yet the names of many of the noble families in Rome during the eleventh and twelfth centuries betray their German origin, and the Sassi, the Astaldi, the Tebaldi, and the Ursini may have been ready to welcome their compatriots. The nobles utilized the emperor as a counterfoil to the Pope, and the *faex Romuli* enjoyed him as a spectacle. The pride of the citizens was gratified by the reflection that the most exalted temporal office in Christendom could only be acquired from them and within the walls of their city, and that it was their gift also which conferred upon the emperor the right of nominating the Vicar of Christ.

A revolution in 1143 offered to the emperors a rare opportunity of converting into a continuous reality the unsubstantial show of power which they intermittently enjoyed in Rome. The burghers rose against the nobility, overthrew them, and established a senate in the capital. A Roman republic was formed which aimed at finally shaking off the temporal dominion of the Pope, and the leaders of the new commune appealed repeatedly to Conrad III. of Germany for help. At last in 1149, having received no answer to their previous communications, the senate addressed to the emperor a most memorable letter. They represented that they had defeated many adversaries of the empire, and had laid a solid foundation for the imperial rule. The fortresses of the nobility, who, supported by Sicily and Pope Eugenius III., had defied the emperor, were now destroyed, but the faithful senate was harried by the Pope, the Frangipani and other nobles. They entreated the emperor to hurry to their assistance. The city was at his command, and he would be able to dwell in Rome, the capital of the world, and to rule from thence over Italy and the German empire more absolutely than almost any of his predecessors. Conrad turned a deaf ear to these solicitations, which would have sounded so sweetly to the heart of Otto III. The emperors definitely rejected the professed alliance of the Roman republic, and thereby helped to confirm the temporal dominion of the Pope. It is perhaps idle to speculate upon the influence which an alliance between the emperor and the Roman republic might have exerted upon Italian, and indeed upon European history. Would the emperors have been permitted to inhabit a palace and to form a court in Rome? Would they have received and continued to receive the imperial crown from the populace of Rome without the intermediation of the Pope? Would the Papacy have been banished to Viterbo or Anagni? Would the temporal power have been annihilated, based though it was upon a series of charters running back into the darkness of the Lombard age, and would the greatest of obstacles to the political unification of Italy have been thus early removed? From our own standpoint it seems almost incredible that Conrad and Frederick, who had both so great a stake in Italy, should have rejected so valuable an ally against the Papacy. But we must remember that no question of medieval politics was ever presented in a naked political form. Religion, symbolism, mystic tradition clouded and environed every step which was not made at the direct prompting of passion.

The Roman republic was founded in opposition to the Papacy and to the temporal power, and Arnold of

Brescia, its austere and eloquent tribune, connected its being with a creed subversive of ecclesiastical wealth. But the essence of the idea of the Medieval Empire was the parity and alliance of the civil and ecclesiastical heads of the Christian world, while the essential fact in the constitution of the German monarchy was the temporal power enjoyed by the prelates. No medieval emperor could espouse the cause of apostolic poverty without loosening the foundations of his power, and running counter to the orthodox ecclesiastical sentiment of his times. To enter into a quarrel with the Papacy upon the lines suggested by the Roman Senate would have been to open an endless chapter of discord, and to seal up for ever the mystic page of the Medieval Empire. Conrad III. was in the hands of pious clerks, and paid no attention to the Roman appeal. Frederick I., in 1155, received the envoys of the Roman Senate and people upon the Monte Mario, only to insult them with a laudation of the German race. "Will you know," for so goes the speech put into his mouth by Otto of Freising,[1] "where the ancient glory of your Rome, the gravity of your senate, the tactics of your camp, the virtue and discipline of knighthood, the stainless and invincible courage in the conflict have gone? Look at our state. All these things are with us Germans. . . . With us are your consuls, with us your senate, with us your soldiery." The Roman envoys appear to have demanded that the emperor, according to custom, should confirm the laws of the republic and distribute the expected largesses to the Roman mob; but Frederick's proud rejoinder, marked by the frank

---

[1] The speech attributed to the emperor by the anonymous writer of Bergamo is less insulting (*Gesta di Federigo I.*, ed. Monaci, l. 630-641).

brutality of the Teuton, was rapidly avenged.[1]   On
June 18, 1155, the young emperor was crowned
among the acclamations of his troops in the Cathedral
of St. Peter, while the bridge by the Castle of St.
Angelo was carefully guarded to prevent an irruption
of the Romans.   But while the ceremony was taking
place, the senators and people of Rome met upon the
Capitol.   When they heard that the emperor had
received the crown without their consent, they poured
across the Tiber, through the Leonine city, to wreak
their vengeance on the Pope and the Germans[2]   The
German troops, overcome with the heat and labour
of the day, were taking a meal in their camp outside
the walls of the city when suddenly the sound of a
great tumult struck upon their ears.   They snatched
up their arms and ran to meet the insurgents.   The
battle lasted from four in the afternoon to nightfall,
and "You might see," says the chronicler, "the Germans slaying the fugitives as if they were saying,
'Receive now, Rome, Teuton steel for Arab gold.
This is the money which your prince offers for your
crown.   Thus do the Franks buy your empire.'"[3]
The Romans lost heavily in the battle, and nearly a
thousand were said to have been slain or drowned,
but the emperor had lost heavily too ; he could obtain

[1] *Gesta di Federigo I.*, ed. Monaci, l. 618 ff :
        "Sed petit ut veterem serves dux inclite morem
        Scilicet ut jures mox intraturus in urbem
        Te servaturum populi decus, urbis honorem,
        Jura senatorum ; nam sic vetus exigit ordo.
        Munera praeterea Romane debita plebi
        Quae solet adveniens huc primum rex dare noster
        Postulat ut tribuas."
[2] *Frid. imp.*, ep. 3, "De ponte Tyberino prosiluerunt et in monasterio
Sta Petri duobus servis nostris occisis et cardinalibus spoliatis papam
capere intendebant."
[3] Otto Fris., *Gesta Frid.*, ii., c. 32.

no provisions from the city, and famine and heat compelled him to withdraw as if he had been the conquered party.[1] Yet the republic of Rome could not afford to dispense with the emperor. When the quarrel between Frederick and Hadrian IV. became acute, they sent [1159] envoys to the emperor; and Frederick, who had been required by the Pope to surrender all authority within the states of the Church, perceived the identity of interest between the republic and himself. He declared himself prepared to recognize the senate, but stipulated that a former prefect should be recalled, and sent an embassy to Rome to arrange a settlement with the republic and the Pope. It is probable that a difference upon points of etiquette would have prevented the German ambassadors from coming to terms with the senate had not the death of Hadrian and the double election to the Papacy opened a new chapter. In the schism which ensued the senate and people of Rome were, in the main, favourable to the imperial candidate, Victor IV., but upon Victor's death in 1164 their sympathies were transferred to the other side. Alexander III. was received into the city, and the Germans found it necessary to avenge the levity and the insult. The thrilling vicissitudes of the summer of 1167 seem to epitomize the whole story of the relations of the empire and the city of Rome. The Romans, attacking in force the hated city of Tusculum, are decimated by the cavalry of two German archbishops [May 29, 1167]. Two months later Frederick appears before Rome, and forces his way into the Leonina, to find the Church of St.

---

[1] The statement of Otto Morena, who says that the loss was heavy on both sides, is clearly to be preferred to that of Otto of Freising, who says that the Romans only lost one man.

Peter's fortified and garrisoned by the papal troops. For eight days the garrison holds out against the German engines; by the order of the emperor, the adjoining Church of St. Maria del Lavoriero was fired, and the flames spread to the Vatican. Then on July 29th, to save the building from destruction, the garrison capitulated, and on the following day the emperor installed his Pope. But the master of the Leonina was again excluded from the city, and Frederick was forced to negotiate with Alexander and the senate. Sicilian galleys brought gold to the Pope, and he scattered it among the Frangipani and his other adherents, but all in vain. Frederick proposed to the patricians that both the contending Popes should abdicate; he promised to interfere no further in papal elections, and to restore his spoils and his prisoners to the Roman people; and the people of Rome believed him, and clamoured for Alexander's resignation. There was now no honourable course open to the Pope except to flee from Rome. Then the senate and people swore fealty to the emperor, promising to protect the rights of the empire both within and without the city, and the emperor recognized the senate as a body dependent on himself.[1] For a moment the republic seemed to be within the palm of the emperor's hand. He caused a new senate to be elected, he nominated a prefect, he took four hundred hostages. Emperor and patrician, lord of a vassal republic, master of a Pope, Frederick stood at the zenith of his power. But the rain fell heavily on August 2, and a hot sun followed. The demon of malaria swooped down upon the German army and

---

[1] "Ut senatus per eum ordinetur et ei subjectus fiat," *Ann. Col.* (SS. xvii., p. 781).

destroyed it, and the emperor re-crossed the Po, with a weary handful of followers and no baggage, leaving the flower of German chivalry withering in that vindictive clime.

Frederick I. never set eyes again upon the scene of his sacrilegious triumph and sudden humiliation. The whole Christian world condemned the desecration of St. Peter's, and the revolt of the Lombard league was the natural sequel to the destruction of the German army For many years to come Frederick was occupied in the north, and to efface the defeat of Legnano in 1176 the emperor was obliged momentarily to concede to the Pope his rights over the Roman prefecture. "Saving all the rights of the empire," all possessions of the prefecture or any other thing which had been taken from the Roman Church are now at the Peace of Venice in 1177 restored to it.[1] But though Frederick, to detach the Pope from the cities, was willing to give renewed sanction to the papal patrimony and to the papal control over Rome, he carefully guarded his concessions. The Italian lawyers were teaching the doctrine that *respublica* meant the republic of the city of Rome, and that the origin and essence of the empire lay in its connection with the city.[2] Frederick had long ago learnt their lesson. " I am called the Roman emperor by

---

[1] Weiland, i., Nos. 249, 250, "*Pax Anagnina*. Possessionem quoque prefecturae urbis dominus imperator libere et plenarie restituet Domino Papae Alexandro et Romanae ecclesiae. Si autem post optentam plenam restitutionem eius dominus imperator aliquid juris in ea voluerit requirere a domino Papae et ab ecclesia Romana, cum hoc postulaverit, paratus erit dominus Papa et ecclesia Romana justitiam ei exhibere." Weiland, vol. i., No. 259, sect. 3, "*Pax Veneta*. Omnem vero possessionem et tenementum sive prefecture sive alterius rei, quam Romana ecclesia habuit et ipse abstulit, per se vel per alios, bona fide restituet ei salvo omni jure imperii."

[2] Gierke, *Genossenschaftrecht*, vol. iii., pp. 199-200.

divine ordinance, yet it is but a shadow of domination
and an empty name, if our power over the city of Rome
be shaken from our hands "[1] It is probable that the
emperor still maintained a party in the city, and that
despite the concessions of Anagni and of Venice, he was
ready to revive his rights on the first opportunity. But
the Papacy, to which he had momentarily capitulated,
had scarcely more control over the republic than had
the empire. The senate steadily developed in strength,
and in 1188 extorted a formal recognition of its constitution from Lucius III. Henry VI. was only able
to obtain his coronation at the price of perfidiously
assisting the Romans to destroy Tusculum. Otto IV.,
like so many of his predecessors, was crowned in the
Leonina, but six thousand men-at-arms could not win
him access to the city or avert the humiliation of a
street fight.

Frederick II. was more fortunate, for his coronation
was marked by a rare tranquillity. But his power over
the city was destined to be no greater than that of any
of his predecessors. When the quarrel broke out with
Gregory IX. he summoned the most powerful citizens
of Rome to his court and the most noble members of
the family of the Frangipani. He then, in 1228, made
a treaty with the Frangipani, according to the terms of
which they were to become vassals of the empire, and
to assist the emperor in all causes. An inventory was
taken of the houses and fields, vineyards and slaves,
which were owned by the family within the city, and
Frederick bought the real estate at the estimated price,
that he might infeoff it to the Frangipani.[2] But the
alliance, though occasionally useful, was essentially

---

[1] Weiland, i., No. 179.

[2] *Chron. Ursp.* SS. xxiii., p. 382 ; *H.B.*, iii., p. 63.

hollow, for Frederick was not prepared to endorse the programme of the republican party, and he was always anxious to recover the favour of the Church. The republic, led by a series of vigorous senators, had now entered into a desperate struggle with the Papacy, which came to a head in 1234. The citizens protested that the Pope was debarred from excommunicating the city or placing it under an interdict; the senate aimed at recovering the ancient Roman duchy and at annexing the patrimony of the Pope, which included the towns of Montalto and Viterbo; while the podestats and senators of the city exacted an annual tribute from the Church. The whole political position of the Papacy in the centre of Italy was gravely menaced. Gregory IX. fled to Perugia, and the Pope and the city appealed alike to Frederick for help. The emperor was no friend of city republics, and at that moment he was anxious to demonstrate his loyalty to the Church. He sent an army to Viterbo, which destroyed the villages, and cut down the vines of the Roman citizens, and inflicted a crushing defeat on a large and disordered force of Romans which marched out to retaliate on the town.[1] The next year Frederick was present in person, and there can be no question that it was due to his support that Gregory was able to return to the city. Although he was afterwards accused of having been lukewarm and treacherous, of having trifled away time in hunting and hawking, which should have been employed in closely pressing the siege of a Roman castle, he answered that he had spent more than a hundred thousand crowns in the papal service, and

---

[1] Matthew Paris estimates the loss on the imperial side at 30,000 *armati*, and says that the Roman loss was heavier still. A gross exaggeration. The computations of a Ghibelline writer are more modest.

that the Pope had made peace with the Romans and left him in the lurch.[1]

As the quarrel with the Pope deepened, Frederick made efforts to regain the favour of the city. " Miles Roma, Miles Imperator," this was the Ghibelline war-cry at Cortenuova in 1237 " We cannot," he writes to the city of Rome when sending them the carrochio taken from the Milanese, " extol the glory of the empire without, at the same time, extolling the honour of the city." In 1240 he asks the Romans to send their pro-consuls to him, that he may appoint them to public offices at the imperial court, that in the antique manner he may entrust to them the administration of regions and kingdoms and provinces. Idle compliments! The emperor might borrow from Roman merchants, and subsidize the Frangipani, but he could never win the confidence of the republic. The Ghibelline senator was never a match for the Guelph senator, or the Ghibelline party for the party of the Pope.[2] When matters looked dangerous, the Pope could appeal to the superstition of the masses; and the most fickle mob in Europe, inflamed by the sight of an ecclesiastical procession, would take the cross to defend the relics of St. Peter against the attacks of an infidel emperor.[3] In four successive years Frederick made a vain attempt to enter Rome. He ravaged the Campagna in the month of August, and pestilence carried off Gregory IX. [21st August, 1241]. His Saracens destroyed the beautiful town of Albano with

---

[1] Richard of S. Germano, 1234-5 ; Matthew Paris, 1234-5 ; H.B., v., 327-340, 254, 297-9 ; vi. 287.

[2] Matthew Paris, 1237, " Eodemque anno procurante domino imperatore Fretherico creatus est alter senatus Romae."

[3] Cf. Matthew Paris, vol. iii., 630-8, for the advance of 1239; Annales Placentini Ghibellini [a most vivid account] for 1240 ; and H.B., vi. 143, for the siege of 1242.

its numerous churches, and pillaged the property of the cardinals. The city within was rent with internal discord.[1] The cardinal, John of Colonna, who had deserted to the emperor, fortified the mausoleum of Augustus. The papal senator Matthew Orsini besieged it and took it. Still Frederick was unable to effect an entrance. Rome leagued itself with Perugia and Narni and the Guelphic towns of Tuscany [1242]. "In truth," said Frederick, writing to Louis IX. of France, "this people has a hard neck, and bears hatred to us for that it has experienced the success of our star. Of old it has shown no reverence to our empire, to which it has transferred all its rights. And it has not feared to attack and to devastate our lieges."[2]   Pride and chagrin mingle in the apology. A hollow peace in 1246 secured no further advantages to the emperor, and he died in 1250, exactly thirty years after he was last permitted to enter Rome.

He had neither strengthened the republic against the Pope nor the Pope against the republic, for in truth his own claims were incompatible with the success of either party. For him a Roman duchy would have been as distasteful as a papal state. And so he was a half-hearted ally, mingling war and diplomacy, compliments and threats, now throwing his weight on the one side, now upon the other. His military force was great, but even forty-five thousand men-at-arms could not bring him into Rome in 1243.[3]   He had the opulence of the Sicilian kingdom at command, but for all that his party

---

[1] Cf. the curious letter written by a French or English clerk from Rome, between 1245 and 1250 [*H.B.*, v. 1077 ; Höfler, *Albert von Behaim's Conceptbuch*, No. 47 ; Gregorovius, vi. 247], "Rome secure qualiter eritis, cum pro diversis adversariis omnibus civibus in diversa diversis sit ibi conflictus continuus inter cives et divisio inter fratres."

[2] *H.B.*, vi. 95.   [3] Matthew Paris, iii. 266-7.

in the city was out-numbered, out-bribed, and over-matched.   In 1246 Innocent IV. won over the Frangi-pani by recognizing their claims to the principality of Tarentum, which had been granted by Constance of Sicily to Otto Frangipani, and which had subsequently been transferred by Frederick to his bastard son Man-fred.   Against the emperor were arrayed the forces of republicanism and of religion, and the memory of the broad river of blood which flowed between Germany and Rome.   The men whose fathers had died at Monte Porzio, the men who had seen the rout of Viterbo, and the Saracen lances scour the Campagna, were ready to resist him to the death.   The time was not far off when they were ready to elect a French prince as their senator [1263-78].

When Goethe first came to Rome all the dreams of his youth sprang at once into living realities.   The pictures and drawings and engravings which had hung on the walls of the old rooms in Frankfort were repro-duced in all their actual shapeliness, and glittered with a touching and romantic beauty in the mellow Novem-ber sunshine.   Wherever he went he found an old acquaintance in a new world.   To the German of the Middle Ages the eternal city was not without its everlasting and mysterious attractions, but its subtle and manifold appeals to the historic memory and to the artistic consciousness were made to empty minds and listless eyes.   The rude soldiery of the medieval emperors cared nothing for the columns of the Forum or the dome of the Pantheon, and the imperial visits to the capital were not productive of a single piece of literature descriptive of the artistic and classical monu-ments of Rome.   The best-educated man who followed a medieval emperor on his coronation journey, while describing the descent of Barbarossa's army from the Monte Mario to the Leonine city, has not a sentence to spare for the magical panorama of castle and column which was spread out before his eyes. The true son of a feudal age, in spite of all his hard-won learning in Paris, Otto of Freising, remembers only to depict the military display of the Germans. " You might see the soldiery shining in the splendour of their arms, terrible as an army with banners. The sun shone upon their shields of gold, and the mountains shone therewith."[1] In this spirit army after army of German warriors marched along the Flaminian way, with their vizors down, in search of the symbol of universal empire, facing malaria and the chances of war in this fickle and enchanted city of abounding perils and unfathomed treasures, and inexhaustible and unsuspected fountains of knowledge and of joy.

[1] Otto Fris., *Gesta Frid.*, ii. 32.

CHAPTER XIII.

IMPERIAL ADMINISTRATION IN ITALY.

THERE is a clause in an imperial ordinance issued from Pavia in 876, which runs as follows : " Let the bishops discharge in their bishoprics the power and authority of our commission." [1] In the tenth and eleventh centuries, when the emperors paid but flying visits to Italy, the Italian bishops were the mainstays of German influence south of the Alps. From 950 to 1060, a period of imperfect records, we can prove the presence of forty-seven German bishops in Italian sees, and the number should probably be more than doubled. [2] The chapter of Goslar, which was only founded under Henry III., supplied two archbishops to Ravenna and bishops to Verona, Padua, Vercelli, and Terni before 1077. [3] The Patriarch of Aglei was almost always a German ; the Archbishops of Ravenna, who had obtained partly by usurpation and partly by papal grant the supremacy of the exarchate, were generally Germans, and held their temporal possessions as imperial fiefs. In Istria, in the Veronese March, in Lombardy, and perhaps also in the Romagna and in Ancona many sees were in the

[1] M.G., *Leg. Sect.*, ii., tom ii., p. 103.
[2] Ficker, *Forsch.*, ii., p. 264.
[3] " Monachi Hamerslebiensis narratio de Basilica Goslariensi eiusque praepositis " (Leibnitz, *Script. Rer. Brunsw.*, ii., pp. 506-7).

imperial gift. " It was an ancient condition of the Italian kingdom, which perseveres to this day," writes Arnulf of Milan in 1067, "that on the death of a bishop of the Church the Italian king should provide successors upon the invitation of the clergy and the people." [1]

These German bishops in the tenth and eleventh centuries wielded political and judicial power within the north Italian cities. They were not overshadowed by a powerful aristocracy, or compelled to submit to the hegemony of an aristocratic advocate. [2] They strengthened themselves by marriage, and founded families, and occasionally received special commissions from the emperor, which widened their judicial prerogatives. The Bishop of Parma—so run the charters of 962, 989, and 1004—shall have "the power of deliberating and deciding and distraining, as if our count of the palace was present. The inhabitants of Parma may not seek any court save the court of the bishop for the time being. But let the bishop have license, as the count of our palace, to distrain, and to define, and to deliberate over all things and families ; and if it should happen that judgment cannot be lawfully given over the aforesaid things and families without battle, we grant to the commissioner or delegate [*misso sive vicedomino*] of

---

[1] SS., viii., p. 23. For an enumeration of Italian bishops who were also princes of the empire, cf. Ficker, *Vom Reichsfürstenstande*, pp. 308-20.

[2] Whereas the advocate of the German see was a powerful noble, who usually robbed the see which he was invited to protect, the advocate of the Italian see was generally a lawyer occupying a very subordinate position. Further, while the German advocate was a judge, the Italian advocate generally represented the bishop as a party. The *vicedominus* appears to have been the judicial delegate of the bishop. It is only exceptionally [*e.g.* in Ravenna and Trent] that the Italian bishops enfeoff whole counties to counts—a procedure frequent in Germany. The title *comes* sometimes merely means an official employed by the bishop. Ficker, *Forsch.*, vol. i., p. 33.

the bishop that he be our commissioner and have the
power of deliberating and defining and judging as **our**
count of the palace." Similar privileges were accorded
to Asti in 969, to Lodi and Lucca in 980, to Novara
in 1014, to Reggio in 1027, to Modena in 1038. It
was to such grants that the bishops owed their
possessions of certain important judicial prerogatives—
the power to decide cases by battle, to appoint tutors
or guardians, to deal with contracts made by minors.

The bishops were not the only persons to receive
commissions from the emperor. Occasionally, but the
occasion is rare, a count or a duke figures as a *missus*.
Sometimes a private individual is made an imperial
commissioner for his own estates, and there must have
been quite a handful of Italian families transmitting
these plenary powers of jurisdiction from father to son.
There were also some permanent judicial commissioners.
In 960 two Milanese citizens, Adelgisus and Azzo, are
given jurisdiction in the county of Milan, and in Milan
and Pavia, two cities in which the prelates do not seem
to have acquired these exceptional powers of jurisdiction,
we find not infrequent traces of such special judicial
commissions. But in the eleventh century almost all
these instances came from Lombardy. We have absolutely no trace of such commissions in Spoleto, or
Verona or Romagna, and even in the twelfth century,
when they are more frequent [in nine Milanese documents, from 1117 to 1156, fifteen different *missi* are
mentioned], they occur nowhere outside Lombardy
except at Lucca. There appears, however, to have been
a permanent imperial commissioner at Rome; there
may have been such another at Ravenna. Besides this,
commissioners would occasionally be sent on special
errands, and it was usual for the sovereign, when he had

resolved upon an Italian journey, to despatch legates before him to collect revenue, to negotiate for provisions, and to make all the necessary arrangements for the visit.[1] It was but a slight fabric, this Italian administration of the tenth and eleventh centuries. The separate Italian chancery, which was established in 962, and which was generally conferred upon some Italian prelate, went in 1031 to Archbishop Pilgrim of Cologne, and from that time onward it continued to be the appanage of the Rhenish archbishopric. In 1066, when there was a question of a legation to Italy, the judgment of the court pointed to Archbishop Anno of Cologne as "the archchancellor and the person through whom above all others the business of Italy ought to be administered." The dignity of Archchancellor of Italy, which had no doubt been originally claimed by the See of Cologne as a counterpoise to the Archchancellorship of Germany, which belonged to the See of Mainz, was a title and nothing more. There was little for an Italian archchancellor to do unless the emperor happened to be in Italy; the functions of the Archbishop of Cologne were generally exercised by deputy, and in the latter half of Barbarossa's reign the connection between the archchancellor and the Italian chancery was almost entirely broken.[2] Few German prelates were less qualified to attend to Italian business than this distant potentate of the lower Rhine, surrounded by a ring of hostile nobles, and absorbed in a territorial and commercial policy which steadily drew them towards Westphalia and the German Ocean.

---

[1] Otto Fris., *Gesta Frid.*, i., c. 12 ; Luitpr., *Hist. Ott.*, c. 2.

[2] Seeliger, *Erzkanzler und Reichskanzleien*, p. 42. The Archbishop of Trèves at the end of the thirteenth century claimed to be Archchancellor of the kingdom of Arles (*ib.*, p. 46).

The archchancellor was but a *nominis umbra*; the Gregorian movement shook the imperial control over the bishops; the communal movement destroyed their political power. The special commissions were in reality from the first so many alienations of imperial prerogative. The bishops who become *missi* are not thereby converted into imperial officials. They are made richer and more powerful. The grant of the imperial commission to lay citizens merely hastens on the development of independent municipal jurisdiction. When a citizen of Lomello may, in virtue of this commission, send litigants to the battle, appoint tutors and guardians, and exercise all forms of plenary jurisdiction, what becomes of the Palsgrave of Lomello? The grant is equivalent to the liberation of the town from a neighbouring lord. When a citizen of Milan gets this commission, then the jurisdiction of the Margrave of Este over that city is doomed. One set of commissions strengthens the bishop, another set strengthens the town. The only good which the emperor derives from his munificence is that his charters keep alive the conception of a Roman *imperium* and the memory of certain imperial prerogatives which might otherwise perish. When we consider the elaborate preparations which were made for the government of Italy in the ninth century: how the country was divided into administrative districts; how the *missi* were to control officials, dismiss incompetent notaries, keep up the royal palaces, see to it that benefices were not deteriorated, protect widows and waifs, maintain highways, bridges, weights, measures, the standard of the mint, not to speak of numerous other duties military and official; when we reflect that during the whole period of the eleventh century there is not a single instruction issued to an imperial commissioner in Italy; that Henry III., who controlled the Papacy more completely than any of his predecessors or successors, spent only sixty-four weeks in Italy out of the seventeen years of his reign, that even during this period he was troubled by rebellious castles in the Campagna and successfully resisted by Benevento, we have some measure of the decline of German administration south of the Alps.[1]

In the century which elapses from the accession of Henry IV. to the accession of Frederick Barbarossa, the political situation in Italy was profoundly changed. A number of free and thriving republics had grasped political power and autonomy, and everywhere except in the sub-Alpine regions the bishops of Northern Italy had capitulated before the might of the communes. In the centre of Italy a great estate, the heritage of the Countess Matilda, comprising the territories of Mantua and Gonzaga, Correggio and Carpi, with the mountainous parts of the counties of Reggio and Modena, and various scattered castles and properties in Lombardy, Romagna and Tuscany, came into imperial hands in 1113. From Rome a revived and active Papacy, freed from the control of the emperor by the Vatican decree of 1059, was in a position to combine and to direct all the forces which were hostile to the imperial supremacy, while in the toe of Italy some Norman adventurers had founded the strongest and most compact military power on the Mediterranean. At the same time, under the influence of Roman law, conceptions of imperial

---

[1] There is an interesting account of Otto of Wittelsbach's attempt to discharge the functions of an imperial legate at Roncaglia in 1068 in the *Annales Altahenses*, SS. xx. 819, "Cum ergo consedissent et res aliqua agi cepta fuisset, Itali, velut natali odio, Teutonicum ducem audire dedignati, incondito clamore cuncta ceperunt turbare et nullo perfecto negotio ducem compulerunt abire."

absolutism were becoming familiar among the cities of
the north, and the same spirit of antiquarianism which
fostered the pride of the communes, invited a more
continuous and systematic display of imperial power.
To manage their estates, to destroy the kingdom of the
Normans, to protect the weaker against the stronger
communes, to quench the flames of inter-communal war,
to restore the imperial authority which had been diminished with the subsidence of the bishops, these were the
aims of the Hohenstauffen emperors of the twelfth
century.   Their presence in Italy was alternately welcome and odious, but in the main they were felt to
embody that principle of impartial justice to strong and
weak alike, which civic factions tended to obliterate.
" We wish you to know," writes Bishop Hermann of
Constance to the men of Crema in 1147, " that our
lord has sent us from his presence into these parts,
and has committed to us the management of the
business of the whole Italian kingdom, to be conducted lawfully and to his honour.   We are to do
justice to all who are oppressed, and especially to
churches ; we are firmly to keep the peace, and to
liberate all who are held captive in the realm ; we
are to put to the ban all rebels and all who disobey
our orders, which are the king's orders ; and we are
diligently to admonish his lieges of his approach and
of his service."[1]   The legate is but the faint reflection
of the emperor.   " He is as the father," says an
Italian of Frederick Barbarossa, " who, hearing of the
excesses of his sons, corrects them and warns them
to lay aside their evil habits."[2]

Home troubles, a disastrous crusade and an early

---

[1] Muratori, *Antiq. Ital.*, iv. 28 ; Ficker, *Forsch.*, i., p. 135.
[2] *Gesta di Federigo I.*, ed. Monaci, l. 200-1.

death, prevented Conrad III. from carrying out his far-reaching schemes in Italy, and it was left for Frederick Barbarossa to make the German once more an active principle in Italian politics. In his reign there was almost a new German invasion of the country. The old policy of leaving the country to the care of the bishops was outworn and discarded, and except in the case of the sub-Alpine sees, where towns were still weak and bishops were still strong, Frederick does not go out of his way to strengthen the hands of ecclesiastics.[1] But in revenge he comes down into Italy with a large army of vassals, part of which is retained to manage the imperial property, to negotiate, to garrison castles, to administer and to fight.[2] Germans are sent all over Lombardy, Piedmont, Tuscany and Romagna. Some of them are prelates like Rainald of Cologne, who was imperial legate from June 1164 to 1166; who makes a contract with the consuls of Lucca concerning the regalia, who is sent to Pisa and to Genoa to stop if possible the war between these two rivals, both so useful to the emperor for his Sicilian enterprise; who holds a court at Piacenza, and orders the inhabitants to receive the imperial pound as their standard money, and to call in the local coin.[3] Cultured, eloquent, provident, affable, munificent and laborious, with a consuming zeal for the imperial prerogative, with a fine complexion and soft yellow hair and well-knit frame, this famous warrior-

---

[1] Charters to Aglei, Trent, Ceneda, Belluno, Feltre.

[2] "Constituit etiam Teutonicos principes ac dominatores super Lombardos et Tuscos ut de caetero ejus voluntati nullus Italicus resistendi locum habere ullatenus possit" (*Vita Alex.*, Watterich, ii. 399); and *Chron. Ursp.*, 1168, SS. xxiii. 355, "Prout opportunitas temporum concessit coepit imperator in partibus Tusciae et terrae Romanae castra ad se spectantia suae potestati vindicare in quorum praesidiis Teutonicos praecipue collocavit."

[3] *Ann. Plac. Guelf.*, SS. xviii., p. 413.

bishop plays a great figure in imperial politics.[1]   He
tours through Lombardy, Tuscany, Romagna and the
Marches.   He fills Tuscany with his Rhineland counts,
and holds a parliament for the Tuscan March at Sarzana.
At one time he administers the Milanese from Monza,
the famous coronation place of the Lombard kings.
When the news comes that Pope Victor IV., the first of
Barbarossa's antipopes, is dead, the active chancellor flies
off to Lucca, elects Guido of Crema Pope in the presence
of a mere handful of cardinals, compels all present to
swear obedience in a common parliament, and is prepared in the following year to force his nominee down
the throats of the German clergy.   Nor is this young
and vigorous Rhinelander a mere diplomatist or administrator.   He is the master of a picked force of men-
at-arms bred and trained in Cologne, who are capable
of giving a good account of themselves in the field.
When the Romans were pressing the Germans hard on
the bloody day of Monte Porzio, the battle was restored
by the steady discipline of the men of Cologne; shouting
the German battle-hymn " Christ is Born," with the
Archbishops of Mainz and Cologne bearing the standards
before them, they drove the enemy back into the city,
and inflicted on him a crushing defeat.

On the day following the siege of St. Peter's on
July 30, 1167, the emperor presented to Rainald, in
the very cathedral which his prowess had helped to
reduce, the revenues of Andernach, " because by the
aid of God the Romans were most gloriously vanquished
by his unconquerable valour and that of the illustrious
militia of the Church of Cologne, and thereby our most
sacred empire has been most indescribably exalted."[2]

---

[1] For a description, cf. *Acerbi Morenae Cont.*, SS. xviii., p. 640.

[2] Böhmer, 2526 ; cf. Gregorovius, iv. 2. 585, English translation

Or again, there is Christian, Archbishop of Mainz, who was not only Frederick's best general, sharing in the victory of 1167, besieging Ancona in 1173, routing a Sicilian army in 1176 at Carseoli, but also the first permanent legate for the whole of Italy. For eleven years, from his appointment in 1171 to his death in 1183, he was the emperor's legate in Italy, building imperial palaces, destroying disobedient towns, fighting hard in Lombardy, Tuscany and the March, making treaties, obtaining revenues. Soldier, judge, ambassador, a great linguist, speaking, so it was said, with equal facility Latin and Greek, the Italian dialects, French and Walloon, Christian was singularly well fitted to deal with the complex situation in Italy. In all the great transactions of the Italian politics he plays a part only second to the emperor himself.

The powers of the legate were indeed both varied and autocratic, nor was there any administrative subdivision of the kingdom until the conquest of Sicily by Henry VI. led to the appointment of a special Sicilian legate. The Italian legates would free towns from the feudal superiority of a duke or a margrave, and subject them directly to the empire; they would wage small wars and cancel municipal privileges[1]; they would exercise sovereign jurisdiction, compel men to swear to a landpeace; sell, augment, administer, or enfeoff the imperial property; permit towns to enjoy imperial rights upon payment of

[1] Cf. *Oberti Annales*, 1172 [SS. xviii., p. 94], "Post multa verba juravit Cristianus archicancellarius Magontinae sedis, qui tunc vicem imperatoris in Tuscia tenebat se guerram pro posse Pisanis facturum ordinatione consulum nostrorum [Genoese] et Lucensium ... et juravit quod mitteret Florentinos in bannum imperatoris et cassaret et destrueret omnia dona et privilegia facta utrisque, videlicet Pisanis et Florentinis."

some stipulated sum[1]; they kept up the show of
a court, occasionally summoned the Italian prelates
and nobility to a kind of parliament, and had the
right to call out the vassals of the empire to war.
Serviceable leaders of *condottieri*, they were invoked
to assist in local feuds. Representatives of the supreme
judicial power, they interposed between city and city,
or decided the cases of individuals. Their rights and
powers were contested as often as they were acknowledged; and as they raised a *corvée* to build a castle,
or pounced down on a town for its regalia, they must
have incurred some of the odium which inevitably
attaches to power.

After the prelates come the nobles and *ministeriales*,
who garrison the fortresses, administer the imperial
property, and watch over the imperial rights. "Invincible swordsmen, trusting in no men except in the
men of their own race, most faithful to their leaders,
they would lose their lives rather than betray their
fealty."[2] How many little knots of self-reliant German
swordsmen were lodged among the fortresses of the
Apennines we cannot say, for the charters only throw a
very faint and intermittent light, and the chronicles are
all but speechless. A complete list of German counts
can be made out for the March of Tuscany from 1115,
when the march came to the empire, until the end of the
twelfth century We may suspect that a German
garrison was lodged at San Miniato, which seems to
have been the official centre of the district, and that the
German counts of Chiusi and Volterra, and Sienna and

---

[1] Ficker, *Forsch.*, ii., pp. 170-17?

[2] *Chron. Ursp.*, SS. xxiii., "Ensibus invicti, in nullis nisi hominibus suae
gentis confidentes, ducibus suis fidelissimi et quibus vitam potius quam
fidem possis auferre.

Florence, and the imperial *nuntii* of Prato and Pistoia were not without a bodyguard of faithful attendants. In the Tuscan patrimony also, which was south of the march, there must have been many German garrisons, for each fortress was contested by the papal party. An imperial palace was built at Viterbo in 1169 ; there was a palace at Montefiascone, a castle built by Frederick I. at Radicofani, and possibly also there was a garrison at Citta di Castello to secure the payment of its annual tribute to the Tuscan *nuntius* at San Miniato. In the later years of the reign we find imperial officers governing the whole of Tuscany : in 1185 Anselm of Kunigsberg, President of Tuscany ; in 1191 Conrad of Lützelhard, Marquis of Tuscany and Romania ; in 1193 Philip of Swabia, who is styled Count or else Duke of Tuscany. There are also German dukes of Spoleto, German margraves of Ancona, a German delegate for Piedmont, Thomas of Annone, who is also magistrate in Turin. There probably was not a town in Northern Italy, however small, which did not at some time during Barbarossa's reign admit a German agent of the emperor sent to collect regalia, or to make a treaty, or to appoint an official.

Frederick scarcely ever put an Italian into a position of extended authority. Conrad of Montferrat, who was probably imperial agent for the Tuscan patrimony from 1172 to 1177, was the most marked exception to this rule ; but as he deserted to the Pope after the Peace of Venice in 1177, waged war upon Christian of Mainz, and once actually succeeded in capturing him, the experiment was not encouraging. In the main, the German rule in Italy was carried out by German administrators. Of the quality of their government we can say but little ; of its quantity we can only say that it must have varied from district to district. In Lombardy, where the cities were large and proud, it was from the first disputed. In Tuscany, where there were many imperial estates, where cities were not yet strong, and where there had been a continuous succession of German officials since the beginning of the twelfth century, the yoke was probably most firmly fixed and most keenly felt. In Piedmont the rights of the Margraviate of Montferrat must have interfered to a certain extent with the work of the German delegates, but the destruction of Asti in 1155 struck terror into the small Piedmontese towns, and more than one can be proved to have received German castellains and financial inquisitors. The successor of Christian of Mainz as legate of the sacred palace in Italy, 1184-1186, Godfrey of Helfenstein, tries and condemns the Count of Savoy, then perhaps the most powerful noble in the land, upon the appeal of the Bishop of Turin.[1] In the Romagna and in the March of Ancona there was always a party for the emperor, as there was always a party against him ; but the imperial power was seldom acknowledged south of a line drawn from Rome eastwards, and as the appearance of the Germans was often the signal for monetary contributions, they were almost invariably resisted.

It is a remarkable fact that this regiment of German soldiers and officials is nowhere felt or declared to be monstrous by the Italian population. In the negotia-

---

[1] The case is described in *Monumenta Historiae Patriae. Chartae*, vol. i., p. 938. The count was accused *per libellum* before the emperor in his palace at Pavia. He refused to appear though frequently cited. The case was then referred to Godfrey, but still the count refused to appear. Judgment was accordingly given for the plaintiff, "plurium sapientum habito diligenti consilio."

tions between Frederick and the Lombard towns, it is never for a moment suggested by the cities that the emperor should reserve Italy for the Italians. There are some towns—Asti, for instance, in Piedmont—which even bargain for a German castellain, and there is one family, the Ubertini, in the valley of the Arno, who stipulate that they shall not be submitted to any Latin city or podestat, but only to the emperor, his son, or a *missus* sent from Germany. A Teuton might be brutal, ignorant of Italian, extortionate, but he was always preferable to a Latin neighbour. He was at worst unentangled in local feuds; at best he represented impartial and intelligent justice, with the prestige and the sword of the empire to drive it home. The evidence would seem to show that the *ministeriales* of Henry VI. were harsh and tyrannical, and certainly at the emperor's death there was something like a popular rising in Tuscany against the Germans. The Pope did all that in him lay to flog up a spirit of Italian nationality. Now was the time to clear the Germans out of Italy. But the Germans clung like limpets to their inexpugnable crags, or lived on prosperously in the towns sheltered by the sunny indifference of the Italian middle class to all things papal and national.[1] The Vatican thundered in vain. The old German officials crop up everywhere—here a burgher of Sienna, there a podestat of Piacenza or Turin[2]—and when Otto IV. came down into Italy to restore the imperial power, it was not the

---

[1] Cf. the vivid description of the indifference of an Italian town in Salimbene, "Quia hi qui in civitate [Parmensi] erant non intromittebant se de negotiis istis quia nec cum ipsis qui venerant, erant, nec pro imperatore pugnabant, sed sedebant trapezitae sive campsores ad teloneum suum, et alii artiste non dimittebant propter hoc quin operarentur in stationibus suis."

[2] Ficker, ii. 271-2.

Italians who failed him. Milan espoused his cause, nobles from Lombardy, Tuscany, Spoleto and Ancona thronged to his court, and the army which he led into Apulia was almost entirely Italian.[1]

A solid national government in Italy could only have been built up in one way; through the medium of a representative parliament mainly composed of town delegates. Municipal co-operation in Italy was not entirely a wild dream. The policy of Frederick I. drove the Lombard towns into a temporary but powerful coalition, and the foundations of a parliamentary system laid by the strong hand, and prompted by the fiscal necessities of Frederick II. were just rising to view in Southern Italy when the fortunes of his house were overwhelmed by death, accident and foreign invasion. But the communion of Italian cities, anywhere outside the kingdom of Sicily, presented enormous and almost insuperable difficulties. The secular hates of neighbouring towns, the jealously guarded varieties of municipal custom, the length of the period during which Italy had enjoyed substantial immunity from German interference, were all formidable obstacles to the formation of an imperial system based upon a regular representation of the towns in a central diet. On the other hand the very keenness of civic jealousies opened out to the emperor a gateway into the affections of many of the cities. The Italian towns were great marts, and they were sufficiently civilized to appreciate the advantages of imperial justice. The twelfth century was not far advanced when some of these towns, Bologna for instance, and Faenza and Reggio and Modena, began to import magistrates or podestats from outside and to assign to these invited guests dictatorial

[1] Ficker, ii. 406-9.

powers for a specified period. It was believed that a foreigner alone who was not involved in the factions of the city could deal out impartial justice ; and the prevalence of this practice might encourage the hope that the whole system of justice within the north Italian cities might fall into alien hands, and if into alien hands, why not into German hands, why not into the hands of men nominated by the emperor who wore the Lombard crown, and was the podestat or foreign judge for the whole of Italy ? Now when Frederick I. held his diet at Roncaglia in 1158, that assembly, not content with assigning to him a long list of fiscal rights—such as tolls, coinage, rights over public ways, streams, harbours, silver mines, treasure trove, fisheries, most of which had long been alienated or else had lapsed—went on to give to the emperor the right of appointing the ordinary magistrates or consuls of the towns. And the story goes that the emperor proceeded to ask the Milanese how he should best retain the loyalty of the Italian towns, and that the Milanese advised him to appoint true men either as consuls or as podestats.[1] Further, we find that the emperor naturally took this advice, that, for instance, in 1162 the men of Piacenza promise to receive such podestats as the emperor shall choose to appoint, whether Teuton or Lombard, and that they swear to stand by their bidding or by the bidding of the emperor,[2] and that, when as a special favour the emperor does allow the existing podestats to continue his office, he is careful to state that the sole power of appointment lies with him.

---

[1] The story is given by Vincent of Prague, p. 675. Rahewin's account differs slightly (iv., c. 9), and is on the whole less credible.

[2] Böhmer, *Acta*, 598 ; Ficker, *Forsch.*, i. 236.

Now this clearly meant a great revolution of things. Imagine two or three men in every town holding the highest offices at the pleasure of the emperor, busied in recovering his antiquated financial rights and in extending his jurisdiction. What a unity is suddenly introduced into the Italian town system! If the experiment should by a miracle turn out successfully, and the Milanese, for instance, should be got to go to the courts of these consuls and to abide by their decisions, what unity may not be introduced into the methods of administering justice! From time to time the emperor or his general legate, having confidence in these imperially governed towns will hold a diet, and the representatives of the faithful towns will attend it and promise money and men. In time there may be something like an imperial parliamentary system for North Italy.

The towns did not object to foreign podestats, nor did Frederick for the most part appoint foreigners. It was, on the contrary, more to his interest to bestow the consulate upon some influential citizen who had a party at his back or a purse in his pocket. Frederick's failure was due to other causes. The towns valued their autonomy. They did not mind foreigners but they wished to choose them for themselves. They feared that the emperor might confer judicial power upon some bishop or influential feudatory, and this would mean that the work of emancipation would have to be done all over again.[1] They knew that together with the judge came the fiscal inquisitor with his odious mission to

---

[1] Cf. Frederick's privilege for Asti, 1159, "Adjicientes quoque constauter statuimus quod praedictam potestatem de civitate et comitatu nulli archiepiscopo, nulli episcopo, nulli marchioni, nulli comiti, nulli potestati unquam concedemus nisi solis nostris fidelibus de ipsa civitate" (Ughelli, *Ital. Sacr.*, iv., p. 366 ; Ficker,. *Forsch.*, i., pp. 236-7).

recover obsolete dues and taxes, and to raise a large and permanent revenue for the emperor, whereas the revenue for many hundreds of years had been slight and occasional. They murmured at the introduction of the German bans, or judicial penalties.[1] The Lombard towns revolted against these decrees of Roncaglia, which threatened alike their autonomy and their tills. During the course of the war Barbarossa was obliged to make concessions to the cities which embraced his side : free choice of consuls and all the regalia to Cremona in 1162 in exchange for a yearly payment of two hundred marks of silver ; full autonomy to Pisa and to Genoa in 1162 ; free choice of consuls to Pavia in 1164, and all the regalia, "except the bridge and the bank"; remission of the regalia, of the Roman, Sicilian, Apulian, Calabrian and Veronese expedition to Mantua in 1164 ; and so on, concession following concession.[2] The upshot of it all was that the cities would not fight for Frederick unless he promised them autonomy and the regalia. They were prepared in return to consent that their consuls should swear fealty, should receive the regalia as imperial fiefs, and pay a fixed yearly sum in exchange for them. The towns in fact became tenants-in-chief of the crown.

This was in reality the basis of the Peace of Constance in 1183, which closed the war between Frederick and the Lombard league. The consuls shall be appointed by the city. But they must be selected from citizens who

---

[1] *Chron. Ursp.*, SS. xxiii., p. 348, "Super quo contra novas institutiones imperatoris murmurare ceperunt Lombardi ; non est enim eorum consuetudo banna solvere, sed ut secundum leges Romanas injuriam passis satisfaciant, secundum quod juraverint laesi se talem velle pati injuriam ; de quibus acquisitis judex tantum vicesimam vel minorem secundum quod ab his decretum est recipit portionem."

[2] Weiland, i., Nos. 218, 221, 212.

have done fealty to the emperor; they must receive
investiture from the emperor or his envoy, and the
investiture must be renewed every five years. All
imperial vassals must receive investiture and do fealty,
and all citizens from the ages of fifteen to seventy must
do fealty likewise. At the same time the fiscal rights
of the empire are circumscribed. The cities of the
league are to enjoy all the regalia which they had
hitherto enjoyed, or which they were then enjoying—
pastures, mills, water, bridges, tolls, the right of forti-
fication, of levying *fodrum* or purveyance, of raising
the host, of full jurisdiction. Only when the emperor
enters Lombardy "to take the crown," they are bound
to give him the royal and accustomed *fodrum*, to restore
the ways and bridges and to provide a sufficient market
for his troops, but the emperor must not make
unnecessary delay in a city or bishopric. Nor was
the emperor permitted to obtain any great measure of
judicial authority in the city. Appeals were allowed to
go to the imperial court in cases where the amount
exceeded 25 imperial pounds, but there was to be
no compulsion to go to Germany. The emperor was
to have his own envoy in every city or bishopric.
The envoy was to be elected by the counsel of the
consuls of the city. He was to swear to examine
"according to the laws and customs of the city within
two months from joinder of issue or the reception
of an appeal," and a clause, which was inserted in the
preliminary negotiations to the effect that the cities
were permitted the *Lex domini imperatoris*, was
omitted in the final draft of the peace.[1] The emperor

---

[1] "Libellariae et precariae in suo statu permaneant secundum con-
suetudinem unius cujusque civitatis non obstante lege nostra quae
dicitur imperatoris Friderici" (Weiland, i., Nos. 293-4; cf. sects. 24-32).

still preserved a nominal suzerainty over the Lombard league, but all the substantial realities of power were ceded to the cities. He had aimed at dividing the cities, but so far he had only united them, and now he was forced to give his written sanction to the continuance of an armed league.

Still Frederick had achieved much. If he was for the moment unsuccessful in Lombardy, he was yet able in Tuscany, in Piedmont, in the Romagna and in the March of Ancona to obtain revenues and to overawe cities. His officials were for the most part real officials, holding office either for life or for a limited period, and not feudatories. Although he had to accept the Lombard league in 1183, three years had not passed before he was able to detach Milan from the allied cities and to fasten it to the imperial cause by an ample charter of privilege. The reign of Henry VI. witnessed a new invasion of German *ministeriales*, but in the disputed election which followed his death the imperial administration must have been completely disjointed. It was not until 1238 and 1239 that an imperial administration was re-established in the north.

There is a letter, proceeding from the chancery of Frederick II., which epitomizes his Italian policy. "We believe," says the writer, "that Providence has thus wonderfully guided our steps to no other end than that, while we rule Jerusalem in the east and the Sicilian kingdom and the people of powerful Germany in deep peace, we should bring back Italy, which lies in the centre of our dominion, to the recognition of our majesty and to the union of the empire." The conquest of Italy falls between the years 1232 and 1238. There were two nobles in the Trevisan March—Eccelin III. and his brother Alberic—who, seeking to carve their way to fortune by entering the Lombard league, came to discover that their hopes were not likely to be realized. Tortured by ambition, condemned to watch the growing power of a rival, Azzo of Este, these two *condottieri* desert to the emperor, and signalize their treacherous accession by doing him a great service. At their instigation, on April 14, 1232, the burghers of Verona revolt against their Lombard podestat and receive a German garrison. Verona was the key to the Brenner Pass, to the great military road between Germany and Italy. Master of Verona, Frederick easily foils the insurrection of his son Henry in 1235, intercepting his traitorous communion with the Lombard league. In 1236 he subdues Vicenza ; in 1237 Padua and Treviso submit to his generals, Mantua deserts the league, and Milan is crushed on the decisive field of Cortenuova. In 1238 follows the submission of Lodi and the conquest of Piedmont, and the north of Italy lay at Frederick's feet. In 1239 Frederick began to organize an administration such as Italy had not seen since the Lombards obliterated the fabric of Justinian. His son, King Enzio, is appointed [July 25, 1239] legate for the whole of Italy. Under him there are a number of provincial governors or general vicars, for the Trevisan March and the Bishopric of Trent, for Lombardy, for the country east of Pavia, for Lunigiana, for the March of Ancona, for the Duchy of Spoleto, for the conquered parts of the patrimony of St. Peter. Beneath them come the vicars and the podestats or captains of the towns, who are nominated by the emperor and salaried according to his directions.[1] In the next year [1240] the high court of Sicily is trans-

---

[1] In the last years of his reign Frederick seems to have everywhere claimed the right to name the podestats (Ficker, *Forsch.*, ii., p. 529).

formed. It becomes a court following the emperor and competent to deal with the cases of the whole empire. It is clear that Frederick intended to weld Italy and Sicily together in a common judicial and administrative system.

The loose administration of Frederick Barbarossa became in the hands of Frederick II. a bureaucracy closely knit and closely watched. The *personnel* had ceased to be German. The emperor came to employ Apulians trained in the rigorous methods and the absolutist doctrines of the Sicilian chancery. For the most part these judges and administrators were selected from the well-to-do aristocracy of the *Regno*, and it was considered important that they should have relations living within its borders to serve as hostages for their loyalty. Constantly changed and shifted from district to district, appointed and dismissed at a nod from the emperor, these Apulians are the most supple instruments of despotism. From 1237 onwards they crowd into the official posts in Northern and Central Italy. They know the language, and therefore they are more acceptable than the Germans. They are foreigners, and therefore they are more acceptable than local men. We find them in the most diverse positions, discharging the most diverse functions. An Apulian knight as podestat of the Bishop of Trent sits at Botzen, and asks for a judgment after the German manner. Knights from the Abruzzi govern the small villages round Viterbo, and the names of the captains and podestats of many of the Piedmontese towns betray a southern origin.

Over and above these Apulian barons, knights and legists come the members and connections of the imperial family—the emperor's sons in the first place; Enzio, legate for all Italy; Frederick of Antioch, general

vicar of Tuscany; Richard of Teate, general vicar
in the March, in the Duchy and in the Romagna; his
sons-in-law, Richard of Caserta, vicar general of the
Holy Empire [1244], through the March, the Duchy
of Spoleto, and from Amelia to Corneto; Jacob of
Caneto, sometime vicar of the land from Pavia to
Asti [1248]; Eccelin da Romano, the real master of the
Trevisan March. A nephew-in-law, Thomas of Savoy, is
appointed general vicar for Piedmont in 1248. One
brother-in-law, Galvano Lancia, is vicar in Roman
Tuscany in 1248; another, Manfred Lancia, holds a
succession of appointments in North Italy, as general
vicar of Lombardy east of Pavia in 1238, as captain
of the sacred empire from Pavia to Asti in 1248 and
1249, as podestat of Lodi and vicar, under Thomas
of Savoy, of Lombardy west of the Lambro in 1250.

The North Italians did not object to the Sicilian
invasion of the thirteenth century as they object to the
Sicilian invasion now. But history had not prepared
them for the despotic methods of the Norman kingdom,
and religion counselled distrust of the despot. The
whole of Lombardy was racked and ruined with war
from 1237 to Frederick's death. "Men could not
plough, nor sow, nor mow, nor make vineyards, nor
live in villages." The husbandmen worked in gangs
with a squad of soldiery to protect them; travellers
were robbed and hanged by the highwaymen; the
wolves, no longer kept down by the rural population,
howled outside the cities and entered at night to
devour the men who slept under the porticos and
in waggons.[1] For some of those who suffered these
horrors the struggle meant the crushing of the in-
famous thing, the fight for all that was holy and

[1] Salimbene, *Chron. Parm.*, p. 71.

safe, the desperate effort to preserve a coherent and comforting scheme of life. To most it was merely the fierce old rage of the communes fought with larger supplies of men and of money. Whether it was religion or a series of accidents, or the carelessness of his supporters, or the better organization of his enemies, or the distrust of despotism, or the treachery of many of his servants which decided the day against the emperor, we cannot say. Probably all these elements were mixed in the cup. But in any case the first administrative and judicial system which had been established for all Italy, since the treachery of Narses was alleged to have opened the Alpine passes to the Lombards, went to pieces in the downfall of his house.

CHAPTER XIV.

THE EMPIRE AND CULTURE.

In 966 Benedict of Soracte, one of the rudest Latinists of a rude age, thus lamented the severities practised by Otto I. within the city of Rome : "Woe unto thee, O Rome, who art oppressed and trodden under foot by so many nations, who hast even been captured by a Saxon king, and thy people put to the sword, and thy strength reduced to nought. Thy gold and thy silver they carry away in their purses. Thou wast mother, now art thou become daughter. That which thou didst possess thou hast lost. Long didst thou fight with foreign nations. On all sides thou didst conquer the world from the north to the south. Thou hast been usurped by the race of the Gauls; thou wast all too fair."[1]

Again and again through the troubled course of Italian history we hear this refrain of wounded pride, in Buoncompagno's history of the siege of Ancona in 1174,[2] in the speeches of the Pope and of the Lombards at the conference of Ferrara in 1177 as given in Romuald of Salerno, when the Pope retails how he has withstood the "Teuton fury," and the cities tell how

[1] SS. iii. 719.

[2] *De Obsidione Anconae Liber*, c. 3 ; Muratori, *Scriptores*, vi. 925, " Nam opinio in hanc me trahit sententiam ut non credam Italiam posse fieri tributariam alicui, nisi Italicorum malitia procederet ac livore ; in legibus enim habetur : ' Non est Provincia sed Domina Provinciarum.' "

they have rejected the offer of the emperor in order to save "the honour and liberty of Italy and the dignity of the Roman Church."[1] We hear it in the letter of Falcandus on the calamity of Sicily;[2] it may have entered as an element into Sordello's cry to Dante ·[3]

> "Ahi serva Italia di dolore ostello,
> Nave senza nocchiero in gran tempesta,
> Non donna di provincie ma bordello."

It sounds in Filicaja's famous lament:

> "Italia Italia o tu cui feo la forte
> Dono infelice di bellezza ond' hai
> Funesta dote d' infinite guai
> Che in fronte scritti per gran doglia porte."

The feeling that Italy, "the mistress of the provinces," was exposed to the ravages of drunken barbarians with uncouth manners and uncivil speech, was mingled with the other feeling which recognized in the empire a great tradition and a present necessity.[4] But

---

[1] SS. xix. 445.   [2] *Ugo Falcando*, ed. Siragusa, p. 175.

[3] *Purgatorio*, vi. 78.

[4] The Bergomask panegyrist of Frederick I. describes the Lombard rumours as to the character of the imperial army in Virgilian phrases:

> "Hunc homines ductare feros qui dentibus artus
> Humanos lanient mordentes more ferarum
> Queis caro cruda cibus, potus cruor, horrida visu
> Corporis effigies" (*Gesta di Federigo I.*, ed. Monaci, l. 1810).

Cf. also *Ann. Alt.*, 1068, SS. xx. 89, "Itali sua superbia elati et velut natali odio Teutonicorum ducem audire dedignati," and Frederick I.'s letter of 1168 in Otto of Freising, SS. iv. 116. On the other hand, see the curious poem written by an Italian on the accession of Henry II. (Dümmler, *Anselm der Peripatetiker*, pp. 72-82):

> "Regnorum robur periit quando Otto cecidit,
> Dum Otto noster moritur, Mars in mundo oritur.
> Mutavit caelum faciem et terra imaginem."

And Villani, *Cron.*, iv. 1, "Questo Otto (Otto I.) amendò molto tutta Italia e mise in pace e buono stato, e abbatte le forze de' tiranni"; and iv. 3, "Parve a Sergio papa ... che lo'mperio fosse alla lezione degli Alemanni, imperocch' erano possenti genti e grande bracchio del Cristianesimo."

the contempt and dislike of Teuton civilization was never sufficiently strong to quench the fire of civic jealousy, to create a national spirit or even to figure as a serious political force.   The coronation of **Arduin** of Ivrea as king of Italy [1014] was but a momentary flicker of patriotism which one Teuton victory was sufficient to extinguish.   The destruction of Spoleto and Milan and the sack of St. Peter's were not sufficient to rouse Italy against Barbarossa.   The Lombards fought not for a united Italy but for municipal franchises, and the jealousy between Milan and Cremona was far more bitter and intense than the hatred of Teuton and of Latin.   The letters of Innocent III., the first Pope who made a serious endeavour to appeal to a common Italian sentiment and to clear the Germans out of Italy, met with but a temporary and a partial response.[1]

Still the persuasion remained that the Germans were an inferior race.   "Their speech," says a Provençal poet of the twelfth century (with but a faint appreciation of the discomforts of the north-western portions of the empire) "seems like the barking of dogs, and for this reason I would not be Lord of Frisia, because I should every day hear the voices of the damned"   There was in fact during the whole of this period very little literary reciprocity between the two countries.   Otto I. imported some Italian scholars into Germany, and bishop Luitprand of Cremona wrote his pointed and intelligent history at Frankfort.   A vainglorious Milanese rhetorician, Anselm the Peripatetic, followed the court of Henry III., and according to his own account secured the applause of Gaul, Burgundy, Saxony, and even of barbarous Franconia for a stupid

---

[1] Cf. the curious evidence on this point collected by Ficker, *Forsch.*, ii. 278.

treatise upon rhetoric, which was justly viewed with disdain by the scholars of Mainz.[1] The emperor himself is said to have been instructed by a monk from Pavia, Almaric, afterwards Abbot of Farfa [1039-46], and perhaps the connection between Germany and Italy was never so tightly drawn as during this age, when the papal chair for a time became a German see, and a large number of Germans were sent to occupy Italian bishoprics.[2] But the wars of the Investitures desolated Germany and stayed the development of German culture. When these wars had passed away France was drawing Italian students to her schools with a magnet whose power increased with the advance of the twelfth century. The culture of Germany and Italy had sprung apart during this epoch of internal struggle and brief and ineffectual imperial raids. When Otto of Freising accompanied Barbarossa on his first journey into Italy, the spectacle filled him with surprise. Despite the Lombard invasions, the immigration of German

---

[1] Some of the Milanese clergy seem to have studied in Germany during the eleventh century, but the general drift of Italian students was to France or Spain (Landulf, *Hist. Med.*, ii., c. 35, SS. viii. 71). For Almario, cf. SS. xi. 559, and Giesebrecht, *KZ.*, iii. 288-361. For Anselm, cf. *Epistula Anselmi ad Drogonem Magistrum*, ed. Dümmler, *Anselm*, p. 57 : " A liberalibus enim vestris disciplinis cum ad capellam me contuli imperatoris et ex vestre philosophiae otio cum seculari me dedi negotio, opus quod apud vos edidi, mecum, ut precepistis, detuli et universis civitatibus quas in eundo perambulavimus vestris litteris aprobatum representavimus. Probanda cuius studia universa consonat Gallia, Burgundia, Saxonia, barbara quidem Frantia. Ex quis Maguntia tandem laudavit ingrata, Droconicam quidem sectam et penitus Italiacam invidens disciplinam." Some lines from the *Rhetorimachia* may be cited :

> " Urbs Augusta probat quod Drogo laude coronat
> Basla nec infirmat quod Parma Placentia firmat :
> Littoribus Reni diadema Maguntia regni
> Digna laude probat quod tellus Italia donat."

[2] For signs of literary correspondence between Germany and Italian clerks in this century, cf. Pflugk-Harttung, *Iter Italicum*, vol. ii.

families, the appointments of German prelates, it was an utterly strange land with an alien civilization. The Lombard had been absorbed by the Latin, as completely as in our own day the German is absorbed by the Anglo-Saxon in America. The wars of Barbarossa instructed the Germans in siege-warfare, and induced a certain number of them to frequent the University of Bologna; but since the armies of the empire were recruited from the feudal class, and the townsfolk were allowed to purchase exemption, there was no fruitful reception of Italian culture.[1] A handful of German administrators acquired a knowledge of the Italian language,[2] which was as yet very slightly removed from Latin. Two Italian poets, the anonymous writer of Bergamo and Godfrey of Viterbo, belonged to the court of Barbarossa, and celebrated his praises in copious hexameters, and Henry II. found in another Italian, Peter of Ebulo, a naive and tasteless encomiast. But on the whole the law and the letters of Germany remained unaffected by the contact. Germany, like Italy, was looking westward for her culture.

In 825 Lothair II., commenting severely upon the decay of Italian education, issued a capitulary to establish schools in nine specified towns in Northern and Central Italy.[3] From 825 till 1158, when Frederick Barbarossa promulgated from Bologna his famous

---

[1] Hegel has suggested that the office of consul may have been derived by some of the German towns from Italy ; *Kieler Monatschrift*, 1854, p. 703. The name first occurs in Rainald of Dassel's charter for Medebach in Westphalia in 1165. The term would, however, as my friend Dr. Keutgen suggests, be the natural translation of the German *Rathgeber*.

[2] A list is given by Ficker, *Forsch.*, ii. 271.

[3] *Cap. Olon. Eccl. primum*, Boretius, i. 327. The towns named are Pavia, Ivrea, Turin, Cremona, Florence, Fermo, Verona, Vicenza, Forum Julii.

privilege known as the Authentic Habita,[1] in favour of the student class of the Lombard kingdom, no imperial ordinance affecting Italian education appears to have been issued. During this long interval of time Italy was recovering her classical traditions. Not a city but fabricates for itself some legendary connection with the ancient world. Padua shows the tomb of Antenor, Milan the statue of Hercules, Fiesole looks back to Catiline. Meanwhile schools steadily multiply and develop. In the tenth century private as well as cathedral and monastic schools are mentioned by Ratherius of Verona. In the eleventh century Milan had two prosperous schools founded by the munificence of her archbishops.[2] Pavia sent Lanfranc to govern England with William the Conqueror ; Aosta produced Anselm ; the school of Parma was famous for the philosophy of its founder Drogo.[3] Under the enlightened patronage of the Abbot Desiderius, afterwards Pope Victor III. [1058-1087], the monastery of Montecassino became a distinguished centre for art, science, poetry and history.[4] The keeper of its archives was Leo Ostiensis, one of the most sober and impartial of Italian historians. Constantinus Afer, founder of the medical school at Salerno and translator of the medical works of the Arabs and the Greeks; Pandulf, a medieval Manilius, who wrote in verse upon mathematics and astronomy;

---

[1] Weiland, i., No. 178; Rashdall, *Universities of Europe in the Middle Ages*, pp. 146-149.

[2] Landulfi, *Hist. Med.*, ii., c. 35 [SS. viii. 71], " In atrio interiori ... philosophorum vero scolae diversarum artium peritiam habentium ubi urbani et extranei clerici philosophiae doctrinis studiose imbuebantur, erant duae."

[3] *Chronicon St. Huberti*, c. 9 [SS. viii. 573].

[4] *Chron. Mon. Cass.*, iii., c. 26 ff. ; SS. vii. 716 ff. for an account of the architectural and artistic energy of Desiderius, who among other things sent to Constantinople for workers in mosaics, reviving an art which had perished in Italy for more than five hundred years.

Alfanus the poet, Amatus the historian of the Norman conquest in Italy, are all connected with this monastic stronghold of the papal party. Wipo, the Burgundian chaplain of Conrad II., drew a frank contrast between the general zeal for education which was characteristic of Italy and the negligent ignorance of the Germans.[1] In the twelfth century the culture of Italy was superior in every point to that of Germany.

As yet there was hardly any vernacular literature in either country, less in Italy, where Latin was still intelligible to the people, than in Germany. But when German vernacular literature did develop itself, it received no hearing south of the Alps. Walther von der Vogelweide, the best of the German lyrists [born 1160-70], who sung at the court of Philip of Swabia and Otto, who received a fief from Frederick II., who wrote short political satires against the papacy, and was the most ardent of imperialists, leaves no trace on Italian literature. He is not referred to by Dante, who shared his opinions, and who was seemingly wholly ignorant that there was such a thing as German poetic literature.[2] The Italians were as ignorant of the literature of the country from which they derived their supreme political rulers as the French contemporaries of Elizabeth and James I. were ignorant of Chaucer and Spenser and Shakespeare. The vernacular literature of Italy rose out of contact with France, not out of contact with Germany. Though the saga of Theodoric of Verona is incorporated in the *Niebelungen Lied*, the great epic

[1] Wipo, *Tetralogus*, SS. xi., p 251 :
        " Hoc servant Itali post prima crepundia cuncti
          Et sudare scholis mandatur tota juventus."
[2] Despite the authority of Mr. A. J. Butler, who traces obligations to Eckart, a German mystic, I think it extremely unlikely that Dante knew German.

is unknown south of the Alps, and in the verse of the Italian *epigoni* even Charles the Great himself is worked up into a champion of Latin culture against Teuton barbarism and guile. The later years of the Hohenstauffen dynasty, while they brought about great changes, constitutional and political, especially within the limits of the Norman kingdom of Sicily, also gave an impulse to manifold developments of thought and literary expression. It was an age of strange contrasts and novelties ; of hardy incredulity and infantine faith ; of monstrous and fantastic forms of religious revivalism ; of quickened scientific curiosity and stern ecclesiastical repression. The whole of the western world seemed to be breaking away from its old moorings. A wave of asceticism, of protest against the whole sacerdotal hierarchy with its pretensions to special gifts, its possession of worldly wealth, its ambition of political power, passed over the north of Italy into Southern France, fed by many long and obscure rills of Oriental belief and practice. In Umbria, where the air had long been filled with mystic prophecy, a new teacher arose in the person of St. Francis, who living in a kind of blithe and inspired communication with nature, rebuked the spirit of morbid and extravagant renunciation and refreshed the Christian religion with his simple and poetic raptures. Lapse of time and the growth of trade had softened the antagonism between east and west, and Arabic science and culture was beginning to influence the mind of the Latins, bringing with it through the Aristotelian commentaries of Averroes a pantheistic philosophy, derived ultimately from a passage in the *De Anima*, which long and profoundly disturbed the even waters of medieval thought. There was in fact an almost universal revolt against the old accepted scheme of life. The autocracy of Latin was breaking down before the pressure of the fresh vernacular romance languages, now for the first time receiving a shapely form, and with this new and delightful instrument of speech, artistic natures won a congenial utterance. Naturalistic ways of looking at life are as old as nature herself, but they cannot be conveniently clothed in the stiff garb of an ecclesiastical language.[1] As well might the convent bell accord with the lay of the troubadour. But with the spread of vernacular literature new fountains of joy were suddenly unsealed. Almost within the limits of a single genera-tion Italy seems to experience a kind of renaissance. Art and literature had escaped from the cloister to the castle and the market-place; Latin had given place to Italian; and lay culture made its first appearance since Rutilius Namatianus wrote his famous lament upon Alaric's siege of Rome. " In 1242 the strenuous and splendid man Azzo of Este caused to be painted a picture by the excellent master of painting, Gelasius   the which Gelasius was in Venice under the discipline of the admirable master Theophanes of Constantinople And he painted the image of our Lady with the blessed fruit of her womb, Jesus, in her arms; also the gonfalon with St. George the knight, with the girl and the fierce dragon slain by the lance. With the said gonfalon was the duke Tiepoli of Venice. In the said picture he portrayed the fall of Phaeton with beautiful colours according to the poet, and a memorable example accord-ing to the psalm : ' Dispersit superbos. Laus Deo, amen.' "[2]

[1] A great genius like Abailard or St. Bernard could infuse passion into medieval Latin ; but the language of the frolicsome Salimbene is already half way towards Italian.

[2] Mouaci, *Crestomazia Italiana*, vol. i., p. 41.

At the same time the forces of repression gathered themselves together to conserve the old order of things. A whole civilization, more cultivated and refined than any which the Middle Ages had yet seen, was within the space of a few years crushed out in Provence. The mighty and ruthless engine of the Inquisition, created for this purpose, spread terror among the hardy and luxurious, while a great and learned German, Albert of Cologne, after protracted study in the schools of Italy, elaborated the gigantic *eirenikon* of the Aristotelian theology, harmonizing, so far as it was possible to do so, the perilous learning of Aristotle with the sayings of the Fathers.

But the new developments of sceptical inquiry and artistic impulse, though they might be trained by the thinker or the inspired mendicant to accord with the traditions of the past, could not be wholly arrested. The exiles of the Albigensian crusades brought their songs, their viols and their hates to the court of Palermo, and there, for the first time since the days of Desiderius of Pavia and Arichis of Beneventum, Italy found a literary capital. Frederick II., who, as the old Italian novel says, "was in truth the mirror of the world in speech and in costume, and loved much delicate speech, and made a study in giving wise answers," was the Maecenas of this new culture. Part Greek, part Italian, part Mussulman, Frederick seems to reflect all the varied lights and shadows of his age. He is cruel as the Byzantine, courteous as the Arab ; tolerant as Gallio, when he obeys his intellect or his temperament, intolerant as the Inquisition itself at the call of policy. He is sensual and treacherous, avaricious and friendless, yet he abounds with high aspirations and intelligent desires. Brought up "in happy Palermo, that trilingual town," he feels the claims of three civilizations, and mediates between the Arab, the Latin, and the Greek. His influence is experienced in all departments of Italian life, in customs and manners, in poetry and learning, in architecture and sport, in philosophical speculation and legal reform. He founded the University of Naples, encouraged the medical schools at Salerno, caused the works of Aristotle to be translated, investigated the origin of language and the anatomy of the human body. There was no subject of human inquiry which he was not willing to attack, and no conclusion which he was not willing to face. The disendowment of the Church, the abolition of the Papacy, the rejection of Christian beliefs, the mortality of the soul, were all familiar ideas within that brilliant and cosmopolitan circle of intellectual Epicureans, where Michael Scott translated into Latin the commentaries of Averroes. and where the study of comparative religions was, for the first time since the birth of Christ, dispassionately pursued.

It is from this court at Palermo that Italian poetry first issues "Those illustrious heroes," wrote Dante, "Frederick Caesar and his well-born son Manfred, displaying the nobility and rectitude of their natures, so long as fortune permitted, followed humane things and disdained the ways of the brute. And so the gifted and the noble-hearted strove to be guided by the majesty of these great princes. so that every work of excellence produced at that time by a Latin author first of all issued from the hall of these great kings. And because Sicily was the royal throne it has come to pass that whatever our predecessors produced in the vulgar tongue is called Sicilian."[1]

[1] Dante, *De Vulgari Eloquio*, i., c. 12.

Versification was a fashionable pastime at the court of Frederick. The emperor himself, his two sons Enzio and Manfred, his chief counsellor Peter de la Vigne all gave themselves up to this elegant pursuit. For forty-six years, from 1220 to the death of Manfred in 1266, there is scarcely a literary man in Italy or Sicily who is not connected with the court.[1] Notaries and judges, advocates and ambassadors relieved the tedium of business with the charms of lyric composition, and perhaps there was no surer passport to royal favour. A story is told that one day, perhaps in Umbria, Fra Pacifico, the disciple of St. Francis, presented himself before Frederick, and singing some of those exquisite devotional lyrics, of which we have specimens in St. Francis's own hymn to the sun, and in the fourteenth century Umbrian lauds, received a crown and the title of *Rex Versuum*.[2] In any case the influence of this royal patronage cannot fail to have been widely felt, and it came at a most critical juncture. Italian vernacular literature was only just trembling into life, for the political distraction of the country had long retarded the growth of any common linguistic canons.[3] The dialects of Italian were numerous and debased, as is

---

[1] Arrigo Testa d'Arezzo died fighting for Frederick II. as podestat of Reggio. Odo della Colonna is probably the imperialist senator of Rome, 1238-41. Rinaldo d'Aquino corresponded with Frederick II. Rugieri d'Amici is probably the ambassador sent to the Saracens, 1240-2. Guidotto da Bologna and Stefano da Messina dedicate works to Manfred Jacopo Mortacci da Pisa is sent on an embassy to Arragon by Manfred in 1260. Percevalle Doria is made by Manfred vicar in the march of Ancona and the duchies of Rome and Spoleto. Giacomo da Lentino and Stefano da Messina are notaries. Cf. Monaci, *Crestomazia*, vols. i. and ii., nd Gaspary, *Sicilianische Dichterschule*, pp. 10-13.

[2] Gaspary, *Geschichte der Italienischen Litteratur*, p. 143.

[3] Boncompagno [1215-26], " Mercatores in suis epistolis verborum ornatum non requirunt quia fere omnes et singuli per idiomata propria seu vulgaria vel per corruptum Latinum ad invicem sibi scribunt et rescribunt."

shown by the fact that Dante counted fourteen main
varieties, and hints that there may be more than a
thousand subsidiary shades of patois. No great writer
had arisen to shape a language or to form a literature.
There was no common Italian hero or national exploit
to celebrate. The most dramatic event of the eleventh
century, the Norman conquest of Sicily, was an achievement of the French race and celebrated in the French
and Latin languages. The revolt of the Lombard
towns, and the naval enterprises of Pisa and of Genoa
produced here and there some vigorous writing, but
all of it in Latin. The Italian panegyrists of the
emperor presumably knew no German. Their own
language was fluid and unformed ; their expected reward was a benefice ; their minds were fashioned by
the Roman poets, and it was besides clearly appropriate to celebrate the Roman emperor in the academic
strains of Virgil or of Lucan.

There were two other languages which vied with
Latin, each of them connected with a special form
of literature, French and Provençal. The epic
cycle of Charles the Great and of Arthur came
to Italy in the flowing and delightful dialect of
Northern France, while the love lyrics and satires
of Provence spread the knowledge of the "more
perfect and sweeter speech" of the south.[1] There was
for a time some danger that the common language
of the Italian people would never force its way
into literature against its three formidable rivals.
Latin was the language of the schools, of public

---

[1] Dante, *De Vulgari Eloquio*, i., c. x., "Allegat ergo pro se lingua *oil*,
quod propter sui faciliorem ac delectabiliorem vulgaritatem, quicquid
redactum sive inventum est ad vulgare prosaicum suum est ... Pro
se argumentatur alia, scilicet *oc*, quod vulgares eloquentes in ea primitus
poetati sunt, tanquam in perfectiori dulciorique loquela."

harangues, of official documents, of polite letter writing, of town chronicles, even of sermons until the days of St. Francis.[1] French was the vehicle of the only medieval saga which the whole people of Italy could appropriate to themselves, while the delicate and intricate workmanship of Provençal poetry, with its curious and gracious artificialities of rhythm and diction and thought, for a long time satisfied the artistic craving for technical perfection. Throughout the whole of the thirteenth century the Langue d'Oil held its own in Northern Italy. The epic cycle of Charles the Great was cast into a language which was still mainly French, though it was partially affected by the Italian dialects of the north-east. Forgotten Italian poets added to the cycle the *Entry to Spain* and the *Capture of Barcelona*. The Carolingian and Arthurian epics had come into Sicily with the Normans, and it is thought that *Aliscans*, undoubtedly the finest poem in the Langue d'Oil after the *Chanson de Roland*, was written in that island.[2] The first great Venetian chronicler, Martin da Canale, who must have died soon after 1275, used the French language because, as he said, "Lengue franceise cort parmi le monde et est

[1] The long Latin poem written by Peter de la Vigne against the political monks who make their profit out of the struggle between the empire and the papacy was clearly intended for general publication, and shows that Latin was still widely understood (Du Méril, *Poésies populaires du moyen age*, pp. 163-77). Florentine ladies, on the other hand, could not make much of verses written to them in that language half a century later (Dante, *Vita Nuova*, 25 ; cf. Gaspary, p. 21). There was, however, a certain amount of letter writing done in the vernacular, as is clear from the *Doctrina ad inveniendas, incipiendas ac formandas materias* composed by Guido Faba or Fava about 1229 in Bologna, which includes some letters in the Bolognese dialect, influenced, however, by Provençal (*Quellen zur bayrischen und deutschen Geschichte*, i. ix., and Monaci *Crestomazia*, vol. i., pp. 32-4).

[2] Gaston Paris, *La Sicile dans la Littérature Française*, Romania, vol. v.

la plus delitable a lire et a oir que nul autre." The
Tresor of Brunetto Latini—the most popular of
encyclopedias—was formed upon a French model and
written in the French language. French leapt to
the lips of St. Francis as he carolled to his rough and
extemporized viol. It was the language in which
Rusticianus of Pisa wrote the travels of Marco Polo, the
language in which Dante read the tales of Charles
and of Arthur and of the Trojans.[1]

The Langue d'Oc was perhaps less popular, but it
exercised a more definite and incisive influence upon art,
just because it appealed to a narrower and a more
scholarly circle. The wide influence of the Provençal
lyric was due to the fact that it provided an artistic
mould for the genuine expression of a personal sentiment. It was through this delicate instrument that the
human heart first outpoured its passion in the Middle
Ages, melting the long frost of Latinity. In the Latin
countries, and especially in Italy, its victory was almost
instantaneous. In the twelfth century clusters of Provençal poets gathered round the small northern courts
of the Margraves of Montferrat and of Este. Some of
them eagerly threw themselves into Italian politics,
as Pier Vidal, who sided with the Pisans against the
Genoese, and Piere de la Caravana, who incited the
Lombards against Henry VI. in 1195. And then came
the exiles of the Albigensian crusade. Scarcely a road
in Italy but must have been traversed by one of these
troubadours, bringing with him a store of song, which
must have seemed to those who heard it a new revela-
tion of human power. St. Francis dreamt of sending

---

[1] *De Vulg. Eloq.*, i. x. The last surviving specimen of this Franco-
Italian literature is the *Aquilon* of Bavaria, a prose piece by Rafaele
Marmora [probably a Veronese], 1379-1407.

out a legion of spiritual troubadours—*joculatores Domini*—who should chant men into righteousness.[1] Italians such as Sordello of Mantua and Albert of Malespina wrote only in the Provençal tongue, and one of the chief Provençal grammars, the *Donatz Provensal*, was composed in Italy, dedicated to two Italians, and intended for Italian use. Long after Sicilian poetry had made its way, men continued to study Provençal models, and to throw off now and again a sonnet in the Langue d'Oc.[2] Dante, when commenting upon the laws of verse, uses indifferently illustrations from the poetry of both lands, and the famous Provençal *trovatore* Arnaut Daniel, meeting the poet in Purgatory, speaks eight lines in his native tongue before he is hidden to view in the refining flames.[3]

The vernacular lyric springs from Frederick's court of Palermo,[4] but the mere fact that lyrics were here first written in the native tongue would not necessarily

---

[1] Sabatier, *Vie de St. François d'Assise*, p. 89 ; and cf. *Riccardus da San Germano ad* 1233, "Eodem mense quidam frater J. vili contectus tegmine tanquam de ordine fratrum minorum ad Sanctum Germanum veniens cum cornu quodam convocabat populum et alta voce cantabat tertio Alleluja, et omnes respondebant Alleluja et ipse consequenter dicebat :

      'Benedictu laudatu et glorificatu lu Patre
      benedictu laudatu et glorificatu lu Fillu
      benedictu laudatu et glorificatu lu Spiritu sanctu.
      Alleluja gloriosa Donna ·'
hoc idem alta voce respondentibus pueris qui erant praesentes."

[2] This was specially the case in North Italy, where Provençal even outlived the Sicilian school. Bartolomeo Zorgi was writing after the death of Conradin. For the whole subject of Provençal influence, cf. Gaspary, *Die Sicilianische Dichterschule*.

[3] *De Vulg. Eloq.*, ii. 6, 10, 13 ; *Purg.*, xxvi., 136 ff.

[4] Probably the earliest known specimens of Italian vernacular verse is the *Contrasto* of the Provençal Rambaut de la Vaqueiras before 1202 [ed. Monaci, *Crestomazia Italiana*, vol. i., n. 11]. A Tuscan *cantilena* [*ib.* n. 7] may be still earlier. But there is no general Italian literature till the literature of the Sicilian school proper.

have been of decisive importance. An outburst of Sicilian patois, however passionate and musical, would never have crossed the straights of Messina. The emperor's court saved the Sicilian lyrics from this fate. It was full of Provençals and of Apulians ; it travelled up and down Italy ; it was interested in classical literature, and steeped in a spirit of universal curiosity which was as favourable to the development of poetic technique as it was fatal to the growth of native lyrical feeling. The poetry of the Silician court was written in a dialect which was remarkably free from insular provincialisms, and scholars debate the question as to whether we now have it in the language in which it was originally composed, or whether it was subsequently transliterated into a dialect of the Tuscan type. It is, however, unlikely that a Sicilian patois would have been tolerated at the imperial court, which was the centre of so many streams of culture, German and Provençal, French and Arabic. The court too travelled with the emperor, who frequently voyaged through every part of Italy, and a compliment paid by King Enzio to the " cortesia " of Tuscany would seem to indicate that the refinements of life were there specially appreciated. The poetry too of the Sicilian school is on the whole shallow and conventional, for it was the product of an aristocratic society, and closely set in the Provençal mould.[1] The forlorn lover is like the swan singing its last song, or the turtle dove who has lost its mate. The flame of love is as proven gold. A smile from the beloved is better than paradise. She is a rose, a lily, a

---

[1] The charming *Contrasto* of Cielo dal Camo [Monaci, vol. i., No. 46] is an exception. It has been translated by Rossetti in his *Circle of Dante*. For other unconventional poems of the Sicilian school, cf. Gaspary, *Die Sicilianische Dichterschule*, pp. 114-116.

star, a mirror of womanhood. She is a basilisk who
slays with her eyes, and he a salamander living in a
perpetual fire of love. If he could only serve God as he
serves her, then assuredly God would put him into
heaven. These are the commonplaces of medieval love-
poetry, and they pervade this literature. But it is form
which preserves. Without this saving and most portable
gift these Sicilian echoes from Provence might have
fainted away among the towns of Northern Italy. The
Sicilian poetry was in fact rescued by its very defici-
encies in realism and local colour. In the hands of the
Tuscan poets its metres were improved and new life was
infused into the mould. The powerful stimulus given
to Aristotelian studies by Frederick II. led to a kind
of philosophical or spiritual conception of love, while
the exciting politics of the Tuscan towns edged the
sirvente with a new reality and bitterness.

> " Barons of Lombardy and Rome and Apulia,
>   And Tuscans and Romagnese and men of the March,
>   Florence the flower which renews itself
>   Call you to her court.
>   For she wishes to make herself King of the Tuscans
>   Now that she has conquered the Germans and the Siennese
>   by force."

So sung Guittone d'Arezzo after the Florentine victory
at Monteaperto in 1260, with all his rough vigour.[1]
On the other side Guido Guinicelli, from the learned
city of Bologna, mingled a kind of deep and religious
spirituality with his ardent passion, such as at times

---

[1] Monaci, vol. i., p. 182. For the Pisan political poems against the
tyranny of Ugolino, cf. Gaspary, *Die Sicilianische Dichterschule*, pp. 21-2.
In the Vatican MS. 3793 there are a number of Florentine political
sonnets, some of which have been printed by Trucchi, i., p. 182, and
others by Cherrier, *La lutte de la Papauté et de les Empereurs de la
Maison de Suabe*, vol. iv., p. 527 ff. ; Gaspary, pp. 22-3.

even suggests comparison with Donne. He is the founder of the *dolce styl nuovo*,[1] whom Dante salutes as his father and the father of his betters "in the sweet and light rhymes of love."

> "The fire of Love comes to the gentle heart
> Like as its virtue to a precious stone ;
> To which no star its influence can impart
> Till it is made a pure thing by the sun :
>   For when the sun hath smit
> From out its essence that which there was vile,
>   The star endoweth it.
> And so the heart created by God's breath
>   Pure, true, and clean from guile,
> A woman like a star enamoureth."[2]

Out of this Tuscan poetry which was called Sicilian, with its varied appeals to love, philosophy and political passion, sprang the first written specimens of literary Italian prose.[3] It also made possible the Divine Comedy. From the intellectual fermentation of the thirteenth century, in which the court of the Swabian emperor played so great a part, sprang the architectonic genius of Dante, the most complete literary witness to the passion and the thought, the memories and the hopes, which were stored up in the conception of the Medieval Empire.

---

[1] For the contrast between the Sicilian school, represented by Jacopo da Lentini and Guittone d'Arezzo, and the later school, represented by Guinicelli and Cavalcante, cf. *Purg.*, xxiv. 15.

[2] Tr. Rossetti.   [3] Dante, *De Vulgari Eloquio*, ii. 1.

CHAPTER XV

CONCLUSION.

THE history of the Medieval Empire has, as we have seen, been fertile in contrasts. By a strange freak of fortune the title and tradition of the Caesars passes to the latest barbarian arrival within the circle of the civilized nations of the west. The Saxon king of a rude race of peasants is required to conserve and to appreciate a conception of government moulded by the genius of the Latin races in a climate of Roman law and Roman religion, and saturated with the spirit of Roman autocracy, that last and most refined distillation of the aristocratic pride of a great city. A barbarian, living in a condition of affable equality with his fellow-tribesmen, is asked to posture as the descendant of Augustus, the masterful and subtle, as the co-equal of those Greek rulers, for whose elaborate court Constantine Porphyrogenitus wrote his massive and curious book upon ceremonies. Yet the difference between the courts of Constantinople and Tribur was as great as that between the court of Versailles, as it was known to the Duc de Luynes, and the highland home of Fergus M'Ivor, as Sir Walter Scott describes it in *Waverley*; and the idea of the Roman Empire, as it was printed upon the Saxon brain of the tenth century, no more reflects the ancient classical conception than the Venus of Botticelli in the Uffizi Gallery renders the spirit of ancient Hellenic art.

By degrees, however, the implications of an idea of which the Teuton sovereigns originally had only apprehended the outward symbols penetrate the minds of men. The revival of classical studies in the twelfth century and the increased contact with Italy revealed some portions of ancient history in a clearer outline, and set the later monarchs of the Hohenstauffen house to dream of autocracy and universal dominion. But the functions of an emperor, as they were understood in antiquity, postulated an economic structure wholly different from that which prevailed in Germany. The Roman Empire of antiquity was a federation of towns; the Roman Empire of the Middle Ages was composed of a loose union between a land of independent communes and a land of isolated self-sufficing rural homesteads. All the engines of autocracy are wanting in this rural state. There is little use of money, and therefore there can be no large surplus. There is little traffic or movement of any kind, and therefore the will of the monarch is but feebly felt. The law of these simple communities is homely and home-made, and therefore the autocrat's legislation is unneeded. The weak armour of offence is no match for the stout walls of the castle. The undrilled, undisciplined population jealously guards its customs, its honour, its personal freedom. To vitalize this huge disjointed rural state and bind it together into a civilized polity must necessarily be the work of many generations. But there are two agencies ready to effect it. There is the Church with its strong Roman tradition of discipline, and there is the native monarchy which is the creation of military needs.

The slow and steady co-operation of these two forces eventually built up Spain and France and England. In Germany too there was co-operation between the spiritual and secular powers, more close, more intimate, and more prolonged than in any other realm in the continent, except the eastern empire. Yet the Church, which was in one sense the buttress of the German monarchy, was in another sense its ruin, for, being the sole depositary of the imperial idea, it favoured the revival and continuance of the Roman Empire. It could not explain to the barbarians what this meant, for the clear significance of the thing was utterly lost, and only to be recovered by deep study. But it tempted them with brilliant symbols, and they deserted the homely task of governing German tribes for impossible schemes of Italian conquest. This brought the rulers of the peasant society into contact with two strange things, the Pope of Rome and the civilization of Italy. Neither the one nor the other was fully intelligible to them. The Pope was the ruler of the real living Roman Empire, of the Catholic Church, which was spread through the western world, which had inherited the spirit and which was organized upon the model of the ancient Roman state. The civilization of Italy was municipal. Otto I. challenged a pope to a duel, Frederick Barbarossa savagely destroyed Milan. Both laboured under a misapprehension, for the conquest of Italy could never be effected by such means. Yet the rulers of the peasant state had something to give to the land of cities; their presence for a moment checked disorder, and, winged as they were in their southern pilgrimages by ecclesiastical ideas, they promoted able and vigorous men to fill that papal

office, the true significance of which they did not
understand. Yet since there was nothing in the
economic condition of Germany which could teach
them the art of government, their visits to Italy were
little better than raids. It was only by degrees that the
German world learnt its Latin lesson, and then it was
too late to put it into practice. The towns had shaken
themselves free of bishops and nobles ; the Church
was penetrated by papal ideas, and the constitution
of Germany had fallen by a natural and unconscious
process into a council of territorial princes. Barbarossa,
who began to realize the Roman character of the
empire, is bound to acknowledge that in Germany
nothing can be done without the consent of the princes.
Henry VI. is ready to consecrate the autonomy of the
magnates who have grown up under the shadow of
a careless rule. Frederick II. actually does so. But
the ironical contrast between theory and practice, idea
and actuality, still pursues the Medieval Empire. The
first emperor who had perfectly learnt the Latin lesson
wrecks his dynasty by very adeptness. Surrounded
by Roman lawyers, steeped in ancient culture, educated
in a land of beautiful and magnificent cities, inheritor
of a strong and well-compacted realm, Frederick II.
first realized what government should really mean,
what the Roman Empire really meant. But to apply
this theory of the empire to practical politics was to
create a revolution. It meant the destruction of the
temporal power of the papacy, the undoing of the
work of Gregory I. "The ghost of the Caesars"
rose up against the Sicilian monarch and destroyed
him, for the existence of the medieval papacy was
incompatible with so literal a transcript of classical
ideas. The attempt to realize a conception of the

empire ruined the political unity of Italy and Germany.

It may be urged in reply that ideals are worth pursuing whithersoever they may lead, and that what Germany and Italy lost in the field of politics they gained in culture and civility. It may be urged that it was something to keep alive the idea of a common polity of the most progressive nations of the world, and to infuse the highest known morality into the conceptions of kingship. The struggle between the empire and the papacy produced, it is true, many physical disasters, and a large crop of fantastic controversy. But although the modern politician will rightly despise the application of analogies from the heavenly bodies to decide the relative position of earthly dignitaries, he must remember that this controversy first lit the flames of political debate in the west, and that sparks from that fire have been burning ever since. The idea of the contractual theory of monarchy on the one hand, and of the divine right of kings on the other, springs from these obscure ecclesiastical tracts which were written during the controversy between Gregory VII. and Henry IV. The question of the relation between Church and State was one which was unknown to antiquity and unknown to Byzantium. But it was raised throughout Latin Christendom in every living between patron and incumbent, in every country between king and clergy, and lastly in a most conspicuous way in the struggle between the empire and the papacy. It was round this, the most conspicuous, struggle that the political literature of Western Europe was gathered.

The apologist of the empire might also urge that the Germans have saved the individuality of Italy by the very fact that they have so little in common with the Italian genius. It was far better for Italy to look to an alien and unsympathetic people for political guidance than to be thrown for help upon the cognate civilization of France. As it was, Italy during the twelfth and thirteenth centuries narrowly risked falling into that intellectual bondage to France which seems to be afflicting her at the present time. If political control had been added to the numerous commercial and intellectual ties which bound her to the western kingdom, would the individuality of the Italian genius have ever asserted itself? Roman law, Teuton domination and the Sicilian court won for the country intellectual independence. By the time that Charles of Valois was established in the Norman kingdom, a new and lovely instrument of speech had been crystallized by half a century of vernacular poetry.

It may be replied that the mutual influence of German and Italian civilization was far slighter during the imperial age than it subsequently became; that the revival of the empire effectually prevented the formation of an Italian kingdom, which was not an impossibility at the end of the tenth or during the first half of the eleventh century, and that political union would have promoted the individuality of the Italian genius. It cannot be denied that the empire ruined the political prospects of Germany; that it may have degraded the German Church; that it arrested the progress of German law; stereotyped anarchy and private warfare; and prepared the humiliations of Westphalia and Lunéville. There can be no more striking commentary upon the statement that history is the biography of great men. Here was a line of rulers extending over a period of three hundred years,

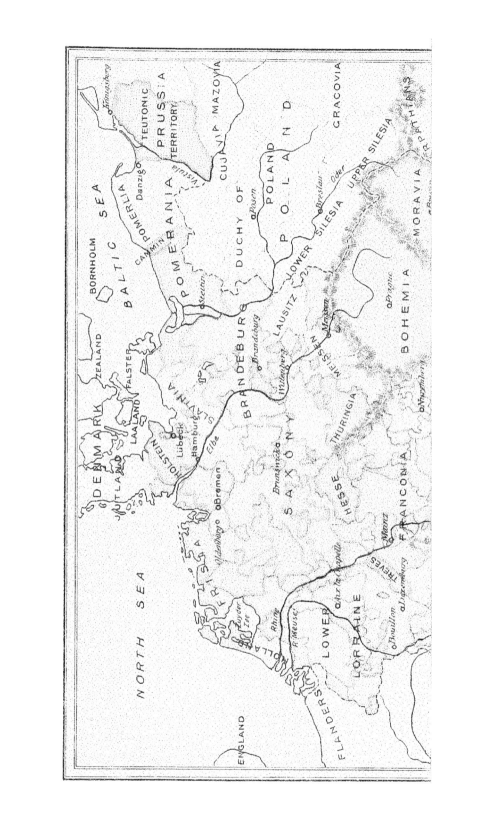

all of them active and zealous, some of them judicious and sensible, some of them imaginative and enthusiastic, one of them a man of genius. They were all governed by a single idea, a single tradition, which became bigger to them and more full of meaning as time revealed the outlines of antiquity. It governed them and it ruined them, for the spirit and the economics of German society were incompatible with autocracy, and the inheritance of the Latin Empire had passed to the Catholic Church and to its chieftain, the Pope.

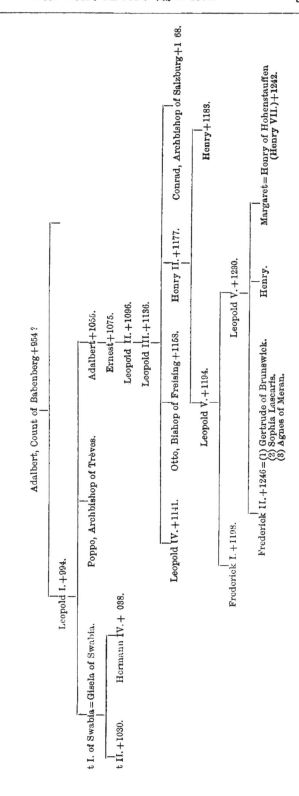

GENEALOGY OF THE HOUSE OF BABENBERG.

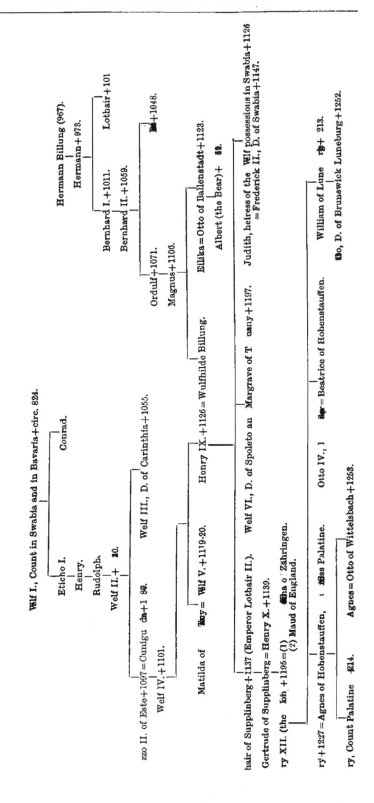

THE WELF AND BILLUNG FAMILIES.

THE DUKES OF SWABIA.

Burkhard I.,	917-926	Ernest II. of Babenberg, -	1015-1027
Hermann I.,	926-948	Hermann IV. of Baben-	
Liudolf of Saxony,[1] -	949-954	berg,	1030-1038
Burkhard II.,[2]	954-973	Henry I., the Black, of	
Otto I. of Saxony,	973-982	Franconia,	1038-1045
Conrad I.,[2]	983-997	Otto II.,[6]	1045-1047
Hermann II.,[3]	997-1003	Otto III. of Schweinfurt,[7]	1048-1057
Hermann III.,[4]	1003-1012	Rudolph of Rheinfelden,[8]	1057-1079
Ernest I. of Babenberg,[5] -	1012-1015	Berchtold of Rheinfelden,	1079-1090

HOHENSTAUFFEN DUKES.

Frederick I., -	1079-1105	Philip, - - --	1196-1208
Frederick II., -	1105-1147	Frederick VI.,	1212-1216
Frederick III.(Barbarossa),	1147-1152	Henry II., -	1216-1235
Frederick IV.	1152-1167	Conrad III.,	1235-1254
Frederick V., - - -	1167-1191	Conrad IV. or Conradin -	1254-1268
Conrad II., - - -	1192-1196		

After the death of Conrad IV. the ducal dynasty disappears, and imperial governors are placed in Upper and Lower Swabia. Towards the end of the thirteenth century the Counts of Wurtemberg became governors of Lower Swabia.

THE DUKES OF BAVARIA.

DUKES.

Arnulf, the Bad,	911-914	Henry IV. (Saxon),[10] -	995-1004
Conrad I. of Franconia, -	914-918	Henry V. of Luxemburg,	1004-1009
Arnulf (returns), -	919-937	Henry IV. (returns), -	1009-1018
Eberhard,	937-938	Henry V. (returns), -	1018-1026
Berchtold,	938-947	Conrad II. of Franconia,[11]	1026-1027
Henry I., the Quarrelsome		Henry VI., the Black, of	
(Saxon),[9]	947-955	Franconia,[12] - -	1027-1042
Henry II.,the Pacific (Saxon),	955-976	Henry VII. of Luxemburg,	1042-1047
Otto I. (Saxon), - -	976-982	Henry VI. (returns), -	1047-1049
Henry III., the Young, -	983-985	Conrad III. of Zutphen, -	1049-1053
Henry II. (returns), -	985-995	Henry VIII. of Franconia,	1053-1054

[1] Son of Otto I. = Ida, d. of Hermann I.
[2] Nephews of Hermann I.
[3] Son of Conrad I.
[4] Son of Hermann II.
[5] = Sister of Hermann III.
[6] Descended from a daughter of Emperor Otto II.
[7] Second cousin of Ernest II.
[8] Nephew by marriage of Ernest II.
[9] Brother of Otto I.
[10] Afterwards Emperor Henry II.
[11] Emperor.
[12] Emperor Henry III.

Agnes of Poitiers,[1] ·	- 1055-1061	Henry X., the Proud, of		
Otto II. of Nordheim,	1061-1070	Este, · ·	1126-1138	
Welf I. of Este,	1070-1077	Leopold of Austria, ·	1138-1141	
Henry VIII. (returns),	1077-1096	Conrad V. of Hohenstauffen,	1141-1143	
Welf I. (returns), ·	1096-1101	Henry XI. of Austria,	1143-1156	
Welf II. of Este, ·	1101-1120	Henry XII., the Lion, of		
Henry IV., the Black, of		Este,	1156-1180	
Este,	1120-1126			

HOUSE OF WITTELSBACH.

Otto I., the Great,	1180-1183	UPPER BAVARIA.	
Lewis I. of Kelheim,	1183-1231	Lewis II., the Severe, -	1255-1294
Otto II., the Illustrious, -	1231-1253		
Lewis II., the Severe, }	1253-1255	LOWER BAVARIA.	
Henry I. }		Henry I.,	1255-1290

[1] Widow of Henry III.

ERRATA.

VOL. I.

p. 32, l. 24.   *For* Pascal *read* Stephen.
p. 34, l. 14.   *For* Henry IV. *read* Henry I.
p. 36, l. 2.   *For* Bold *read* Bald.
p. 44, l. 15.   *For* Ivrea *read* Friuli,
p. 99, l. 10.   *For* Lothar *read* Lothair.
p. 134, l. 26.   *For* niece *read* daughter.
p. 183, *n* 3. l. 3.   *For* Cont *read* Count.
p. 241, l. 20.   *For* Bertolf *read* Bertold.
p. 267, l. 27.   *For* Lewis XIX. *read* Lewis XIV.
p. 289, l. 22.   *For* Raske *read* Raspe.
p. 291, l. 19.   *For* Henry IV. *read* Henry I.
p. 339, l. 18.   *For* Ekbert *read* Eckbert.

ERRATA.

VOL. II.

p. 21, l. 4.   *For* Pribislav of Bohemia *read* Pribislaw of Brandenburg.
p. 163, *n* 1, l. 1.   *For* partition *read* petition.
p. 181, l. 11.   *For* Civita-nova *read* Civita-nuova.
p. 189, l. 8.   *For* immoral *read* immortal.
p. 258, l. 22.   *For* Lothair II. *read* Lothair I.

The author wishes to apologise heartily to his readers for some inconsistencies in the orthography of proper names which escaped his notice until it was too late to correct them. His object has been to give the proper names in the forms which are most familiar to English readers.

INDEX.

308 THE MEDIEVAL EMPIRE

Lightning Source UK Ltd.
Milton Keynes UK
UKOW05f1912290317
297858UK00016B/211/P